MASTER CLASS

Guitar Soloing

The Complete Guide to Blues Lead Guitar Techniques, Concepts, and Styles

by KEITH WYATT

To access audio visit:
www.halleonard.com/mylibrary

Enter Code
6365-6624-6710-9083

ISBN 978-0-7935-7129-1

7777 W. Bluemound Rd. P.O. Box 13819 Milwaukee, WI 53213

Visit Hal Leonard Online at
www.halleonard.com

Table of Contents

Introduction

W.C. Handy, a bandleader, composer, and arranger who became known as the "Father of the Blues," tells in his memoirs of hearing a strange new style of music for the first time when, in 1903, he encountered a man sliding a knife blade up and down the guitar strings while he sang mysteriously about "going where the Southern cross the Dog." Handy was so inspired that he devoted the rest of his career to documenting and promoting the music that would become known as the blues.

It was a few more years before blues found mainstream recognition. In 1912, Handy was one of the first to publish a blues-style song in sheet-music form ("The Memphis Blues"), but it was not until 1920 that the first commercial blues recording, "Crazy Blues" by Mamie Smith's Jazz Hounds, achieved massive success and launched the first commercial blues craze. In 1923, slide guitarist Sylvester Weaver cut the first blues guitar recording, "Guitar Blues" b/w "Guitar Rag," and 1925 saw the commercial debuts of both Blind Lemon Jefferson and Lonnie Johnson, guitarists who respectively epitomized the "down home" (rural) and "uptown" (urban) streams of the blues style. Around 1936, companies first began producing single-pickup hollow-body "electric Spanish" guitars for the general public, and in 1939, Charlie Christian's phenomenal recordings and appearances with popular bandleader Benny Goodman made him the first bona-fide electric guitar star. The same year, an electric slide guitar was heard on "Floyd's Guitar Blues," a commercial hit featuring guitarist Floyd Smith fronting Andy Kirk's Clouds of Joy. But it was in 1942 that T-Bone Walker truly launched the era of electric blues lead guitar when he featured the instrument on his single "Mean Old World."

In the decades since, electric blues has remained a primary source of inspiration and innovation for guitar players of all styles. The sound of music never stops changing, but if you want to express yourself with the guitar, there's still no better way to do it than by learning to play the blues.

What This Book Provides

This book presents an organized, progressive method for learning the skills, concepts, and stylistic awareness you need in order to understand how great blues soloists play and how to create your own solos in a variety of different styles of blues. Detailed written explanations are accompanied by hundreds of examples notated in music notation and guitar tablature, recorded demonstrations, and play-along rhythm tracks. Specific skills and concepts include:

- How to understand and organize blues melody, including blue notes, blues tonality, and dozens of useful one- and two-bar phrases in every position on the neck.
- How to develop a blues touch, including legato, picking technique, dynamics, sliding, bending, and vibrato.
- How to organize your ideas into expressive solos, including call-and-response phrasing, pickup phrases, intros, turnarounds, endings, breathing, and texture.
- How to solo over 12-bar, 8-bar and other standard blues progressions, typical chromatic and substitute changes, and different tempos and rhythm feels.
- Influential soloing styles and techniques and examples of classic solos.
- Specific practice guidelines and listening references.

Here's a brief overview of the contents:

Part 1: Techniques and Patterns

This section covers the fundamental concepts and techniques of blues melody and phrasing. Chapters 1–6 focus on phrasing within one octave of a single fingering pattern. In Chapter 7, you learn how to expand the same concepts to cover the entire neck.

Part 2: 12-Bar Soloing

The 12-bar medium shuffle is the essential blues progression. Skills presented in Chapters 8–9 include strategies for playing over chord changes and how to organize your phrases into expressive solos. Chapter 10 presents ideas and techniques for expanding your 12-bar soloing vocabulary.

Part 3: Beyond the 12-Bar Shuffle

The final chapters explore strategies for soloing effectively over different progressions and chord changes, at different tempos, and in a variety of different blues-related styles.

Appendices: Sound; Style and Influences

These sections provide an overview of factors that contribute to a classic blues sound as well as capsule introductions to the great musicians and recordings that formed the electric blues guitar tradition.

At the end of each chapter, you will find a practice guide and specific recommendations for listening (almost all specific recordings are available online via streaming services such as YouTube). In order to really understand blues, it's essential to listen not just to the audio demonstrations but to the artists and recordings that inspired them.

IMPORTANT!

To help you absorb and apply techniques and concepts more quickly and efficiently, almost all examples in this book are presented only in the key of A. Fortunately, one of the great advantages of the guitar is the ease with which you can transpose (change keys), so you can quickly apply everything you learn in the key of A to other keys as needed (Chapter 1 includes methods for practicing in different keys). Also note that the key signatures aren't included on most of the examples to keep the accidentals to a minimum.

If You Are an Intermediate or Advanced Player

Depending on your experience and skill level, you may already be familiar with some or even most of the content presented in the first section, but the information is presented progressively, so it is highly recommended that you at least scan through all of the material from the beginning to be sure that you're familiar with the techniques and ideas you'll encounter in later chapters. Every aspect of blues guitar playing provides challenges at different technical and conceptual levels, and even advanced players can always improve specific skills or learn new soloing concepts.

If You Just Started Playing the Guitar

This book does not require you to have much experience with guitar playing in general or blues in particular, but it is not a comprehensive beginning guitar method. Before you begin using this book, it is recommended that you learn a few basic guitar playing skills and concepts, including:

- How to tune the guitar
- How to hold a flatpick
- How to play common major, minor, and dominant seventh chords in both open and moveable (barre chord) voicings
- The names of the notes on at least the first, sixth, and fifth strings
- How to read guitar tablature

If you're just starting out, here are some recommendations for books that provide basic techniques and concepts of guitar playing and music in general as well as explanations and exercises that will prepare you to grasp the material presented in this book (all are available in stores or online from MI Press/Hal Leonard Publishing):

Guitar Basics by Bruce Buckingham: An all-around introduction to guitar-playing techniques.

Harmony and Theory*, the Essential Guide* by Keith Wyatt and Carl Schroeder: Explains scale and chord construction as well as the musical concepts that underlie all forms of popular music, including blues.

Blues Rhythm Guitar by Keith Wyatt: To reach your full potential as a soloist, you also need to develop your rhythm-playing abilities; this book is the ideal companion to *Blues Guitar Soloing*.

How to Use the Audio Examples

To access the audio examples that accompany this book, simply go to **www.halleonard.com/mylibrary** and enter the code found on page 1. This will grant you instant access to every example. The examples that include audio are marked with an audio icon throughout the book.

Since the beginning, blues has been mainly an "ear" style, and listening is absolutely required in order to capture the subtleties of blues phrasing. The audio demonstrations that accompany this book provide details of style and touch that can't be captured in music notation, so listen to every example while you follow the notation to see string and fret locations before you attempt to perform it. Here are some features and tips:

- A number of the audio tracks demonstrate examples at different tempos and are arranged in a call-and-response format.
- Additional music-minus-one (play-along) tracks are provided so you can practice the examples or jam on your own.
- If a recorded example is too fast for you to keep up with, divide it into short musical phrases, practice each phrase individually, connect it to the phrases around it, and gradually work it up to the tempo of the track.
- Play along with the recorded examples to learn the timing and touch and then play over the rhythm tracks on your own to confirm the details. Once you have an example memorized, you own it—like all of the great players before you, you can shape everything you learn to your own taste and style.

Part I

Techniques and Patterns

Mance Lipscomb once described the guitar style of his fellow Texas bluesman Lightnin' Hopkins as follows: "Lightnin' Hopkins' [is] a E man, E and a little A, only type he try to play. He can play E chord good as he want to. And everything he going to play that have any kind of sense to it, he going to play in E. And maybe some time in A."

Lipscomb's observation raises a very important point about playing blues: what counts isn't how many different things you know how to play, but how well you play what you know. Lightnin' Hopkins is one of the most-recorded blues performers in history and a profound influence on generations of guitarists; he may have been proficient in only two keys, but there was no limit to his powers of expression.

In this section, you will learn the fundamental playing skills that are common to all styles of electric blues guitar soloing and then look in detail at note choices, rhythmic organization, and expressive techniques. As noted in the introduction, everything will be presented in just one key (A) and, at least for now, will be applied over just one chord (A7). Once you know how to phrase effectively over one chord, you will quickly be able to transfer that ability to other chords and keys. Until then, different keys and chords are just a distraction; before you go wide, you have to go deep.

1 Essential Skills

All great blues soloists share two essential qualities: confidence and control. Every note is chosen for a purpose and is played with a solid rhythm and distinctive touch. This sense of assurance is traditionally developed through years of playing experience, but on a purely technical level, it involves such fundamental guitar-playing skills as maintaining a firm grip on the strings, a strong picking attack, and reliable coordination between the hands, each of which can be developed through focused exercises. In the first few chapters we'll look at how to develop effective fretting-hand techniques, and then we'll turn to building your blues vocabulary and picking skills.

> **NOTE:** Although this book begins by teaching basic playing techniques related to blues phrasing, it is not designed as a comprehensive introductory guitar method. If you are a complete beginner, you are urged to supplement this book with a basic guitar method and/or guitar lessons.

The Minor Pentatonic Scale

The best melodic platform for developing blues soloing technique is the *minor pentatonic scale*. This scale not only shares many notes in common with traditional blues melodies, but when it is laid out on the guitar neck, it forms a very convenient fingering pattern.

As the name suggests, the minor pentatonic scale contains five notes; specifically, these are the tonic, minor 3rd, 4th, 5th, and minor 7th, which are numbered 1, ♭3, 4, 5, and ♭7, respectively. (Scale steps are numbered in comparison to the major scale; "♭" means "flat," or "lowered by one half step" and "8," the octave of the scale, is also the "1" of the next octave.)

The figure below shows a one-octave minor pentatonic scale fingering that is often referred to as the "home" pattern or "box" pattern due to the squared-off configuration of notes on the neck.

Fig. 1: A Minor Pentatonic Scale

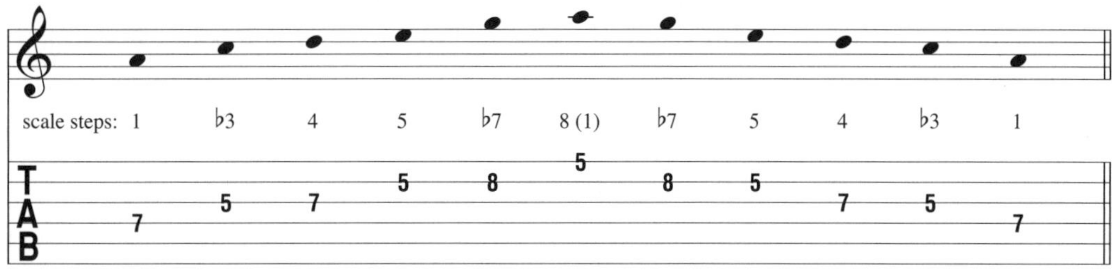

When you play this or any other scale pattern, observe these general rules of fingering and picking:

1. **Fingering:** Use the "one-finger-per-fret" approach; i.e., use your index (first) finger for any note at the fifth fret, your second (middle) finger for any note at the sixth fret (there are none in this pattern), your third (ring) finger at the seventh fret, and your fourth (little) finger at the eighth fret.
2. **Fretting-Hand Thumb:** Classical guitar technique calls for placing the thumb behind the neck opposite the first finger, but most blues guitarists use a baseball bat-style grip with the thumb sticking over the top of the neck, which is the grip recommended here. The "thumb-over" grip is also most effective when you play standing up with the guitar on a strap; most electric blues guitarists perform standing up most of the time, so it's essential to spend at least some of your practice time standing so you get used to it and develop the techniques that are effective in that position.

3. **Picking:** The most flexible and efficient flatpicking technique is *alternate picking* (that is, alternating down- and up-strokes as opposed to using only down-strokes). As a general rule, use alternate picking exclusively regardless of which strings the notes fall on or the order in which you play them. (We'll look at various blues picking techniques in Chapter 4.)

Techniques of Touch

Albert King, one of the greatest blues guitarists in history, picked up an unusual nickname—"Velvet Bulldozer"—during his early years in the construction trade due to his finesse in controlling the massive machine; reportedly, he could use it to lift a carpet from the floor without scratching the wood underneath. The name also perfectly summarizes his approach as a guitar player, which rested not on speed or complexity, but rather on his ability to combine power and precision to control the smallest nuances of each note—in other words, his *touch*.

Touch is one of the most important components of a blues style, and the following exercises are specifically designed to provide you with the tools to develop your own.

Supportive Fingering

Legato ("tied together") is the musical term that best describes the polished, flowing sound that is a hallmark of accomplished blues soloists like Albert King. A legato sound relies on accurate, consistent fretting technique with precise control over the duration of each note and its connection to the notes around it. An effective method for developing legato technique is to practice *supportive fingering*, or fretting each string with more than one finger whenever possible. Supportive fingering improves your touch by strengthening your grip on each note and reducing the amount of finger movement required to fret the next note (it is also a crucial component of techniques like string-bending and vibrato, which will be presented later in this book).

The following exercise applies supportive fingering technique to the A minor pentatonic scale pattern shown in Fig. 1 (**NOTE:** This exercise is meant to be played *extremely* slowly; the emphasis is entirely on precision, not speed):

Exercise 1: Supportive Fingering

1. Fret A on the fourth string, seventh fret with your third finger while simultaneously fretting the same string with your second finger at the sixth fret and your first finger at the fifth fret. Pick the note.
2. While keeping your second and third fingers in position, move only your first finger to the next note in the scale (C) on the third string, fifth fret and pick that note.
3. Hold your first finger in place while you simultaneously lift and move your second and third fingers from the fourth to the third string, placing your third finger at the seventh fret (D) and second finger at the sixth fret. When both fingers are solidly in place, pick the note.
4. Hold the second and third fingers in place while you move your first finger to the second string (E) at the fifth fret and pick the note.
5. Hold your first finger in position as you move your second, third, and fourth fingers simultaneously to the second string, with your fourth finger fretting the eighth fret (G) and the other fingers placed one fret apart on the same string; pick the note.
6. Holding your second, third, and fourth fingers in place, move your first finger to the first string (A) and pick the note to complete the one-octave scale pattern.
7. To descend through the scale, apply the same fingering in reverse, taking care to place each finger with precision and without lifting any finger from a string until necessary.

When you first sit down to practice, perform this exercise up and down the pentatonic scale for a few minutes (the same technique can be applied to any scale). The exercise is extremely painstaking and requires the utmost concentration, but when you're done with the exercise, don't think about the technique at all—by devoting regular, short periods of hyper-conscious focus to the smallest details of your technique you will, over time, develop unconscious reflexes that free your mind to concentrate on the music rather than the mechanics.

The Finger Roll

Another very practical legato phrasing technique is the *finger roll*, which applies whenever you play two consecutive notes on adjacent strings at the same fret, such as in the following minor pentatonic melody:

Fig. 2: Minor Pentatonic Phrase

At four points in this phrase, the same finger is required to play consecutive notes on adjacent strings. When this happens, the natural reflex is to lift your finger from one string and re-set it on the next. But when your finger momentarily breaks contact with the string, it also interrupts the flow of the phrasing. At the same time, if you fret both strings simultaneously with the same finger (called a *barre*), you give up control over the individual notes. The best solution is to *roll* the finger from one string to the next, transferring the pressure from the side to the tip of the finger or vice versa, depending on the direction of the roll.

The following exercise describes the finger roll technique in detail:

Exercise 2: Finger Roll

Ascending:

1. Fret the fourth string, seventh fret (A) normally with the tip of your third finger and pick the string.
2. While still fretting the fourth string, roll your finger onto the third string, seventh fret (D), fretting it with the side of your finger. When you roll your finger over, A will stop sounding just as you make firm contact with D. At the instant this happens, pick the third string so there is no interruption or overlap between the notes.
3. Roll your finger back to its original upright position on A. As soon as you break contact with the third string, pick the fourth string so that again there is no interruption or overlap between the two notes.
4. Practice rolling back and forth between these two notes until the sound is consistently legato.

Descending:

1. Fret A on the first string, fifth fret with the side of your first finger—about a half-inch from the tip—and pick the string.
2. Roll your finger onto its tip to fret the second string at the fifth fret (E). If you position the side of your finger properly on A, when you roll it over onto E, you should land on the same part of your fingertip that you normally use to fret the note. Pick the second string as soon as you break contact with the first string—no interruption, no overlap.
3. Roll your finger back onto A and pick the string.
4. Practice rolling back and forth between these two notes until the sound is consistently legato.

Fig. 3 shows the finger roll technique applied to the minor pentatonic box pattern. When you descend through the scale, you must anticipate each finger roll by fretting the higher note with the side of your finger, allowing enough room for your fingertip to roll onto the lower note. Practice this technique by going through the pattern slowly and precisely in both directions for a few minutes a day until you can maintain consistent, accurate legato technique throughout with no hesitation.

Fig. 3: Finger Roll Exercise

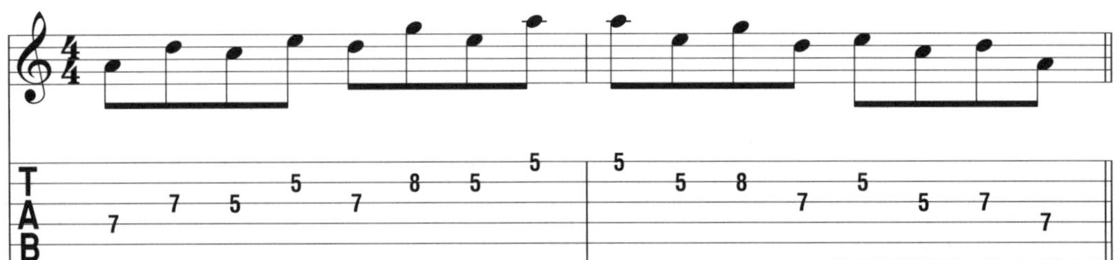

The key to being a great blues soloist is to control the smallest detail of every note, including how long you sustain it, how you connect it to the next note, how hard you pick it, and how you bend, slide, or use any other technique to give it personality. The most efficient way to develop this level of control is by identifying and isolating each specific skill and practicing it with focused intensity. With this thought in mind, apply the following principles of practicing not only to the exercises in this chapter, but to all of the exercises and examples presented in this book.

Principles of Practicing

Howard Roberts, the great guitarist, musician, and educator, had a favorite saying: "Speed is the byproduct of accuracy." Accuracy simply means giving each note its full musical value, and if you practice accurately, you'll ultimately be able to play at any tempo while maintaining the full quality of every note. On the other hand, practicing inaccurately—typically by attempting to play faster than your technique will support—reduces the value of each note and the overall musical value of a phrase. To solo convincingly, you need to practice convincingly, so keep these ideas in mind as you move through this book.

Warming Up

When you first pick up the guitar, take a few minutes to play single notes and short phrases slowly on different strings and different parts of the neck. Concentrate on accurately fretting and picking each note with perfect left/right hand coordination and maintaining maximum musical value. (Exercise 1 is very good for this purpose.) It doesn't matter what key or position you play in; the idea is simply to get your hands re-acquainted with the instrument.

Setting Tempo

A metronome is essential for developing accurate playing skills. Far from making your playing sound "mechanical," a metronome is the most effective way to develop the accurate and consistent feel for time and rhythm that are essential for expressive phrasing. Here are some tips for using a metronome effectively:

1. *Before* you turn on the metronome, play each exercise at the fastest tempo at which you can execute it perfectly.
2. Set your metronome to match that tempo at one note per beat (quarter notes) and play the exercise along with the metronome. If your pick attack is precise, the metronome will seem to "disappear" behind the notes; if you pick too early or too late, the note and the metronome will be out of sync. The goal of practicing is 100 percent accuracy.
3. Each day, set the metronome according to your skill level on that day. The tempo won't always be faster than the day before, but over time, the tempo will increase along with your skill level. Don't "chase" the metronome by setting it faster than you can play perfectly and then trying to catch up—that simply reinforces bad technique.
4. When the tempo at which you can perfectly execute quarter notes reaches above 100 bpm, reduce the tempo to 50 bpm and play the exercise using two even notes per beat (straight eighth notes). Continue increasing your tempo from that point (later we'll look at *shuffled* eighth notes—the basic rhythm of blues).

How Long to Practice

Practicing is a process of gradual development, and practicing for a short period every day is better than skipping days and trying to make up for it by "cramming." Muscles don't respond well to that approach. For any specific exercise, as little as 10–15 minutes of concentrated practice every day will yield results over time, but obviously the more time you devote to developing your skill properly, the more quickly your skill level will increase.

If you're playing for recreation, play whenever you can and always look forward to the next opportunity. Reaching a professional level obviously takes considerable time and dedication, but no matter what your goals may be, the more concentrated effort you are able to give to your playing, the greater the rewards will be in terms of your confidence and expressive ability.

What to Practice and When to Move On

Scientists who study the learning process have identified several key factors related to mastering a subject that certainly apply to blues guitar soloing. One is that in order to retain knowledge or skill for a long period of time, you must over-practice; in other words, you need to continue practicing a skill long after you have first mastered it. Continuous, long-term practice is required in order to move knowledge from "working memory," or conscious thought, into "automatic memory," or reflex. Before you can organize your ideas spontaneously—i.e., improvise—you need to develop a strong repertoire of reflexes so your mind isn't overloaded with technical problems and you can instead listen to what you play, what other musicians are playing, and what you hear in your imagination. It's also important to keep challenging yourself by moving beyond your current comfort level. In other words, practice familiar material in order to develop your unconscious reflexes, but also turn your conscious focus to the next example. Musical growth is a continuous process of overlapping the reinforcement of existing skills with the development of new skills.

This book is organized progressively, with each idea or technique preparing you for those that follow, so in order to get the most comprehensive results, move forward in the order presented. The early exercises, which emphasize basic techniques that are the foundations of your playing, will pay off when you tackle the stylistic examples later in the book. Even if a subject looks familiar, go through each exercise and example to see how it may benefit you. Depending on your skill level, you may move through parts of the book very quickly, and whenever you have mastered a skill well enough to match the audio demo accurately, it's time to take on the next challenge. All techniques are applied again and again in various settings, so you have many opportunities for reinforcement.

Setting and maintaining a good practice schedule is subject to many factors—musical and otherwise—and most people find it difficult to assess their own progress and figure out what they most need to work on next, so if possible, meet at least from time to time with a private teacher who can help you adjust your priorities.

Practicing in Different Keys: Transposing and the Cycle of Fourths

Lightnin' Hopkins may have needed to know only a couple of keys, but he was also playing only his own music. In order to streamline the learning process, everything in this book is presented in one key, but if you play along with records or jam with other people, you definitely need to know how to *transpose*, or play in other keys.

Fortunately, transposing on the guitar is easy compared to other instruments. For example, to transpose the minor pentatonic box pattern to a key other than A, find the tonic of the new key on the first or fourth string and play the same pattern of notes; e.g., to play in the key of C, locate C on the first string (eighth fret) and fourth string (10th fret) and duplicate the fingering pattern from Fig. 1. The pattern is identical in every key; the only difference is the change in position.

A classic, highly effective method for learning to play in all 12 keys is to practice all exercises in the *cycle of fourths*. In other words, play the exercise in the first key (e.g., A) and then move four steps of the major scale up the neck to the next key (D) and repeat the exercise. Then move up again to the key a 4th above that (G) and so on until the cycle finally returns to A. (When the next key is located too high on the neck to be playable, move it down 12 frets and continue.)

Here is the cycle of fourths beginning on A (after E, the cycle returns to A):

A D G C F B♭ E♭ A♭ D♭ G♭ B E

The same approach that applies to technical exercises will also apply to phrases and solos as you progress through this book, and almost everything that is demonstrated in the key of A is applicable to every other key.

Practicing Blues: Beyond Technique

Good technique is essential, but it's still only one aspect of becoming a good blues soloist. Traditionally, blues guitarists learned their craft by listening to records, transcribing by ear, observing other players, learning songs, and playing with other people. Each of these is also a form of practicing, and each is necessary in order to develop a complete blues style. A method like this one provides an organized system for developing your guitar skills, but beyond licks and solos there's no substitute for learning complete songs, including rhythm patterns, melodies, form, and lyrics. A great solo is not just a collection of licks, but an extension of the song and an expression of a larger tradition, so the more songs you know, the better all-around musician and soloist you will be.

Chapter 1 Summary

1. **Minor Pentatonic Scale**
   a. One-finger-per-fret
   b. "Thumb-over" grip
   c. Alternate picking
2. **Techniques of Touch**
   a. Supportive fingering
      - As a general rule, fret each note with more than one finger.
      - Hold unused fingers close to the strings.
   b. Finger roll
      - When moving from string to string at the same fret, roll your finger from tip to side or vice versa and maintain contact with the first note until you pick the next note.
      - Avoid "string-hopping" with your fingertips.
3. **Principles of Practicing**
   a. Speed is the byproduct of accuracy; practice with precision and don't chase the metronome.
   b. Shorter, regular practice sessions yield better results than longer, infrequent sessions.
   c. Learn how to transpose by practicing exercises in all keys using the cycle of fourths.
   d. To become a better soloist, learn complete songs—not just licks and solos.

2 Blue Notes

If you analyze a traditional blues melody and line the notes up in order of ascending pitch, the resulting pattern will often be similar to the minor pentatonic scale. But blues melodies also include regular variations that go outside this scale. These *blue notes* are deliberately shaded slightly sharp or flat in relation to the 12 equally-divided (equal-tempered) tones represented by the keys on a piano (or the frets on a guitar) and give blues melody its distinctive emotional quality.

Research into the origins of blues has identified melodic inflections in the music of certain pre-slave-trade North African cultures that can be traced through time to field hollers—the unaccompanied songs of African-American slaves—and ultimately to African-American ensemble styles including blues, jazz, and gospel. Today, blue notes are everywhere, but to early-20th-century ears, they were exotic enough to prompt even W.C. Handy (the "Father of the Blues") to describe blues as "...the weirdest music I had ever heard."

The Blue 3rd

The traditional Western European system for organizing harmony and melody (the *diatonic system*) divides music into major and minor keys (*tonalities*) based on the size (*quality*) of the third scale degree, and a piece of music is usually written entirely within a specific tonality—e.g., G major or F minor.

In blues, however, the barrier between tonalities is extremely porous; blues melodies can include major and minor qualities as well as an in-between quality: the *blue 3rd*. In written music, the blue 3rd is notated as a *quarter tone*, which you produce by bending the string to a pitch halfway between two adjacent frets on the guitar:

Fig. 1: Minor, Major, and Blue 3rd

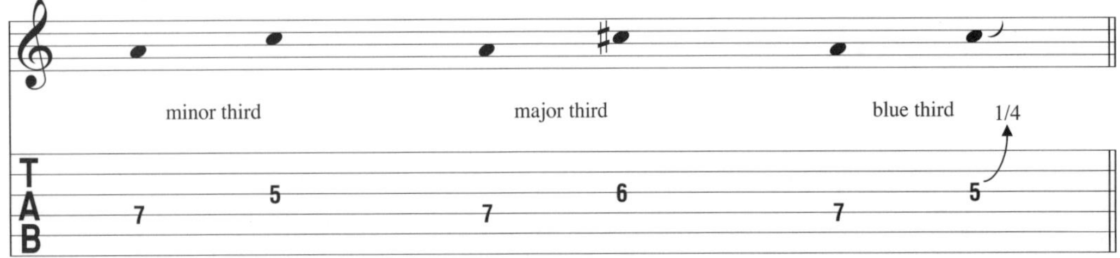

In addition to the quarter-tone bend, you can create the sound of a blue 3rd on the guitar by combining major and minor 3rds as described in the next example.

Fig. 2: Blue-3rd Phrasing Techniques

Performance Notes

NOTE: *Grace notes*, the small notes preceding the normal-sized notes on the staff, have no measurable time value and are not meant to be heard as distinct tones. After you pick a grace note, instantly hammer-on, slide, or bend into the next note to create the effect of a single, blended note.

1. **Quarter-Tone Bend:** This is the technique that most closely resembles the way vocalists inflect the blue 3rd. Fret C with your index finger and then bend the string downward (i.e., pull the string toward the floor) slightly toward C♯. The center of the blue 3rd is halfway between the two pitches, but you can also bend slightly more or less to vary the effect.

2. **Hammer-On:** Fret C natural with your index finger, pick the string, and instantly hammer onto the C♯ with your middle finger. Although the major 3rd (C♯) receives the emphasis, combining it with the minor 3rd suggests the in-between quality of the blue 3rd.
3. **Slide:** Fret C with your first finger, pick the string, and slide the finger instantly up to C♯ (in notation, a slide is indicated by a slanted line between two notes). At a distance of one fret, a slide sounds almost identical to a hammer-on and has the same melodic effect, but each technique has different applications that we'll explore later in the context of solo phrasing.

The sound of the blue 3rd is also built into the relationship between blues melody and blues harmony (Chapter 8 includes a more thorough discussion of blues harmony).

Briefly, in the diatonic system, melody is synchronized with harmony of the same quality; i.e., a major melody goes with a major triad, and a minor melody goes with a minor triad. In blues, however, the quality of the melody, which varies from minor to "blue" to major, is matched with a system of harmony based on the dominant seventh chord, which contains a major 3rd degree. The built-in "friction" between a minor or blue 3rd in the melody and the major 3rd in the harmony is another characteristic that gives blues its distinctive sound.

Fig. 3: Dominant Seventh Chord, Minor Pentatonic Scale, and Blue 3rd

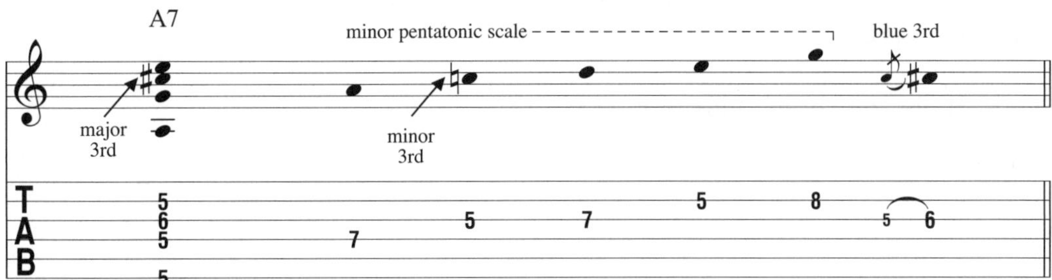

One of the most basic techniques of blues phrasing is to manipulate the various shades of the 3rd degree. The next example shows how different blue-3rd techniques are applied within a blues melody.

Fig. 4: Blue-3rd Melodies

Performance Notes

1. **Hammer-On:** Whether the melody is ascending or descending, always fret with your first (index) finger followed instantly by your second finger—treat the two fingers as a team.
2. **Slide:** Ascending, slide from C to C♯ with your first finger and fret D with your third finger. Descending, slide from C to C♯ with your first finger and fret A on the fourth string with your third finger. (Using your third finger rather than your second finger keeps your hand in position for the following phrase.)
3. **Bend:** There are several different shades of "blue" within a half step; listen carefully as you play to avoid over-bending.

Demo 2-1
(0:00)

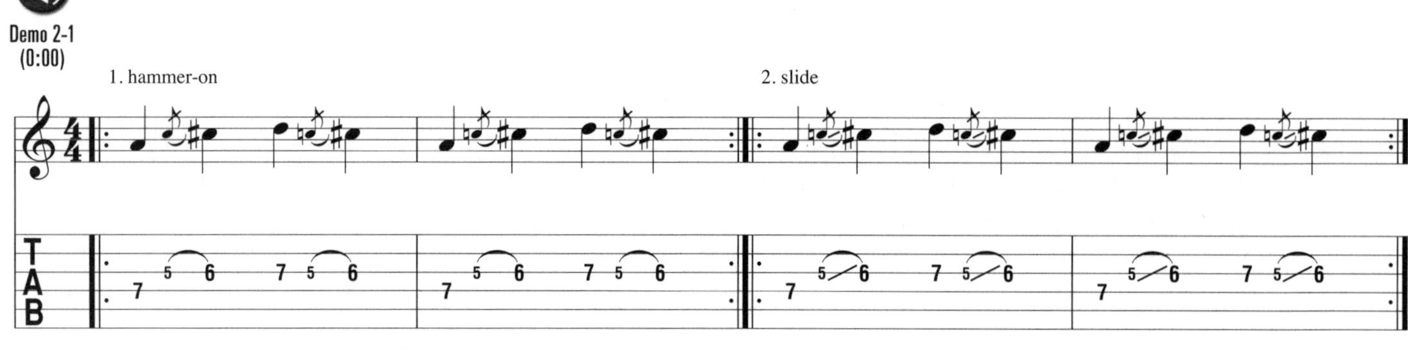

The ♭5th

The half step between the fourth and fifth scale degrees, commonly called the ♭5th, is another basic ingredient in blues melody and one that carries considerable musical baggage. In medieval music theory, its dark, dissonant quality was associated with impure thoughts and labeled *diabolus in musica* ("devil in music"). Blues itself has often been called "the devil's music," so it's only fitting that the ♭5th is a fundamental part of the sound.

Fig. 5: Minor Pentatonic Plus ♭5th

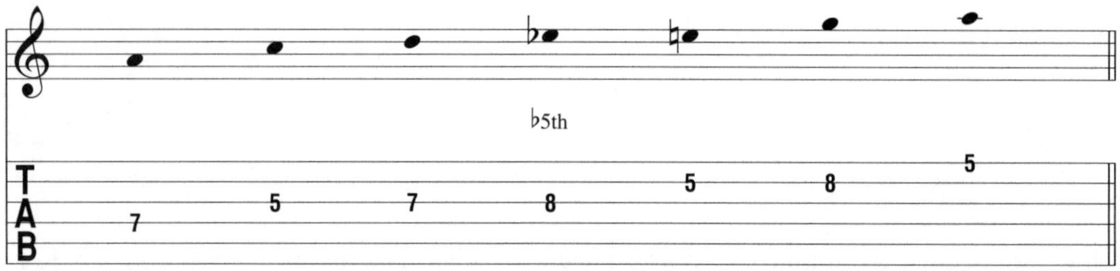

Phrasing the ♭5th in this fingering pattern requires using the third and fourth fingers. Hammer on or slide into it from one fret below or bend the fourth degree between a quarter and a half step (like the blue 3rd, the exact pitch of the flat-5th bend is flexible).

Fig. 6: ♭5th Phrasing Techniques

The next example applies the same techniques to both the blue 3rd and ♭5th when they are combined in a phrase. When you are comfortable with each technique, of course you can mix them up within a phrase any way you like—e.g., slide into the 3rd and bend into the ♭5th. Each technique creates a subtly different effect that gives the phrase a distinct personality.

Fig. 7: Phrasing with the Blue 3rd and ♭5th

Performance Notes

1. **Hammer-On:** Both ascending and descending, hammer on from your third to your fourth finger.
2. **Slide:** Ascending, slide from C to C♯ with your first finger, fret D with your third finger, and slide to E♭; descending, slide from D to E♭ and back with your third finger.
3. **Bend and Release:** Ascending, bend from D to E♭ and let go of the note before you pick E on the second string; descending, fret D, bend it toward E♭, and then release it without picking again. (For both bends and slides, picking or not picking the second note in the combination is a matter of choice.)

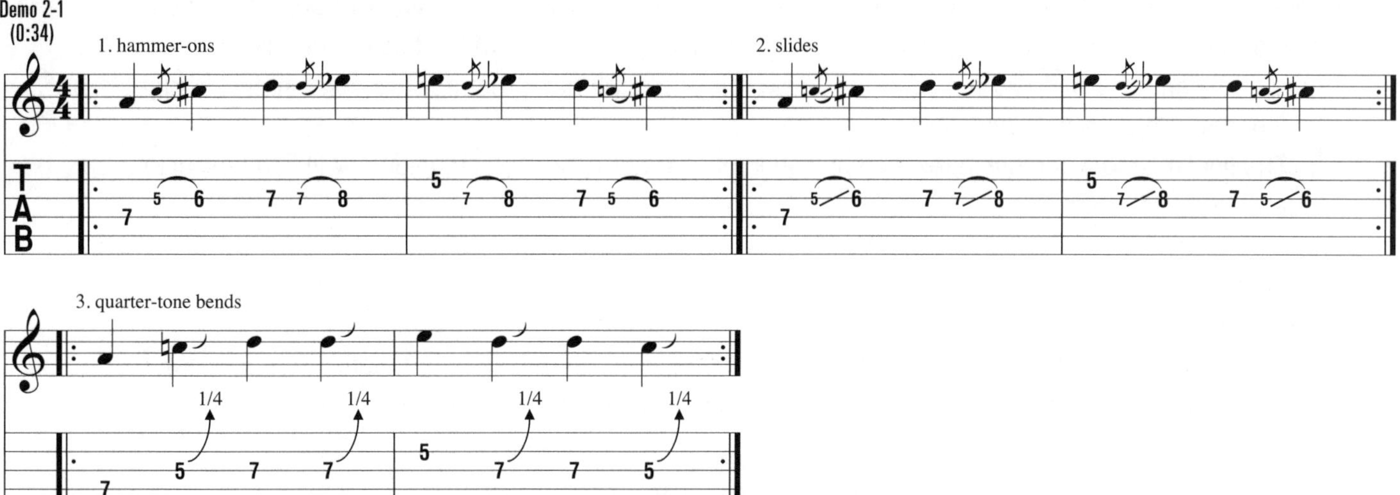

The ♭7th

The remaining blue note is the ♭7th (technically minor 7th). The ♭7th belongs to both the minor pentatonic scale and the dominant seventh chord, and the blue-note effect is achieved by bending it approximately a quarter tone sharp (the hammer-on and slide techniques don't apply to the ♭7th because they over-emphasize the major 7th, which clashes with dominant seventh harmony in a non-bluesy way).

In the one-octave A minor pentatonic pattern, the ♭7th is located on the second string. The "one-finger-per-fret" rule suggests using your fourth finger to fret this note, but because the blue-note bend requires some extra strength and control, many players prefer to use the third finger (or third and second fingers together) instead. In either case, be especially careful to avoid over-bending.

Fig. 8: Minor Pentatonic Scale with Blue 7th

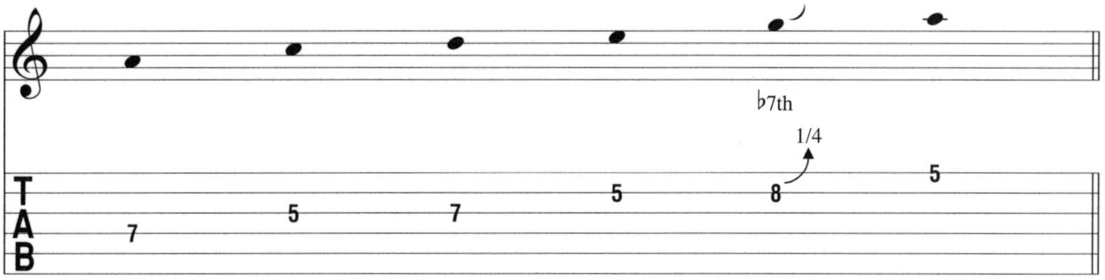

♭7th

1/4

The next example includes all three blue notes phrased with quarter-tone bends.

Fig. 9: Minor Pentatonic Scale with Blue 3rd, ♭5th, and ♭7th

The Blue-Note Pentatonic

Phrasing the minor pentatonic scale with all of the different blue-note inflections creates the melodic vocabulary that is at the heart of blues melody, and if you analyze a collection of traditional blues melodies and line the notes up in order within a single octave, most will fit within this pattern. Since blue notes greatly expand the melodic range of the basic minor pentatonic structure, the combination suggests a new name: the *blue-note pentatonic.*

The final example demonstrates a combination of blue-note phrasing techniques within a typical four-bar blue-note pentatonic phrase.

Fig. 10: Blue-Note Pentatonic Phrase

Performance Notes

1. Blues phrasing is complicated to read, and many of the details defy notation, so the best way to learn examples like this is to listen to the audio demonstration first and treat the printed music mainly as a reference.
2. Bar 2, beat 3: Use a finger roll between A and E.

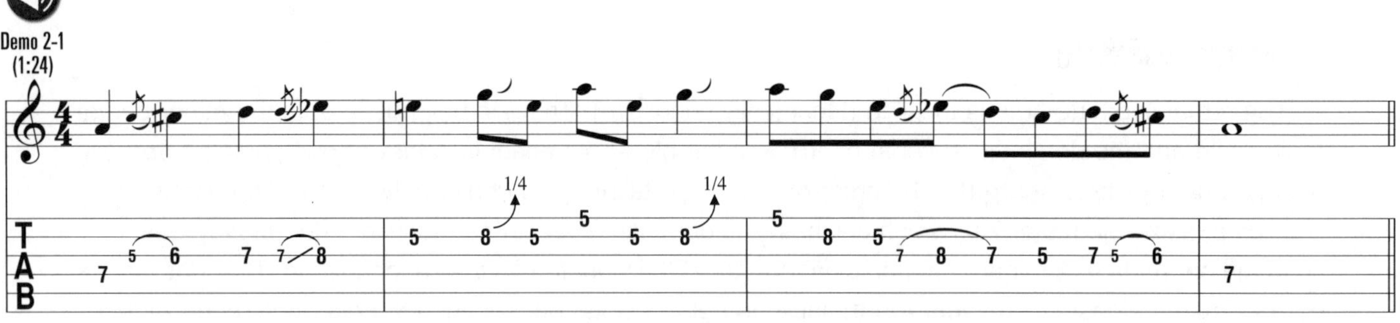

Chapter 2 Summary

1. Blues melody includes distinctive African-influenced vocal inflections called blue notes, specifically, slight alterations in the pitch of the third, fifth, and seventh degrees of the minor pentatonic scale:
   - Blue 3rd: A tone between the minor and major 3rd scale degrees
   - ♭5th: A tone between the fourth and fifth scale degrees
   - ♭7th: A quarter tone above the minor seventh scale degree
2. On the guitar, standard blue-note phrasing techniques include:
   - Quarter-tone bend
   - Hammer-on
   - Slide
3. The core melodic vocabulary of traditional blues is encompassed by the blue-note pentatonic, or minor pentatonic scale with blue-note phrasing.

Practice

1. **Figs. 2, 6, 8:** Repeat each specific phrasing technique until you can execute it quickly and accurately.
2. **Figs. 4, 7, 9, 10:**
   - Listen to each audio track to hear the proper phrasing.
   - Practice each example at a tempo at which you can execute it perfectly; if that's slower than the audio demo, repeat the exercise until you can match the audio tempo. When you can match the audio perfectly in tempo, move on—the same techniques will be used throughout this book, so you'll have many opportunities to apply them in different settings and at different tempos.

Listen

Recording technology was not invented until well after the end of slavery, so probably the closest approximation we have of what slave field hollers might have sounded like are Southern prison songs. Many of these were recorded decades later by Alan Lomax, who made field recordings of various American music styles in the 1930s and 1940s:

Prison Songs: Historical Recordings from Parchman Farm 1947–48 (Rounder Records)

Lomax also assembled a collection of field recordings of "down home" (rural Southern African-American) blues to accompany his book of the same name:

The Land Where the Blues Began (Rounder Records)

The first blues recordings were made in the early 1920s, and the influence of guitarists and vocalists from this decade was still strongly felt when the electric guitar era began two decades later:

Blind Lemon Jefferson, the first commercially successful male guitarist/singer/songwriter, cut dozens of records beginning in 1925. Check out "Matchbox Blues" and "Black Snake Moan."

Bessie Smith, one of the best-known of the "classic" blues singers of the early 1920s, cut one of the most famous versions of one of the most famous blues songs of all time in 1925 with W.C. Handy's "St. Louis Blues," featuring Louis Armstrong "answering" Smith with his horn.

Lonnie Johnson, the most versatile, virtuosic, and influential blues guitarist of the acoustic era, cut dozens of records beginning in 1925. Check out "Away Down in the Alley Blues."

Blind Willie Johnson was a gospel singer/slide guitarist, but gospel and blues are musically very similar in terms of blue-note inflections. Check out his slide/wordless vocal masterpiece "Dark Was the Night, Cold Was the Ground" from 1927.

3 Shuffle Phrasing – Rhythm and the Blues

Blue-note melodies are an essential part of the blues sound, but to create a *phrase*, or complete musical idea, we have to combine melody with rhythm. In this chapter, we'll look at how to create the basic style of phrasing that's at the heart of every great blues solo.

The Shuffle

The phrasing of a solo is inseparable from the feel of the rhythm, and the traditional rhythm of blues is the *shuffle*. The shuffle is derived from the *eighth-note triplet*, a rhythmic figure that consists of three equal notes in the space of one quarter note (or beat). When you play just the first and third notes of a triplet, the resulting lopsided rhythm is known as a *triplet shuffle*.

Fig. 1: Eighth Notes, Triplets, and Triplet Shuffle

Performance Notes

Tap your foot or set a metronome to a medium tempo (not too fast) and play a bar of even eighth notes, a bar of triplets, and then a bar of shuffled eighth notes. When you play the shuffle, count three notes per beat (tri-puh-let) but pick only the first and third notes of the triplet (tri-[ ]-let).

Repeat the sequence until the transition from one rhythm to the next is smooth and reliable (if you need help with understanding concepts like note values and meter, consult any basic music theory book).

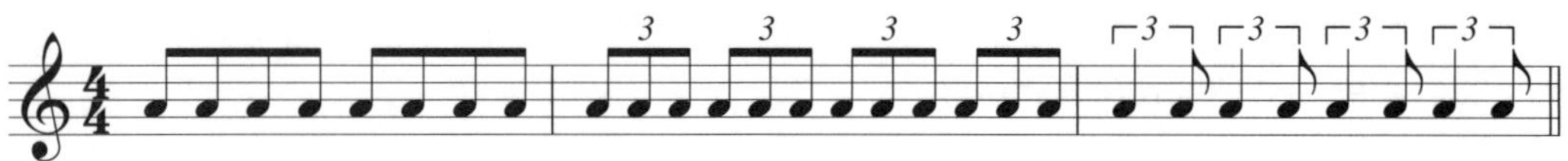

When you can transition seamlessly between rhythms on a single note, the next step is to play the minor pentatonic scale ascending and descending while you alternate between straight and shuffled eighths without pausing between rhythms, as shown in the following example:

Fig. 2: Minor Pentatonic Scale with Straight and Shuffle Rhythms

"Shuffle Feel"

As you can see from Fig. 2, triplet shuffle notation adds visual clutter to the staff. In order to make shuffle-based music easier to read, a more common approach is simply to include the word "shuffle" or "swing" at the beginning, indicating that, although the rhythms are written as straight eighth notes, you should interpret them with a shuffle feel (triplet notation is still used whenever the melody includes actual triplets). All examples from here on in this book will be notated in straight eighths but are to be played with a shuffle feel except where otherwise indicated.

Call-and-Response Phrasing

The basic rhythmic building-block of a blues solo is the two-bar phrase, which is (not coincidentally) also the standard length of a blues vocal phrase. Fig. 3 illustrates an example of blues lyrics arranged in a typical two-bar phrase.

Fig. 3: Typical Blues Lyric Phrasing

A standard line of blues lyrics consists of two one-bar phrases separated by a slight pause for breath. This is a natural, conversational cadence like the beginning and end of a thought—a question and answer—or, as it is usually described in the context of blues, *call-and-response*. Two-bar call-and-response phrasing is the basic unit of organization that is used in every form of blues to arrange individual ideas into a complete musical story.

One-Bar Phrases

The following listening and playing exercises are designed as introductory "conversational blues" lessons based on the classic call-and-response format. Each exercise provides a series of short, practical phrases for you to repeat in exact detail so that you gain fluency with notes, timing, and inflections. The phrases are based on the same ingredients you hear in actual blues solos, but the melodies are limited to just the one-octave blue-note pentatonic box pattern and employ only the blue-note phrasing techniques that have been presented so far in this book.

Notation is provided, but use it only for reference; this is an "ear" exercise designed to be played in tempo along with the audio track. Depending on your level of experience, you may need to repeat each exercise a number of times before you can match each phrase accurately in tempo. Feel free to keep moving ahead through the book, but come back to these exercises regularly until you are able to repeat the phrases in tempo with a high degree of accuracy. In addition to playing the exercise along with the recorded guitar, a separate rhythm play-along track is provided minus the guitar so you can also practice phrasing on your own.

Exercise 1: One-Bar Call-and-Response Phrases

Performance Notes

1. Start the audio track, listen, and repeat each phrase in tempo during the bar of rhythm that follows.
2. Repeat each phrase exactly as played, matching not only the notes but also the rhythms and details of the melodic phrasing.

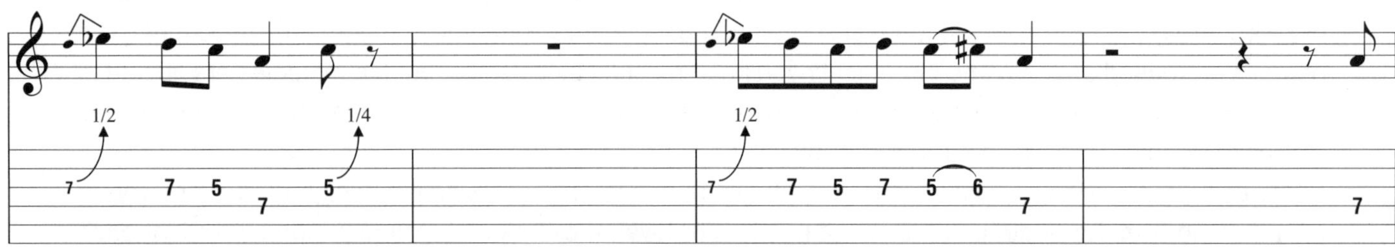

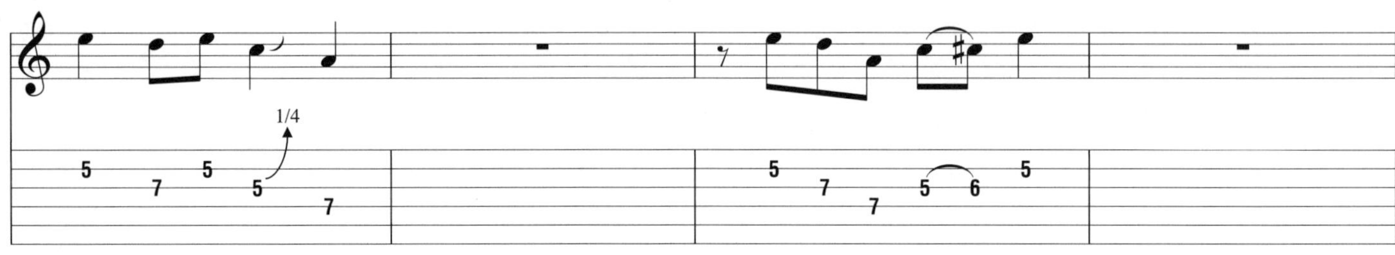

BM19IA QP110D86

BK Y M C

Serial Number	WBNK104496
Firmware Version	BM19IA.16.73
Color Pages	3399
B/W Pages	2023
Blank Pages	83
Total Pages	5505

1793

Dec 1 - Neutrality
Dec 2 - Peace

1800

Dec 4 - more intervention
Dec 5 - (back to being alone)
Dec 3 - peace

1820

Dec 7 - 130 again

Peace
Dec 1 ✓
2 ✓
3 ✓
5
7

Not
Dec 4

Rhythm, Melody, and Resolution

Effective one-bar phrases (and phrasing in general) depend on creating the right mix of two ingredients: rhythm and melody. We'll be working on this process throughout the rest of this book, but for now here are a few guidelines.

Rhythm

Blues phrases are almost invariably *syncopated*; i.e., rhythmic accents vary between downbeats and upbeats, but the placement of accents is more intuitive than technical. The rhythm of a phrase should feel complete apart from the melody. While you listen to the groove, hum or clap a one-bar rhythmic phrase; when the rhythm has a natural flow, combining it with just one or two notes is enough to turn it into a complete melodic idea.

Melody

The final note of a phrase completes the idea, and in general, the strongest choices are those that match the harmony—i.e., chord tones. In the A minor blue-note pentatonic, every note corresponds to a dominant seventh chord tone except the 4th (D) and ♭5th (E♭). When a phrase ends on one of these notes, it sounds *unresolved* (incomplete), as if you're putting a question mark at the end of a sentence instead of a period.

To illustrate, play the following two phrases and compare how they end:

Fig. 4: Resolving a Phrase

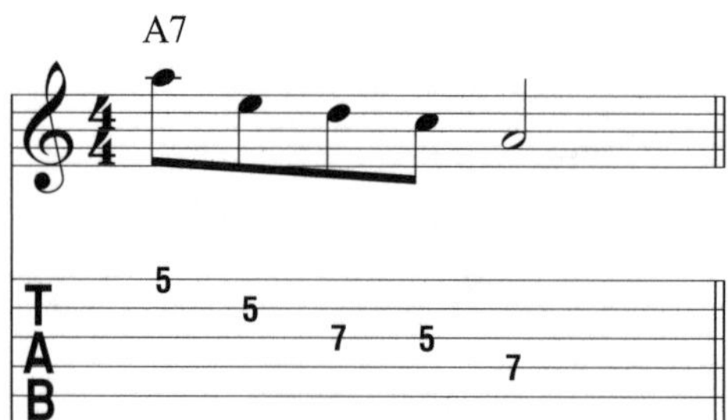

The first phrase, which ends on the 4th, sounds as though it is left "hanging" (in musical terms, *suspended*), while the second phrase, which ends on the tonic, sounds "finished" (*resolved*). You can hear the difference immediately, but a common mistake among guitarists is to choose notes with your eyes and fingers rather than with your ears. Since at this point the phrases are all limited to one position on the neck, a practical blues-style solution is simply to close your eyes when you play and let your ears take over.

Two-Bar Phrases

The next exercise introduces a series of two-bar phrases based on the same fingering pattern and techniques. Aside from additional practice in phrasing skills, these examples also test your ability to retain larger amounts of musical information. Follow the same procedures as for Exercise 1.

Exercise 2: Two-Bar Call-and-Response Phrases

Demo 3-2

Play-Along 1

1/4
1/2
1/4
3
1/4
3
1/2
1/4
3
1/4
1/4
1/4
3
3
1/4
1/4
3
3
3
1/2
1/4
1/4
3
1/4
1/4
3
1/4
1/4
1/4

Vocalization

Blues originated as a vocal style, so it makes sense that one of the quickest, most effective and intuitive ways to improve your soloing is to *vocalize*—i.e., sing or hum along with your guitar lines. As B.B. King put it, "I do feel that I'm still singing when I play. When I'm playing a solo, I hear me singing through the guitar" (*Rollin' and Tumblin': the Postwar Blues Guitarists*, by Jas Obrecht). Vocalizing acts as a sort of reality check on the musical value of a phrase and many, if not most, great blues guitar soloists vocalize, whether audibly or not (Albert Collins, for one, made it part of the show by vocalizing into the microphone while soloing).

When you practice a phrase on the guitar, you establish connections between your brain and your fingers that become stronger with time and repetition. Memorizing a phrase means creating a connection strong enough that you can retain and accurately repeat an idea in your mind, and what we call improvising is largely a process of recalling those memorized ideas on the spot. The goal is to hear each idea accurately in your mind *before* you play it and transmit it directly to your fingers without interference. When you vocalize, your voice acts as a physical link between your imagination and your fingers, helping to eliminate distractions and giving you better control over the timing and feel of each phrase. Since vocalizing is primarily a matter of breath control, it doesn't matter whether or not you sing in tune (even grunting works); likewise, vocalizing doesn't prevent you from playing fast, but it will help assure that your fast licks make musical sense.

You can practice vocalizing by singing along with the call-and-response exercises in this chapter as you play the "answers." Beyond that, apply the process to any phrase that you memorize—sing it first and then simultaneously sing and play it in tempo.

Visualization

Along with vocalization, another factor that has a great long-term impact on your soloing ability and your overall development as a musician is the process of *visualization*, or "seeing in your mind." The concept has been applied to fields from sports to science to business, but in relation to guitar soloing, it means replaying a phrase in your mind while you picture your hands playing it on the fretboard, including all of the fingerings and techniques.

Playing the guitar involves a lot of physical skill, but a great deal of what goes into being a successful musician is mental. The goal of visualization is to create an internal model of the guitar—a sort of virtual instrument that you carry with you at all times. After you memorize the sound of a phrase, you convert it into a mental movie of your hand playing the phrase on the neck so you can anticipate all of the technical challenges without actually touching the instrument. If your visualization is accurate, when you pick up the guitar—assuming your physical skills are equal to the task—you will be able to execute it perfectly the first time.

It's important to point out that you don't need to know the actual key of a piece of music before you visualize it. One of the beauties of the guitar is that, when you learn a fingering in one key, you can easily transpose it by moving up or down the neck. Over time, you may begin to "hear" common guitar keys like E and A, but *perfect pitch* (the ability to identify a pitch by name without an outside reference) is not a requirement for successful visualization.

To begin developing your ability to visualize, follow these steps:

1. Watch your fingers as you play any phrase that you know well and note the technical details: which finger you use on each note, how your fingers move from string to string, and so on.

2. Close your eyes and replay the phrase in your head, note for note, replicating each fingering detail.

3. Play the phrase again and compare your physical performance to your mental movie, working out any differences until they match perfectly.

Now apply this approach to a short phrase from a recording that you haven't already memorized but that sounds as though it is within your capabilities as a player (pick something from Exercise 1 or 2, for example):

1. Listen to the phrase and sing it (listen as many times as necessary to memorize it).
2. Close your eyes and visualize how you think it should be fingered, running it through in your mind while finding and solving any technically tricky moves.
3. Pick up the guitar and play the lick the way you visualized it. If your picture was accurate, it will closely match the original. If not, then repeat the process until you have a reliable internal model.

Make visualizing part of your regular routine when you learn new phrases. For example, rather than groping through a tabbed-out solo or trying to pick out licks from a recording by trial and error while making endless mistakes, take a moment to study the phrase, sing it, and visualize it before you attempt to play it. Again, it is not important that you visualize in the actual key; if you accurately hear and visualize the relationships between the notes (known as *relative pitch*) in one key, you can play it in any key.

Visualization is a skill that takes time to develop, but once you have created your internal model, you can learn new ideas more quickly because you can practice anywhere and at any time with or without an instrument.

Chapter 3 Summary

1. A **shuffle** rhythm includes the first and third notes of an eighth-note triplet.
2. **One-** and **two-bar phrases** are the basic building blocks of blues soloing, equivalent to the length and structure of standard blues vocal lines.
3. A **complete phrase** combines melody and rhythm with a strong resolution.
4. **Vocalization**—i.e., singing or humming along with your playing—is an intuitive blues-style way to improve your phrasing.
5. **Visualization** is a powerful learning technique that closes the gap between your hands, ears, and mind.

Practice

1. **Rhythm:** Repeat Figs. 1 and 2 until you can switch between rhythms accurately at a medium tempo without hesitation.
2. **One-Bar Phrases:** Play along with the audio track in two ways:
   a. Play one time through the exercise in tempo and match as many of the phrases by ear as you can without stopping; don't worry about mistakes.
   b. Go back to the first phrase that you didn't match precisely and isolate it.
      - Refer to the notation as needed to work out each detail of the fingering.
      - Visualize the phrase. Close your eyes and picture your fingers playing the phrase perfectly at a slow tempo.
      - Play the phrase slowly while vocalizing until you can execute it perfectly in tempo.
      - Repeat the same process for each phrase until you can match them all in tempo.
3. **Two-Bar Phrases:** Follow the same routine as for one-bar phrases.
4. **Vocalization:** Develop the habit by vocalizing the phrases in Exercises 1 and 2.
5. **Visualization:** Visualize each phrase in Exercises 1 and 2 until your mental picture accurately matches the fingering.

Listen

One- and two-bar phrases are the building blocks of all styles of blues, and all accomplished blues guitarists play them practically all the time. Some players, such as Albert King or B.B. King, typically separate their phrases with intervals of silence that make it easy to identify where they begin and end, while others, such as Johnny Winter, early Clapton, or Stevie Ray Vaughan, often connect one phrase to the next with little or no space between them. The breathing points are still there, but they're less obvious. The tendency to use "sparse" versus "dense" phrasing is one aspect of a player's overall style, but either way, good blues phrasing starts with a clear rhythmic structure.

Check out "Night Stomp" by Albert King (*Live Wire/Blues Power*) for a great example of how a master blues guitarist strings together clear one- and two-bar phrases, maintaining rhythmic momentum even without accompaniment.

4 Legato, Picking, and Dynamics

A musical phrase consists of three basic ingredients: melody (notes), rhythm (how notes are arranged in time), and touch (expressive techniques). So far, we have concentrated mainly on melody (the blue-note pentatonic) and rhythm (call-and-response shuffle phrasing), but in this chapter and the next we'll take a detailed look at the third and equally important ingredient: *touch*.

Touch is a catch-all term that includes all of the techniques that we use to add expression to a phrase or even a single note. This includes legato technique, picking technique, dynamics, sliding, bending, vibrato, and tone. In the blues guitar tradition, most players tend to use very similar melodies and rhythms, so a distinctive, personal touch is a highly-prized commodity and the mark of a true stylist. First, we'll look at the most common legato fretting techniques in blues.

Legato Phrasing

In Chapter 1, we looked at two techniques of legato phrasing—supportive fingering and the finger roll—but the most common legato techniques on the guitar are *hammer-ons* and *pull-offs*. While certain styles like jazz, fusion, and metal place a high value on fast, synchronized picking skills, legato remains the most common technique among blues guitarists.

Hammer-Ons and Pull-Offs

Legato technique shifts much of the responsibility for sounding notes from the picking hand to the fretting hand, and considerable fretting-hand finger strength is required to maintain the technique throughout the length of a solo. The following exercises are designed to build strength and endurance by applying legato techniques to the minor pentatonic scale (the pattern is extended across the neck to the sixth string).

Fig. 1: Hammer-On Exercise

Performance Notes

1. Use one-finger-per-fret fingering; this means using your fourth finger to hammer on notes at the eighth fret. (For certain techniques, the third finger is preferable, but your fourth finger is an essential part of versatile legato technique.) Apart from the main exercise, you may need to put in additional hammering practice with your fourth finger in order to develop and maintain a volume level that is consistently equal to the other fingers.
2. When practicing legato technique, position your fretting-hand thumb behind the neck opposite your fingers in order to maximize the vertical downward pressure with each finger. Once you build up some strength and endurance, you may allow your thumb to hang over the top of the neck.
3. Hammer-ons are indicated by a *slur* (curved line) connecting two different notes; pick the first note, and then sound the next note by bringing your finger squarely down on the string with authority so the hammered note equals the volume of the picked note. Do not use distortion when playing this exercise, as it covers up flaws in your technique by artificially compensating for variations in finger strength.
4. Maintain a strict triplet rhythm (three equal notes per beat) throughout.
5. The recorded example is performed at a moderate tempo in order to demonstrate how the technique should sound. To establish your own tempo, set your metronome to the tempo at which you can play the exercise perfectly and concentrate on playing with precise rhythm and even volume. Do not set the metronome faster and try to catch up. If you practice

properly, your "perfect" tempo will naturally increase over time; if you don't practice properly, you're just teaching yourself to play mistakes.

6. If you begin to feel any pain in your fretting hand, wrist, or forearm, stop and relax until the pain is gone before resuming. Muscle strain or tendonitis that results from over-practicing or improper technique will bring your playing to a complete halt, and the idea that you should "play through the pain" is a destructive myth. If you encounter persistent pain, you may need to seek medical advice and/or have an experienced private instructor evaluate your technique.

Demo 4-1 (0:00)

Fig. 2: Pull-Off Exercise

Performance Notes

1. Before you execute a pull-off, position both fingers on their respective frets (e.g., first finger at fifth fret, first string, and fourth finger at eighth fret, first string). Pick the note at the higher fret and then pull the finger sharply to the side, sounding the lower note at equal volume.
2. A pull-off is indicated by a slur; pick the first note and pull off to the next note.
3. Follow the same overall procedure as for Fig. 1.

Demo 4-1 (0:12)

Fig. 3: Combination Hammer-On/Pull-Off Exercise

Performance Notes

1. Both hammer-ons and pull-offs are indicated by slurs.
2. Execute each note of the hammer-on/pull-off combination at an equal volume.
3. Follow the general procedure for Fig. 1.

Demo 4-1 (0:24)

Picking Technique and Dynamics

Dynamics are variations in volume and intensity within or between phrases. Dynamics are such a natural part of singing and speech that we often notice them only when they're missing, as in the sound of a computer-generated voice. Dynamics are also essential ingredients in natural-sounding musical phrases, and the flatness that results from neglecting them is a real blues vibe-killer.

On the guitar, we control dynamics with the picking hand, and even if you mainly use legato phrasing, your picking technique has a big impact on your overall sound. Here is a survey of blues picking styles and how they affect your sound.

Flatpicking

Flatpicking is the most common electric blues picking technique. The pick is normally held between the thumb and index finger. Curl your index finger so the first joint is approximately parallel with your thumb, insert the pick with the tip perpendicular to the thumb and finger, and allow between 1/8 and 1/4 inch of the tip to protrude. The most versatile picking technique is to alternate down-strokes and up-strokes, known as alternate picking. For beginning players, down-strokes are easier to execute, but alternate picking greatly improves efficiency, and with practice, down- and up-strokes are equally easy to play.

Flatpicks come in dozens of sizes, shapes, and materials, and each variation influences the sound and feel. There is no universal ideal pick, but the shape favored by many players is the medium-sized "tear-drop" (triangular with rounded corners) about one millimeter thick. The size and shape should be big enough to grip comfortably but not so big as to be unwieldy, and for maximum dynamic range it should be thick enough to allow you to hit the strings hard with a minimum amount of flex. Thinner picks produce a brighter sound but also flex and crack more easily; thicker, rounded picks move across the strings more easily but sacrifice "bite," which is a significant factor in dynamics. Whatever type of pick you currently use, check out a few different shapes and sizes. They're inexpensive, and even a small change in size, shape, or weight can have a big effect on the sound and feel.

Flatpicking Dynamics

Many exercises designed to develop flatpicking technique concentrate on maintaining an even attack—i.e., maintaining the volume of the notes on every string at an equal, moderate level whether using down- or up-strokes. While technical consistency is a good thing in general, blues requires a wide dynamic range. The force of your attack is directly related to emotional intensity, so to uncover your full range of expression, you must learn to hit the strings both much harder and softer than average. The following exercises are designed to give you control over both ends of the spectrum.

Fig. 4 is an exercise in dynamic control with a flatpick; the notes are the same as in Fig. 1, but legato technique is replaced by alternate picking. The most intuitive place to use dynamic accents is on down-beats, but the exercise also requires you to put accents in unusual places in order to develop control over your picking. The exercise is fairly challenging, so before you perform it, prepare by following these steps:

1. Fret A on the fourth string at the seventh fret and play triplets against a slow metronome pulse using alternate picking technique. Maintain a steady down-up-down-up pattern so that the first triplet begins with a down-stroke, the second with an up-stroke, the third with a down-stroke, and so on.

2. When the picking pattern and triplet rhythm are consistent, add each of the accents indicated in Fig. 4. Practice each accent pattern—accenting the first, second, or third note of each triplet—until you can play it with complete accuracy. Changing accents is challenging, so it's essential to absorb the feel and sound of the dynamics on a single note before you attempt to apply them to the scale.

3. Next, using alternate picking, play through the scale without accents until the picking pattern is consistent. When your picking and fretting hands are completely synchronized, it's time to move on to the actual exercise.

Play the exercise as slowly as necessary in order to maintain absolute accuracy. The audio track accompanying the exercise is played at a moderate tempo to demonstrate the results, but you will need to set your own tempo as you did for the legato exercises.

Fig. 4: Flatpicking Dynamics

Performance Notes

Begin the exercise with a down-stroke and maintain strict alternate picking throughout, regardless of where the accents occur.

1. Play the exercise once, accenting only the first eighth note of each triplet.
2. Play it again, accenting only the second eighth note of each triplet.
3. Play it again, accenting only the third eighth note of each triplet.

Demo 4-2

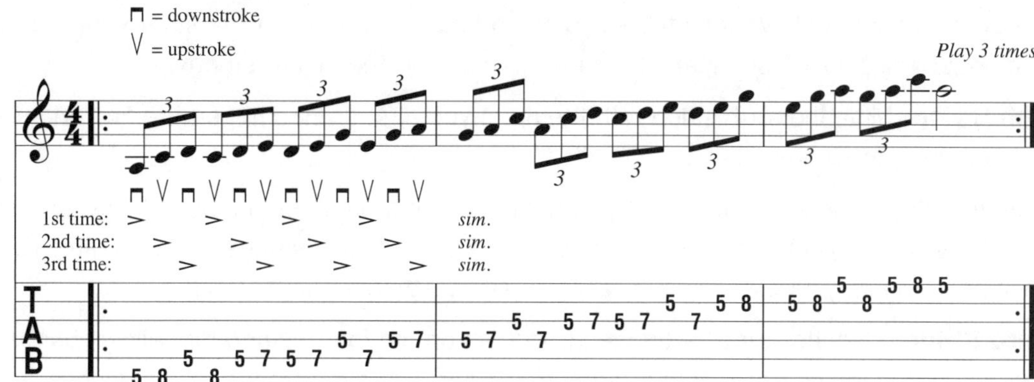

Like the legato exercises, this exercise in dynamics is very technical and not at all bluesy, but the point of all of these exercises is to gain control of your touch by focusing on the most miniscule details. Over time, through regular, brief periods of intense concentration, these techniques will become intuitive, and you won't need to think about them while you play. The results, however, will be obvious.

The Slap

The amount of energy we perceive in a phrase is directly related to the intensity of the attack, and the harder you hit the strings, the more intensity you create. *Slapping* means exactly what it says: increasing the energy by slapping at the strings with a larger motion that comes from the wrist and forearm rather than using a tight, focused pick attack. When you slap the strings, you strike not only the string you're aiming for but also the strings next to it. In order for the technique to be effective, your fretting hand must isolate the target string and mute the others. Stevie Ray Vaughan, for one, routinely used an aggressive attack that included slapping, and the technique is also applied in a number of the solos throughout this book. Here's the basic technique:

1. Fret A with your third finger on the fourth string, seventh fret.
2. Mute the fifth string by positioning the tip of your third finger so that it just touches the string.
3. Mute the top three strings by letting the first finger of your fretting hand lie lightly across them.
4. Using the "baseball bat" thumb-over grip, mute the sixth string with the side of your fretting-hand thumb.
5. Slowly drag the pick across all six strings; if the strings are properly muted, the only pitch you hear will be the fourth-string A surrounded by the percussion of the muted strings.
   If you hear any other notes, adjust your fingers as needed. When all strings are properly muted, slap the pick sharply across all six strings with a down-stroke. Only the A note should ring out clearly, while the other strings simply add sonic "weight."

When you learn to apply this technique quickly and accurately, you can attack the strings with all of the power at your disposal and still hear the melody clearly. It's certainly not necessary or desirable to constantly slap all six strings, but as with other techniques, the more control you have over the details of fretting-hand muting, the more freedom you will gain with your picking hand.

With a few adjustments, you can apply the same technique to any note on any string. Play the A minor pentatonic as follows. Since the essence of the technique requires accurate muting and coordination between hands, play it slowly and with complete accuracy. The notation shows the ascending scale only, but the same techniques also apply when descending.

Fig. 5: The Slap

Performance Notes

1. **Sixth String:** Fret A with your first finger and let the side of the finger lie lightly across the rest of the strings while your thumb stays behind the neck. Fret C with either your fourth or third finger while your first finger continues to lie across the higher strings.
2. **Fifth String:** Mute the sixth string with the tip of your first or third finger; the first finger still mutes the upper strings.
3. **Fourth String:** Use the same fretting technique as on the fifth string, but allow your thumb to curl over the top of the neck to mute both the fifth and sixth strings (if this is difficult, you'll need to aim your pick more carefully to avoid hitting the fifth string).
4. **Third String:** Use the same fretting technique as on the fourth string, but allow your thumb to curl over the top of the neck to mute both the fifth and sixth strings (if this is difficult, you'll need to aim your pick more carefully to avoid hitting the fifth string).
5. **Second String:** Mute the third string with the tip of your fretting finger (fret G with your third finger rather than your fourth—since the third finger is bigger, it makes a better mute). It's difficult for the thumb to mute the fourth string, so aim the pick more directly at the second string. For the clearest sound on the highest strings, combine the slap with picking-hand muting as described below (the rake).
6. **First String:** Mute the second string with the tip of the fretting finger and aim the pick at just the top two strings.

Demo 4-3

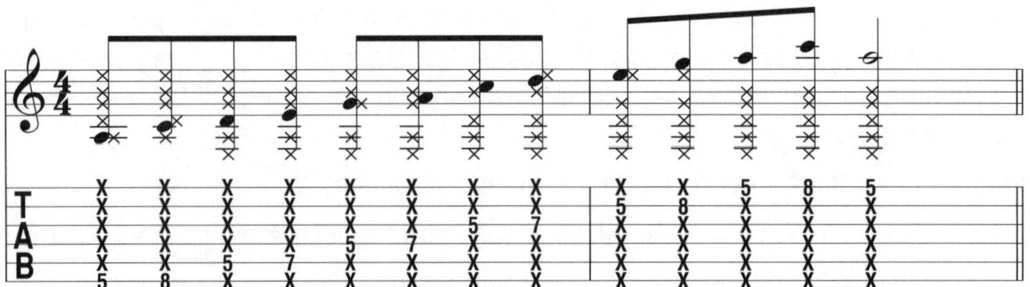

(**NOTE:** Audio is played twice—once at half speed as quarter notes, and once as written with eighth notes.)

The Rake

A technique related to the slap is the *rake*, a dynamic flatpicking technique that is also a stylistic trademark of B.B. King. To perform a rake:

1. Fret a note on the first string (e.g., A at the fifth fret).
2. Rest the heel of your picking hand on the strings slightly in front of the bridge; position your hand so your skin mutes all except the first string.
3. Position the pick on the sixth string and rake (or sweep) the pick across the muted strings with a fast, continuous down-stroke. A rake can also include fewer strings; the number of strings involved affects the speed and intensity of the effect.
4. Finish by striking the un-muted high string.

When executed properly, a rake sounds somewhat like taking a quick breath before singing a loud, clear note. Depending on the intensity of your pick attack, how quickly you execute the rake, how many strings are involved, and how much emphasis you place on the muted strings, you can make a rake sound more prominent or more subtle, but like most embellishment techniques, the rake works best when used as an occasional effect rather than as a constant feature.

For more practice, apply the technique to the call-and-response phrasing exercises in Chapter 3. Examples later in this book also incorporate raking in the context of solos.

Fig. 6: The Rake

Bare-Finger Picking

Most electric guitarists today learn to use a flatpick from the very beginning, but a number of major electric stylists, such as Albert King, Albert Collins, Gatemouth Brown, Guitar Slim, and Johnny "Guitar" Watson, built their musical personalities around the distinctive sound of a bare-handed attack.

If you use a flatpick, switching to bare fingers may feel like a step backward in terms of technique. But what you lose in speed, you gain in tone and dynamic control. Because the sound is so distinctive, some players who normally use a flatpick switch to their fingers on occasion (holding the pick in their teeth or tucking it away in their picking hand) in order to take advantage of the added dynamic range. A few players end up abandoning the pick altogether.

You don't need to follow any particular method to develop bare-handed technique; simply devote a portion of your practicing and jamming time to playing without the pick. Unlike classical guitar technique, which uses all five digits and demands an extremely precise balance between skin and fingernail, bare-handed blues picking technique usually requires only the thumb and index finger, with the bare skin as the main point of contact (calluses will develop over time).

To explore the feel and dynamic range of bare-finger picking, play the pentatonic triplet sequence on the next page by alternating between your thumb (indicated by "t") and index finger ("i"). Create accents by hooking your index finger under the string and snapping it against the fretboard on the release. For more practice, play the call-and-response exercises in Chapter 3 with bare fingers; a number of examples later in this book are performed with bare-finger or hybrid picking (see next page) as well. Developing a versatile picking attack is one of the best investments that you can make in your style.

Fig. 7: Bare-Finger Picking

Hybrid Picking

Hybrid picking combines flatpicking with bare-finger picking. In other words, while you hold the pick in the usual manner between your thumb and index finger, you also pick with your bare second and/or third fingers. The advantage of hybrid technique is that you can seamlessly switch from pick to fingers or combine the two to increase the dynamic range within a single phrase.

To practice hybrid technique, play Fig. 7 again but use your pick to attack the notes marked "t" and your second or third finger (either one is OK; the choice is a matter of preference) to attack the "i" notes. The accents will happen almost without trying, as hybrid picking is dynamic by nature.

Once you have developed a basic feel for the technique, the best way to expand your hybrid skills is simply to substitute one of your fingers for the pick within phrases you already know (such as the call-and-response exercises in Chapter 3). Once comfortable with the technique, you can choose either picking method based on sound.

Thumb-Picks

Acoustic finger-picking guitarists have long used thumb-picks to get a bigger sound compared to the bare thumb. Muddy Waters, for example, switched from bare-handed technique to a thumb-pick when he first moved from Stovall's Plantation to Chicago because he discovered that he needed to play louder just to be heard in crowded urban bars. Among electric guitarists, Freddie King (who also wore a metal finger-pick on his forefinger), Magic Slim, and many other Chicago guitarists, were known for their use of the thumb-pick.

The advantages of the thumb-pick for a finger-style player are that it provides a sharper attack on the low strings than the bare thumb and also offers the advantages of hybrid technique. Although the feel of the thumb-pick is considerably different from a flatpick, you can treat the thumb-pick somewhat like a flatpick by gripping it with your forefinger. To experiment with thumb-picking technique, play the triplet exercise in Fig. 7 or the call-and-response exercises in Chapter 3 using a combination of thumb-pick and fingers.

Eventually, almost all players settle on a single primary picking technique, but many players switch between different techniques in order to get different sounds. The point of any technique, after all, is simply to produce the sound you hear in your head, and as that sound evolves, your technique can evolve right along with it.

Chapter 4 Summary

1. **Legato Technique:** Using hammer-ons and pull-offs to create a smooth, flowing style.
2. **Dynamics:** Variations in volume controlled by the picking hand.
3. **Picking:** There are four main picking methods:
   a. Flatpick: The most common technique in all styles, including blues.
      - Alternate picking is the most efficient and versatile flatpicking technique.
      - The slap is a technique for creating maximum dynamic intensity with the flatpick.
      - The rake is a dynamic accenting technique favored by B.B. King.

   b. Bare-Finger Picking: Provides great dynamic variety and tone.
   c. Hybrid Picking: Combines the flatpick with bare fingers to gain the advantages of each.
   d. Thumb-Pick: A variation on bare-finger technique.

Practice

1. **Legato Technique:** Perform Figs. 1–3 for five minutes each per practice day. Set the tempo each day at the point where you can perform the exercise perfectly; there is no final upper limit, but a useful medium-tempo range is between 80–100 bpm. Compare your playing to the recorded examples for accuracy. These techniques apply to almost every blues solo, so consistency and accuracy of execution are essential for developing a reliable and versatile blues technique.
2. **Pick Dynamics:** Repeat Fig. 4 until you are able to execute the scale pattern accurately with dynamic variations at a steady tempo. Treat each dynamic variation as a separate exercise, developing each one until you can perform them all accurately at the same tempo.
3. **Slap:** Practice the technique as a scale exercise (Fig. 5) and then incorporate it into phrases like those from Chapter 3. Slapping provides intensity and dynamic variety, so to be effective, don't use it all the time—just when you really want to make a point.
4. **Rake:** Practice the phrases and gradually increase the tempo until you can match the tempo and execution of the audio demo for Fig. 6.
5. **Bare-Finger, Hybrid,** and **Thumb-Picking:** Perform the exercises with each technique to gain familiarity with the sound and feel. Study the sound and picking technique of the players you most admire; picking technique is a major component of every player's sound and style.

Listen

Every mainstream blues guitar influence relies primarily on legato fretting technique, but there are many variations in picking technique. Here are a few examples of each; listen to each one and focus your attention on the sound of their attack.

- **Flatpicking:** T-Bone Walker, B.B. King, Buddy Guy, Otis Rush, Jimi Hendrix, Stevie Ray Vaughan
- **Bare-Finger Picking:** Albert King, Albert Collins, Gatemouth Brown, Johnny "Guitar" Watson, Guitar Slim
- **Hybrid Picking:** Hybrid picking is by definition a variation on flatpicking technique, and many, if not most, flatpickers incorporate bare fingers at least occasionally.
- **Thumb-Picking:** Freddie King (combined with finger pick), Magic Slim, Muddy Waters, Jimmy Rogers, Johnny Winter, Jimmy Vaughan
- **Slapping:** You can hear this technique clearly in Stevie Ray Vaughan's "Cold Shot" or "Pride and Joy," but it's used by almost all flatpicking mainstream players from time to time. Check out B.B. King's "Worry Worry" (*Live at the Regal*) for a prime example of dynamics in action.
- **Raking:** This is a B.B. King trademark (check out "The Thrill Is Gone," where he executes a subtle rake on the very first note), but many other players use it to add dynamic emphasis to a high note. Once you learn the technique, it becomes easy to recognize it in other players.

5 Sliding, Bending, and Vibrato

Blues guitarists were among the first to explore the electric guitar's potential for vocal-style expressive techniques like sliding, string-bending, and vibrato. In this chapter, we'll take a detailed look at each of these essential ingredients of touch.

Sliding

In the early days of electric guitar, the only string sets sold in music stores were equivalent to acoustic strings—what we now consider heavy-gauge (typically .012 or .013 for the high E with a wound third string). Bending such heavy strings was difficult at best, so to add "grease" to their phrases, players would instead slide from note to note along one string. Eventually, lighter strings allowed string-bending to flourish, but finger-sliding remains an essential blues technique (*slide* or *bottleneck* guitar is a different technique altogether).

In addition to blue-note slides (Chapter 2), slides are also common between notes of the minor pentatonic scale. Fig. 1 shows some standard one-bar phrases that include ascending and descending slides based around the minor pentatonic pattern. The accompanying audio track demonstrates each slide slowly and then again at a medium tempo; the one-bar gaps allow you to repeat or answer each phrase.

Fig. 1: Sliding

Performance Notes

1. Bar 1: Sliding from the 4th to the 5th followed by the ♭7th is one of the most common phrases in blues. In the box pattern, it requires a temporary position shift—i.e., slide up two frets with your third finger, fret the ♭7th with your second finger, and then slide back down with your third finger.
2. Bar 3: This is the same phrase with slightly different rhythm.
3. Bar 5: Slide up the third string from the 4th to the ♭5th, pick the second string, and then slide back down the third string and pull off in one continuous motion (another extremely common technique).
4. Bar 7: Slide from the 4th to the ♭5th and back in one continuous motion followed by a pull-off. Execute the final slide from the minor 3rd to the 4th and back with your first finger.
5. Bar 9: Add some "grease" to the tonic by sliding into it from below with your third finger. Use the same finger to slide up the third string and back.
6. Bar 11: Here's another common sliding variation ending with an octave jump from the fourth to the first string. Add extra "ping" to the last note by picking it with the bare third finger of your picking hand (hybrid technique).

Bending

String-bending can be heard on some of the earliest acoustic blues guitar recordings—particularly those by virtuoso stylist Lonnie Johnson—but the technique was limited by the heavy strings, high action, and limited sustain of acoustic instruments. After the introduction of the electric, blues guitarists like B.B. King figured out that by replacing the high E of a store-bought set with a banjo string and moving the rest of the set over a notch—i.e., moving the E string to B, etc.—they could perform bigger, vocal-style bends. This trend culminated with the no-limits string-stretching of players like Albert King, Buddy Guy, and Hendrix. However you use string-bending in your own style, a few fundamental techniques are essential for accuracy and consistency.

Whole-Step Bends

The most common bend in blues (after blue-note inflections) is the whole-step bend, which is the equivalent of two frets on the guitar. A basic technique for maintaining pitch accuracy and endurance when bending is to fret the string with multiple fingers (*supportive fingering*). While most of the strength required to bend a string is provided by the wrist muscles, supportive fingering ensures that the string stays firmly clamped against the fret.

Fig. 2 shows whole-step bends within the minor pentatonic scale in home position. Follow the fingering instructions below carefully before you play the examples.

Fig. 2: Common Whole-Step Bends

Performance Notes

1. Before each bend, fret the note you're aiming for (up two frets) to establish the correct pitch—inadvertently bending out of tune is a mortal musical sin.
2. Execute all bends with the first, second, and third fingers working together. Position your third finger on the note to be bent with the second and first fingers behind it on adjacent frets and use all three to push the string up (toward the ceiling). Hook your thumb over the top of the neck to provide leverage (you can also bend the third string by pulling it down, but the upward bend is more common).
3. As you bend, push the adjacent strings aside while keeping the string that you're bending under your fingertips, slightly separated from the others.
4. In bars 1–6, each bend is played slowly and then fast (indicated by grace notes); the technique is the same for both, but since a grace note has no measurable time value, the bend is essentially instantaneous.
5. When you bend the second string from the ♭7th to the octave and the first string from the minor 3rd to the 4th, shift your hand up one fret while keeping the three fingers grouped together (some players bend these strings with the fourth finger, but the third finger is more common).

6. When the note reaches the correct pitch, mute the string with the side of your picking-hand thumb to avoid hearing it go flat when you release the bend (unless the release is deliberate, as described below).
7. Bars 13–16: It's very common to follow a whole-step bend on the third or second string by playing the same note on the next higher string. Before you pick the higher string, mute the bent string with the side of your picking-hand thumb. When E (second string) and A (first string) are played back-to-back within bending phrases like these, it's common to use a first-finger barre rather than a finger roll.

(**NOTE:** The audio track is performed with hybrid picking—i.e., plucking the higher strings with bare fingers. This creates a punchier attack as well as a warmer tone, similar to the bare-fingered sound of Albert King.)

Releasing a Bend

Audibly returning a bent string to its starting point is called a *release*. When you release a string, you need to avoid sounding the adjacent open strings as your fretting hand breaks contact with them. You can eliminate most of the unwanted sound with accurate bending technique, but your picking hand also plays a role by applying *palm muting* (the same technique used for the rake). When you bend, rest the heel of your picking hand on the lower strings near the bridge; if you inadvertently sound an open string while releasing a bend, the palm-mute will deaden the sound.

Fig. 3: Releasing Bends

Performance Notes

1. Bars 1–6: Bending is often accompanied by a rake. The same palm-muting technique applies to both the rake and the release. Vary the tone and dynamics by using bare fingers instead of the pick.
2. Bars 7–14: A release is often followed by a pull-off. Pick the first note of each group and then execute the bend, release, and pull-off in a continuous motion.

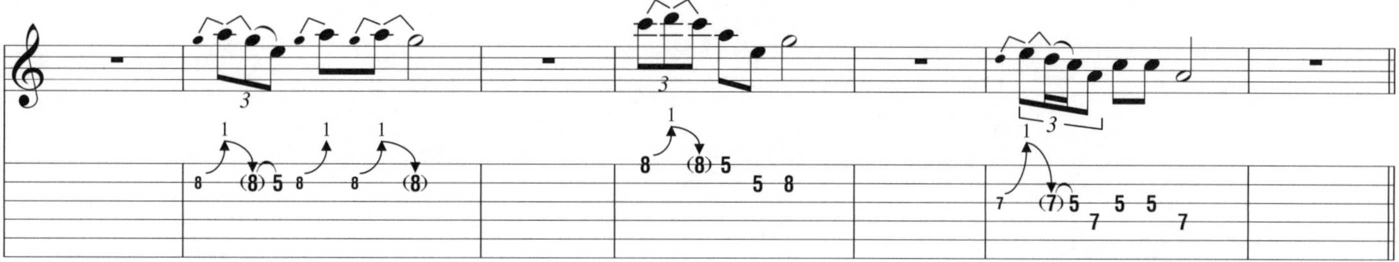

Pre-Bending

An excellent way to improve the pitch accuracy of your bends is to practice bending the note exactly to pitch *before* you pick it—a technique known as *pre-bending*. Accurate pre-bending depends on knowing exactly how much strength it takes to bend the string to a certain pitch; in other words, you feel the pitch before you hear it.

To practice pre-bending, play the bends from Fig. 2 using the following technique:

1. Play the "target note" (e.g., E on the third string, ninth fret) to hear the pitch for which you're aiming.
2. Fret the same string two frets below and bend it (don't pick), estimating how far you need to bend and how much strength it takes to match pitch.
3. Pick the note to find out how close you came.
4. Repeat until accurate.

With practice, you will know the precise amount of strength it takes to hit a given pitch accurately on your guitar without trial-and-error (the feel will vary from one guitar to the next depending on set up and string gauges). Apart from its value as an exercise, pre-bending has a unique sound when you combine it with vibrato. Hendrix, for example, made pre-bending one of his stylistic trademarks.

Half-Step Bends

Within blue-note pentatonic phrases, the most common half-step bends are slight extensions of the quarter-tone blue-note bends covered previously. Half-step bends require a very light touch, so use the pre-bending exercise in order to develop precise control and avoid over-bending (also see Fig. 5 on the next page). Since less strength is required, small bends can be managed with one finger, but supportive fingering is still recommended whenever possible. (Phrases that incorporate half-step bends are included in various solo examples later in this book.)

Fig. 4: Half-Step Bends

Performance Notes

1. C to C♯ (third string): This bend is usually accomplished with the first finger alone, but you can also move your hand down a fret and use the first and second fingers combined for greater control.
2. E♭ to E (third string) and C to C♯ (first string): Use the third finger backed up by the second.

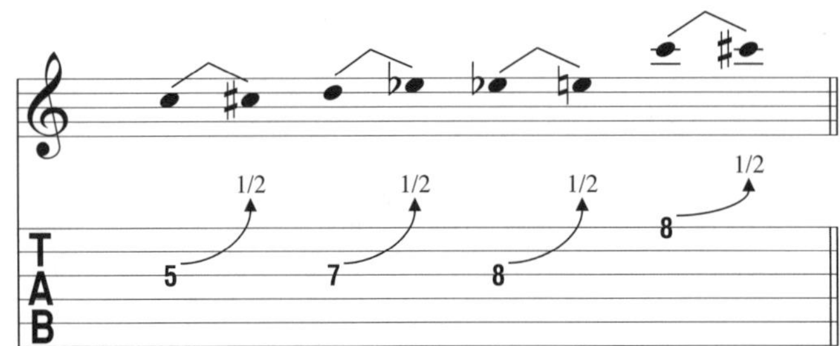

Big Bends

T-Bone Walker set the early standard for electric blues string-bending in the 1940s, and B.B. King expanded the vocabulary in the 1950s, but in the mid-1960s, Albert King literally took the technique to new heights with bends of as much as two whole steps.

Like many of his rural Southern contemporaries, when he was young King played a *diddley bow*, a traditional one-stringed instrument assembled out of wire, nails, and wood that's played by sliding a bottle along the string. After he graduated to a real guitar (ultimately, a Gibson Flying V), King continued to echo the slippery sound of the diddley bow with a technique that combined ultra-wide string bends and extremely subtle pitch shading.

King's guitar setup was definitely non-standard. A left-hander, he turned right-handed guitars upside-down without reversing the strings, used an unusual open tuning, strung his guitar with a light-gauge set, and picked with his bare fingers—all factors that combine to make his sound very challenging to duplicate. However, countless players have been inspired to adapt his style to more conventional setups, and his phrases are widely quoted in both blues and rock to this day.

King executed most of his bends on his high (thinnest) string, but on guitars with standard tuning and string gauges, accurately bending the high E string two whole steps is difficult at best. In the following example, these wide bends are transferred to the second string to take advantage of its lower tension. Bending accuracy is also affected by your setup; a floating vibrato tailpiece, for example, will tend to counteract bends and require proportionately greater effort to stay on pitch. When you practice big bends, your fingertips will very likely get sore, but this will diminish as your calluses thicken. It takes time to build up the necessary strength, so if you begin to feel any strain in your hand, wrist, or forearm, take a break to avoid injuring delicate muscles.

Fig. 5: Two-Step Bend/Release Exercise

Performance Notes

1. Place your index finger on A on the second string, 10th fret. This note is the tonic of the key and also your primary visual reference point for this pattern. To transpose the same phrases to any other key, locate the tonic with your index finger on the second string (e.g., G at the eighth fret).
2. To "tune" your ear in preparation for bending, play the series of half steps between C (2nd string, 13th fret) and E (17th fret) ascending and descending.

3. Fret the second string at the 13th fret (C) with your third finger backed up by the second and first fingers. As noted earlier, string-bending muscle power originates in the wrist, but bigger bends require more finger strength to keep the string clamped firmly against the fret, so for accurate bending, you will need the strength of all three fingers working together.
4. Bend the string in successive half steps: first to C♯, then D, D♯, and finally E, which is two whole steps above the starting note (pick with a bare finger to more closely emulate Albert King's sound).
5. Gradually release the bend, pausing briefly at each half step, until you return to the original, un-bent C note. Releasing bends in tune is actually more challenging than bending in tune; it requires a very gentle touch combined with a precise sense of pitch.

Demo 5-4
(0:00)

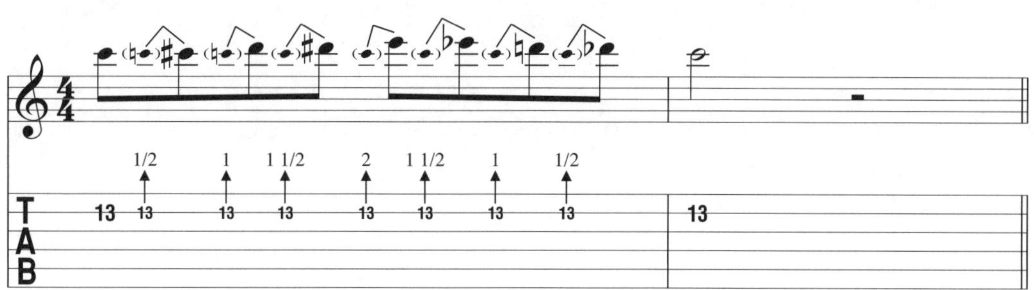

The next exercise involves bending and releasing half steps between A7 chord tones, also on the second string. Bend from one chord tone to the next and release the bend in half steps. Then shift your third finger (supported by the first and second) to the next chord tone and repeat.

Fig. 6: Chord Tone Bend/Release Exercise

Demo 5-4
(0:18)

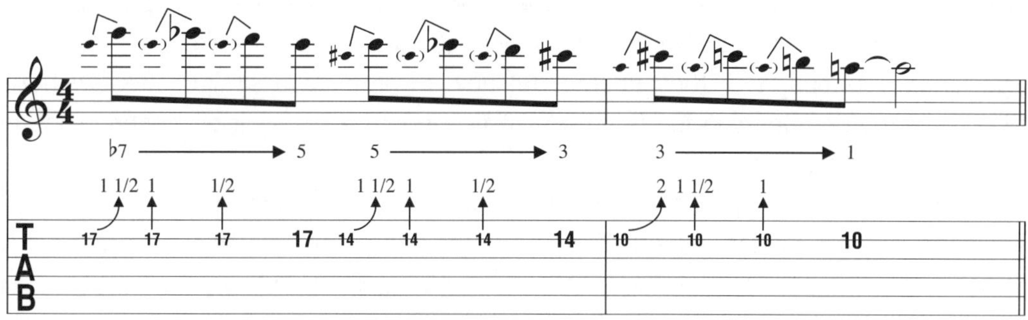

The final example demonstrates different combinations of bent notes. The notation is provided for reference, but this is mainly an "ear" exercise. Listen and match the phrases multiple times until you both feel and hear the details. Increase your accuracy by applying the pre-bending exercise to these larger bends. King routinely pre-bent strings with micro-tonal precision.

Fig. 7: Phrasing with Big Bends

Performance Notes

1. Bar 11: One of King's trademark techniques was to bend past a note and then partially release the string to come into a pitch from above rather than below (a "reverse bend"). This creates a crying effect that was especially powerful on slow blues. This type of bend is difficult to notate, but you can hear it on the accompanying audio.

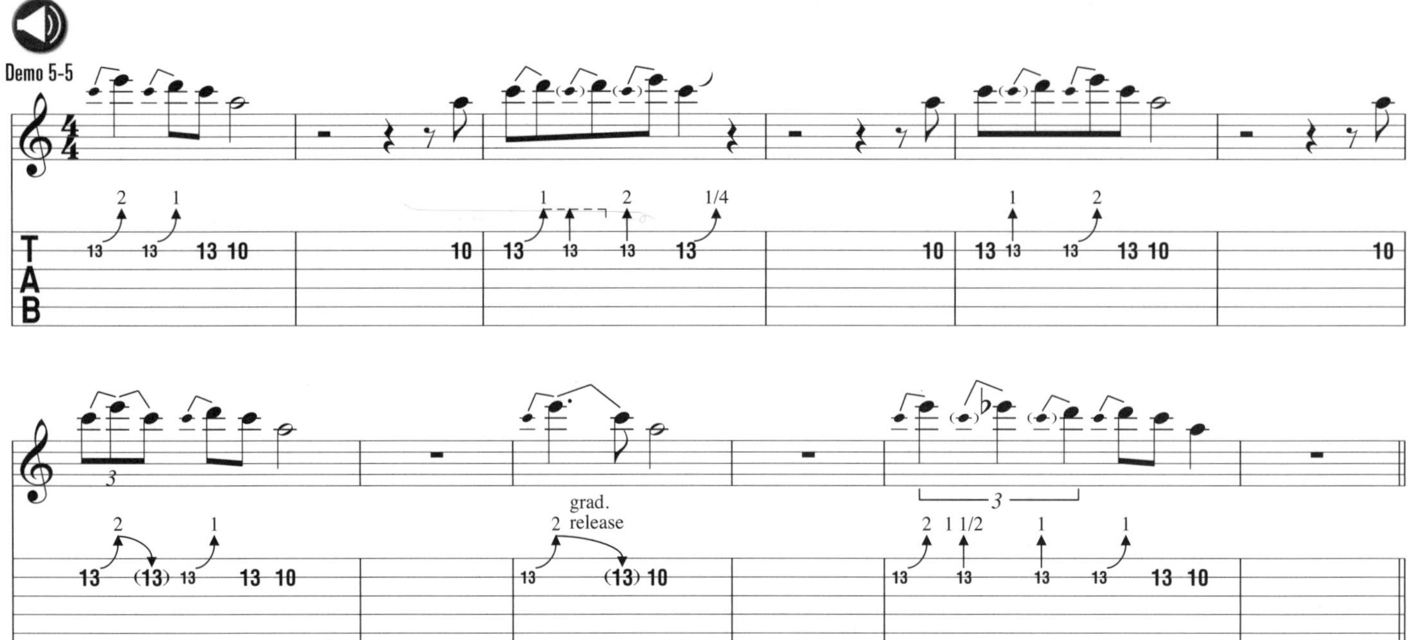

Vibrato

From the biggest bend we now turn to the smallest—the subtle, rhythmic variation in pitch known as *vibrato*. (This term is often confused with *tremolo*, which is a rhythmic change in volume—not pitch). Like vocal vibrato, guitar vibrato sustains and polishes the end of a phrase, allowing you to hold a note with confidence and arrange your phrases more economically. When mastered, vibrato is one of the most expressive techniques in the blues guitar repertoire.

The vibrato technique that we use on the standard electric guitar today was popularized in the 1950s by B.B. King. Inspired by the vocal-style vibrato of acoustic slide guitarists like his cousin Bukka White and Chicago kingpin Tampa Red, King figured out how to produce a similar effect without the slide and combined it with string-bending to create a stylistic signature that quickly became one of the core elements of electric blues guitar.

There are three basic techniques for producing vibrato on a stringed instrument (not counting the vibrato bar, which is a mechanical effect). The first technique, known as "violin vibrato," is created by rocking the finger back and forth along the length of the string. This works well on a fretless instrument like the violin, but on a guitar, the fret limits the amount of pitch-change and makes the effect too subtle for blues. The remaining two techniques, *finger vibrato* and *wrist vibrato*, are the techniques used by blues guitarists.

Finger Vibrato

Finger vibrato is created by pulling a string slightly downward (toward the floor) and essentially wiggling your fingers in a controlled manner. Vibrato consists of two elements: rate (how quickly the note changes pitch) and width (the amount of pitch change). The key to effective vibrato is to develop complete control over both. It takes a fair amount of time and effort to develop the necessary coordination; here's a good exercise.

Fig. 8: Finger Vibrato
Performance Notes

1. Fret D on the third string, seventh fret with your third finger backed up by the first and second. Hang your fretting-hand thumb over the top of the neck to provide a fulcrum.
2. Pick the string and pull your fingers down (toward your hand) just enough to raise the pitch about a quarter tone. Release the string to its starting point and repeat the bend several

times while the note sustains (without picking again). This is the fundamental technique of finger vibrato.

3. Set your metronome to a tempo of 60 bpm.
4. Bend and release the string evenly on each beat in a pattern of eighth notes. Pick on every other beat (i.e., beats 1 and 3) and maintain the rate and width of each bend with absolute consistency.
5. When the eighth notes are consistent, increase the rate to eighth-note triplets (bend-release-bend), then 16th notes (two bends and releases per beat), 16th-note triplets (three per beat), and finally 32nd notes (four per beat). Do not increase the rate until you have established complete control at the previous rate. A natural-sounding, vocal-style vibrato falls somewhere in the range of 16th-note triplets or 32nd notes at 60 bpm (the exact width and rate of your vibrato is a stylistic choice).
6. To take it faster, raise the tempo one click and repeat the sequence of rhythms; when the rate becomes too fast to count, listen for overall consistency. Once you have control of the technique, you don't need to think about the rhythmic values; the singing quality is what counts.

Demo 5-6

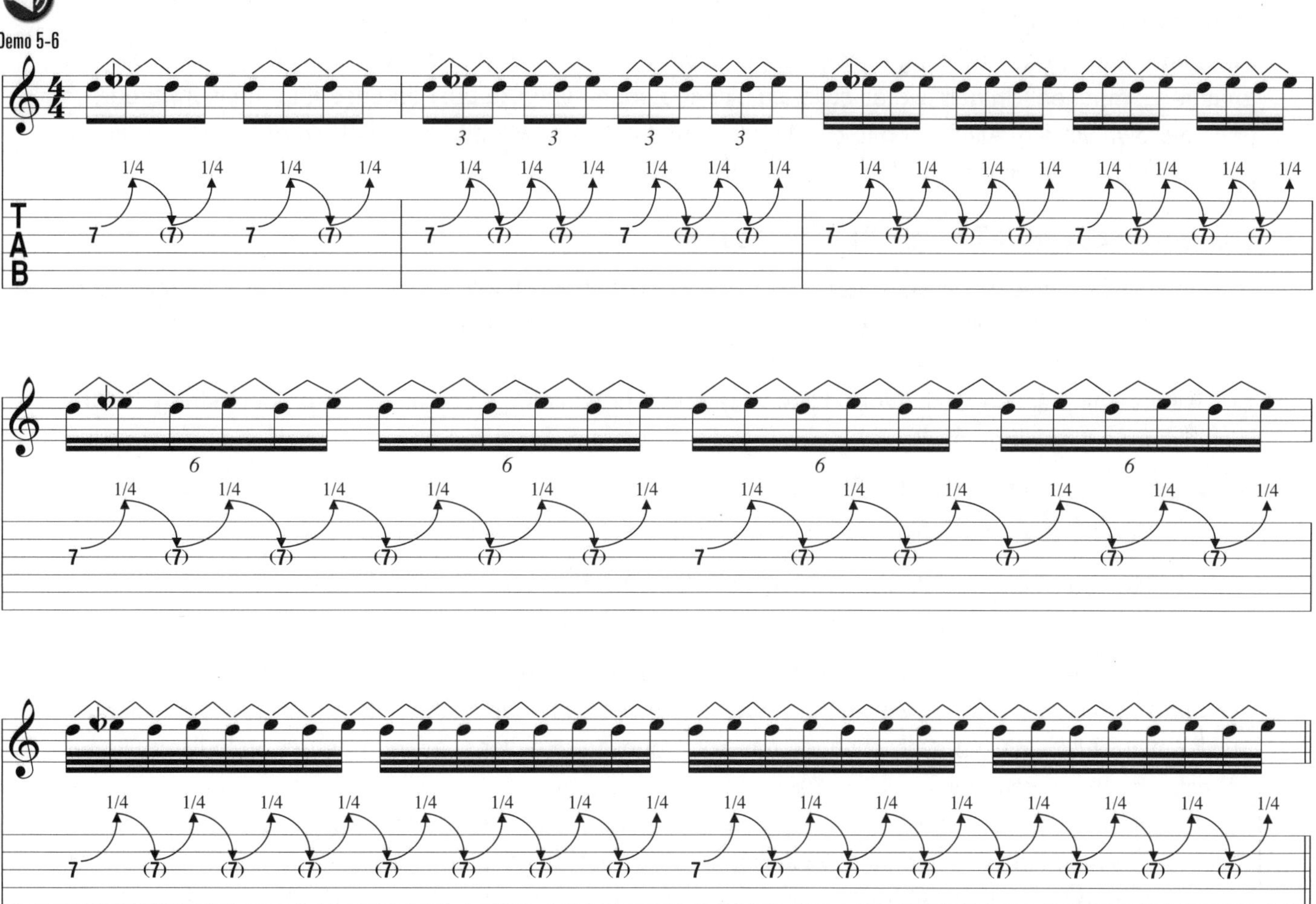

Finger vibrato is useable on the third string and below, but on the two highest strings (E and B), pulling the strings downward tends to take them right off the edge of the fingerboard. On these strings, you need to use *wrist vibrato* (described next) unless you're a left-hander playing a right-handed guitar turned upside-down like Albert King or Otis Rush—both, incidentally, renowned for their vibrato—in which case the opposite is true.

Wrist Vibrato

Wrist vibrato is produced by pushing the string up (toward the ceiling) rather than pulling it down, so it is the ideal technique for adding vibrato to notes on the first and second strings. However, when you change the direction of the bend, you bring a different set of muscles into play. So, while the results sound the same, the technique is quite different. To see how, place your third finger (backed up by the first and second) on D at the third string, seventh fret. Bend the string upward and carefully observe what happens: your wrist cocks upward and pushes your fingers across the neck, taking the string along with them. While your fingers hold the string against the fret, it's actually the muscles in your wrist that are doing the work of bending—hence, *wrist vibrato.*

The exercise for developing wrist vibrato is the same as for finger vibrato: fret a note, push it up a quarter tone, release it, and repeat at increasingly faster rates while maintaining absolute consistency. Wrist vibrato involves a more complex muscular interaction than finger vibrato so you should expect to spend more time mastering the technique, but the same disciplined approach will gradually train the muscles and neural pathways to act together. Like other guitar-playing skills, what may be awkward and uncoordinated at first will become natural and unconscious over time.

Along with a methodical approach to mastering vibrato, it's also very important to keep a target in mind—i.e., your ideal vibrato. There is no universal standard for what constitutes the perfect vibrato. B.B. King's wrist vibrato, for example, is faster and narrower than Albert King's finger vibrato, but Hendrix (who was left-handed but played right-side up) perfected a wide, slow wrist vibrato. Each player's vibrato is a natural component of their overall style, so pick the sound you like best and use it to measure progress on your own vibrato. Also, listen to good singers and notice how they use vibrato to round off and polish the ends of notes; vibrato is, after all, a vocal technique applied to the guitar.

Bending Plus Vibrato

One of the most expressive ways to use vibrato is to combine it with a string bend. You can apply either finger vibrato or wrist vibrato to a bend, but since the sound is particularly effective on the high strings where wrist vibrato is required, that's the first technique to master.

The overall practice routine for adding vibrato to a bend is the same as for an un-bent string, but the details are a little different:

Adding Vibrato to a Bend

1. Bend D to E by pushing the string up (toward the ceiling) with three fingers.
2. Release the bend by a quarter tone, bend it back to pitch, and repeat the motion, progressing through the rhythms as described in Fig. 8.

On an un-bent string, vibrato is created by bending the note slightly sharp and returning to pitch. When you add vibrato to a bend, however, the vibrato is created by releasing the note slightly and bending back up to pitch. Although the pitch changes move in opposite directions, as long as the underlying pitch is consistent, the vibrato sounds in tune either way.

To gain full control of your vibrato, you need to train your muscles to respond unconsciously and without hesitation anywhere on the neck. Apply vibrato exercises to other strings and positions. Practice vibrato on bends of various sizes from blue notes to two-step, Albert King-size stretches or add vibrato to the end of a slide (a signature technique of Albert Collins). It is likely to take some time before your vibrato becomes completely reliable, but once you master it, it will serve you for as long as you play.

Chapter 5 Summary

1. **Sliding** from note to note along one string is a classic technique for adding "grease" to a phrase.
2. **Bending:** Bends can extend from quarter-tone blue-note inflections to half steps, whole steps (the most common), and radical, two-step bends like those perfected by Albert King.
3. **Vibrato** is produced by two main techniques:
   a. **Finger vibrato** is produced by pulling the string down (toward the floor) using the finger muscles; it's not effective on the top two strings.
   b. **Wrist vibrato** is produced by pushing the string up (toward the ceiling) with the wrist muscles; it's the most effective technique on the top two strings and in combination with string-bending.

Practice

1. **Sliding:** Practice each phrase in Fig. 1 until you can perform it accurately in tempo with the accompanying audio track.
2. **Bending:** Figs. 2–7 demonstrate specific string-bending techniques. Each audio track demonstrates the examples at a slower tempo and again along with a rhythm track at a medium tempo. The spaces included allow you to "answer" each phrase. Work out the details of each phrase by listening, singing, visualizing, and practicing at a tempo where you can execute it perfectly, and then play along with the track.
3. **Vibrato:** Vibrato technique takes time to develop. As with any physical fitness routine, muscles respond gradually. Repeat the brief exercise just a few times a day but don't be discouraged if you don't perfect the technique quickly; the result is worth whatever time and effort it takes to achieve it.

Listen

Slides

Every blues guitarist uses sliding to some extent, but the technique was most widespread in the earlier days of electric blues and is still the norm in jazzier blues styles. Check out Stevie Ray Vaughan's "Stang's Swang" or Kenny Burrell, one of Vaughan's jazz-blues influences ("Chitlins con Carne," among other tracks) for good examples of sliding combined with legato technique. Among more straight-ahead blues stylists, Albert Collins generally favored slides over bends; his signature lick was a razor-sharp slide/vibrato combination that he featured in most of his solos.

Bends

Almost every post-B.B. King electric blues guitarist uses whole-step bends as part of their core style, so examples are everywhere, but in particular check out Freddie King's "Going Down" for a classic demonstration of minor pentatonic whole-step bends.

Most players also use half-step bends on occasion, but T-Bone Walker made them a personal trademark. Check out his "Mean Old World" for classic half-step phrases.

Albert King built his style around wide string bends, and you can hear them in every one of his solos. Check out "Personal Manager" and "Blues at Sunrise" (*Live Wire/Blues Power*) for some especially hair-raising examples (the latter track includes "reverse bends" like those demonstrated in Fig. 7).

Vibrato

Vibrato is a central part of most blues guitarists' musical personality. When you hear a vibrato that you especially like, find out if they play upside-down; if not, they are almost certainly using wrist vibrato, particularly on high, bent notes.

6 Blues Melody – Core and Color

The formal definition of a melody—"a succession of tones forming a line of individual significance and expressive value" (*Harvard Brief Dictionary of Music*)—applies to a good blues lick just as well as it does to a symphonic motif. In this chapter, we'll look more deeply into how to organize the notes you play, evaluate their emotional effect, and expand your melodic vocabulary in order to set the stage for creating phrases that are both individual and expressive—exactly what a blues guitar style is all about.

Blues Core

All of the phrases presented in this book so far are contained within the blue-note pentatonic scale, which combines the minor pentatonic with blue notes to encompass the *blues core*, or the core melodic vocabulary that most blues soloists play most of the time. This scale has been derived by analyzing a variety of blues melodies to find the notes they have in common, and like all scales, it is essentially a tool for organizing the notes you play most often so you can retrieve them efficiently.

Most guitar teaching methods approach blues soloing from a different direction; rather than a single scale, they present a combination of scales, such as minor pentatonic, major pentatonic, Dorian, or Mixolydian along with various rules for how and when to apply them over a blues progression (see Wikipedia or any standard music theory source for an explanation of these scales). Since this method for explaining blues phrasing is so common, it's important to examine some basic assumptions about blues melody to understand why this book takes a different approach.

Melodies and Scales

To be useful as a melodic tool, a scale must accurately reflect the sound of the music you want to play. If you play minor-key music like rock, minor-scale melodies have the right sound; likewise, if the music is in a major key, major scales provide the right fit. Wherever there is a clear division between major and minor tonalities, choosing the appropriate scale is very straightforward. This may seem completely obvious, but much of the difficulty that guitar players encounter in learning to play blues stems from trying to use the wrong scale for the job—like trying to drive a screw with the wrong screwdriver.

The basis for confusion lies in the fact that blues doesn't play by European rules. Unlike the clear either/or division between major and minor sounds in the European system, blues melodies move freely between them. For example, the typical blues phrase below includes minor, major, and blue 3rds that, according to traditional theory, shouldn't coexist in a single tonality. But when you listen to the phrase, your ears will tell you that they clearly do:

Fig. 1: Blues Phrase – Major or Minor?

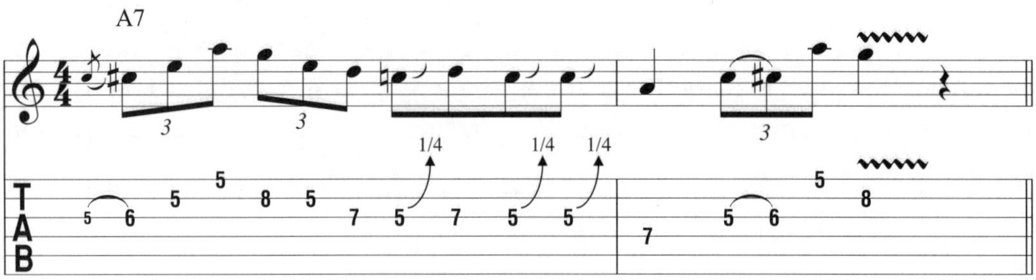

Trying to explain the way blues melodies sound by applying the either/or rules of diatonic theory almost invariably leads to a list of major and minor scale options (see below) along with formulas for how to apply them, such as: "Play major pentatonic on the I7 chord and switch to minor pentatonic on the IV7 chord." However, great blues soloists clearly do not exhibit this sort of thought process when they play. And, more to the point, it does not describe what we hear when we listen to blues.

Typical Blues Soloing Scale Options

Scale	**Scale Steps (in relation to major scale)**
Minor Pentatonic	1 ♭3 4 5 ♭7
Dorian	1 2 ♭3 4 5 6 ♭7
Major Pentatonic	1 2 3 5 6
Mixolydian	1 2 3 4 5 6 ♭7

Each of these scales is a very valuable tool in the right circumstances, but when it comes to blues, none of them does what a scale should do, which is to accurately reflect the sound of the music you want to play. Traditional theory says that a scale must be *either* major or minor, but our ears tell us that blues melody is both major *and* minor. Rather than trying to describe blues phrasing in terms of continuously switching between two tonalities, it is more musically accurate to understand it on its own, unique terms as *blues tonality*.

Blues Tonality

Blues tonality describes the combination of blue-note melody and dominant seventh-based harmony (see Chapter 8) that distinctly set blues apart from diatonic tonalities. This concept is derived from listening to a wide range of blues melodies and solos and identifying common traits, including:

- What combinations of tones players use more or less often—i.e., "core tones" and "color tones" (see next page).
- Which tones are used to express standard blues attitudes and styles, such as "down home"(the salty, rough-edged sound of rural blues), and "uptown" (the sweet, smooth sound of jazz-influenced urban blues).
- How players separate or blend these various melodic ingredients.

Within a blues phrase, going from "salty" to "sweet," for example, does not require changing from a minor scale to a major scale; it's essentially a matter of shifting the melodic emphasis from the minor 3rd to the major 3rd. In other words, you change the mood of a solo not by changing to a different tonality but by choosing among the different shades of expression that are already contained within the blues tonality.

The concept of a comprehensive blues tonality provides a more accurate framework for understanding how blues melody works than a collection of different scales, but blues always has been and will remain an "ear" style. You can't learn it from a page, and patterns and formulas won't tell you how to express yourself. The freedom of choice that is built into blues phrasing puts the player in charge of creating the mood, so in order to take control you need to look deeply at the connection between the notes you play and the feelings they evoke.

Notes and Feelings

Putting aside the technical challenges of playing the guitar, the primary goal of a blues solo is to create an emotional connection with listeners—in other words, to connect what we feel to what we play and express it with enough clarity that the audience feels it too. It's surprisingly easy to play guitar without really listening to yourself, but if you want your audience to feel what you play, you have to establish your own connection between the choices you make and the feelings they elicit.

An emotional message is affected by a wide variety of different factors, but among the most important are the specific notes we choose. The following exercise examines the connection between notes and feelings at the most basic, one-to-one level:

1. Record an A7 chord played in steady quarter notes at a tempo of 60 bpm for two minutes.
2. While the chord accompaniment plays back, play each note in the A blue-note pentatonic scale over it in steady eighth notes for 15 seconds apiece.
3. When you hear each combination of note and chord, check your emotional response. Which feel sweet? Edgy? Strong? Expectant? There is no technically right or wrong answer—concentrate on your emotional reaction to each note (write your responses in the space provided).

Note	**Response**
Tonic	
Minor 3rd	
Blue 3rd (quarter-tone bend)	
Major 3rd	
4th	
♭5th	
5th	
♭7th	

This exercise is something you may only do once, but making judgments about the relationship between notes and feelings is a permanent, ongoing part of the soloing process, and your perceptions will continue to evolve through time, experience, and circumstance. Each note has a particular character, a scale is a collection of these characters, and phrasing is the process of arranging the different characters to tell a story. Of course, when we solo, we don't choose notes one at a time any more than we speak one word at a time, but just as we choose our words carefully when we want to say something important, at the very heart of blues is the principle that every note is there for a reason, so spending a little time alone with each note is time well spent.

Expanding the Blues Tonality: Color Notes

The blue-note pentatonic comprises the core of the blues tonality, and every blues soloist—from the most down home to the most sophisticated—draws from it constantly, but most players also add certain other tones to their melodies to expand the range of emotion and style. Rather than thinking of these notes as belonging to different scales or tonalities, it is more musically accurate to think of them as additional musical colors within the blues tonality—i.e., *color notes.*

The 6th

The 6th (more precisely, the major 6th, corresponding to the sixth degree of the major scale) fills the melodic gap between the 5th and ♭7th of the pentatonic scale. In addition to smoothing the melodic line, the 6th adds a "sweet" quality to the melody, particularly when phrased in combination with the major 3rd.

Fig. 2: Blues Core Plus the 6th

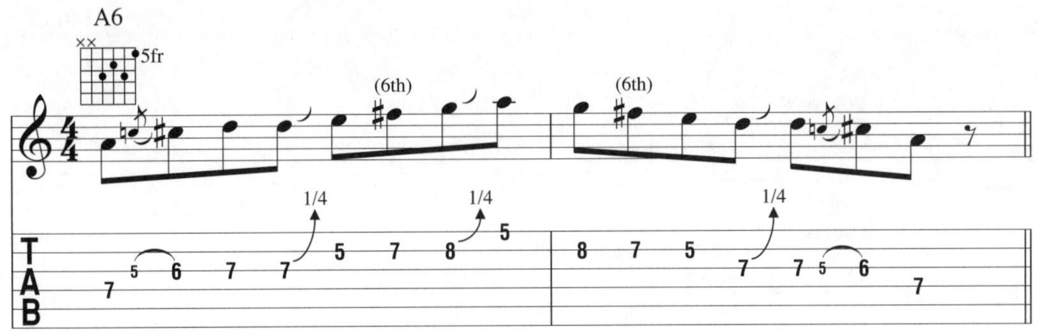

NOTE: The accompanying chord diagram shows a major sixth chord voicing. This chord echoes the use of the 6th in the melody and is very common in blues rhythm guitar arrangements, but the melody may include the 6th whether or not it's present in the harmony.

The next figure shows a few examples of blues phrases that include the 6th. To judge the relative sweetness of the 6th, replace each 6th with the ♭7th and notice how the phrases instantly become harder-edged or "bluesier."

The 6th is particularly common in the smooth, jazzy phrases of T-Bone Walker and his disciple B.B. King (fittingly, both are known for their romantic approach to blues). Once you become familiar with the sound of the 6th in your own playing, it's easy to recognize when used by others.

Fig. 3: Phrasing with the 6th

Performance Notes

1. Bars 1, 14: If you want to add vibrato to A immediately after fretting E on the second string, use your second finger to fret the A rather than rolling your index finger from E to A.
2. Note the numerous slides used at the end of phrases—a characteristic sound in this more "uptown" style.

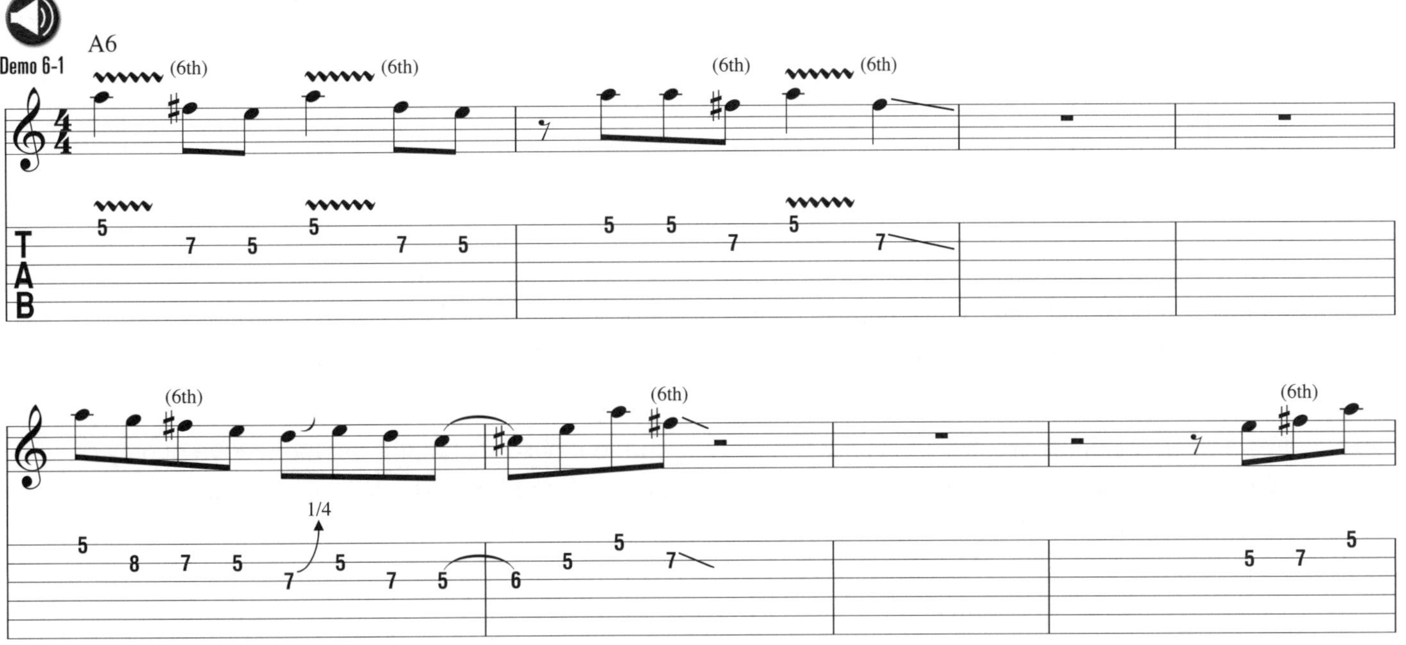

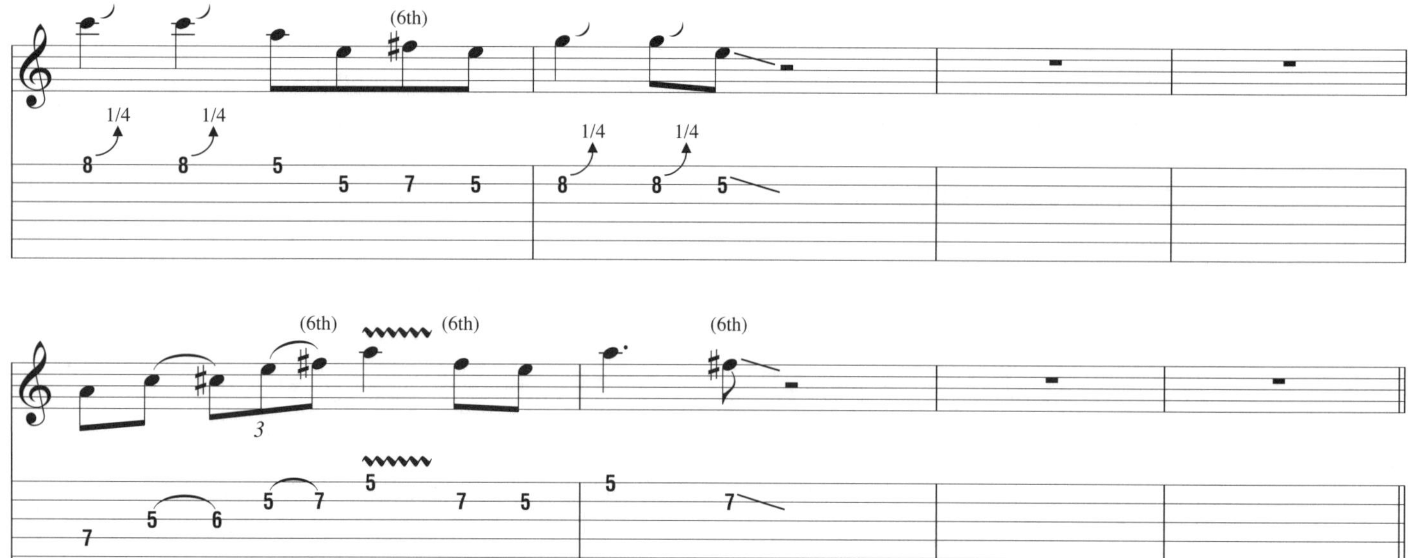

The 9th

The 9th (or major 9th, equivalent to the second degree of the major scale) is located between two very powerful melodic tones: the root and the 3rd. When the 9th is emphasized in the melody, it adds a subtle feeling of unresolved tension that pulls in either direction. This sophisticated, jazzy quality is favored by uptown blues soloists like T-Bone Walker as well as jazz-blues guitarists like Kenny Burrell. But the 9th has also been integrated into the blues-rock vocabulary by players like Jimi Hendrix and Stevie Ray Vaughan.

Fig. 4: Blues Core Plus the 9th

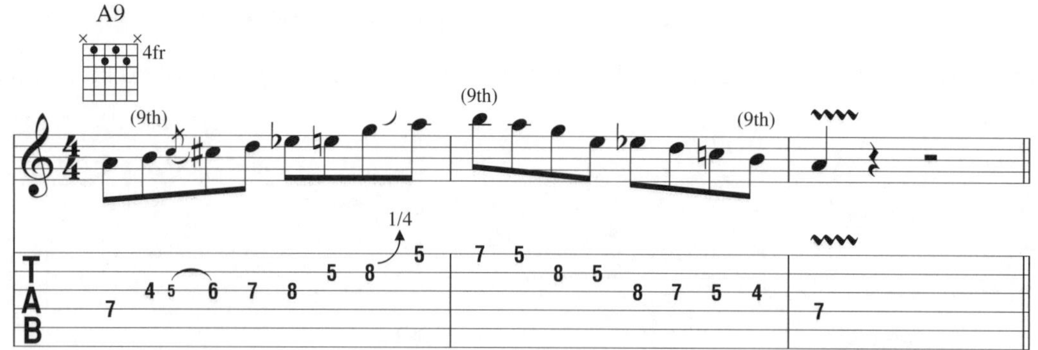

NOTE: The common voicing for A9 shown in the chord diagram does not include a root; in a band arrangement, the root is virtually always provided by the bass. Like the 6th, using the 9th in the harmony reinforces the sound of the 9th in the melody, but the two can be (and are) used independently.

In stepwise melodic lines, the 9th fills the gap between the tonic and the 3rd, but the unique quality of the 9th comes through most clearly when it is accented on a strong beat. The following phrases include examples of both.

Fig. 5: Phrasing with the 9th

Performance Notes

1. Bars 5–6: This T-Bone Walker-derived phrase has been used and modified by generations of blues guitarists including Hendrix and Stevie Ray Vaughan. Practice it in tempo very slowly to learn the triplet phrasing and maintain rhythmic accuracy when applying the hammer-ons and pull-offs.
2. Bars 7–8: This phrase is a staple of T-Bone Walker's soloing vocabulary; practice carefully to maintain the even triplets.

The 6th and 9th are frequently combined within melodies as shown in the following two-bar examples. Color notes not only add expressive subtlety to your phrasing, but they also extend your range to encompass the whole spectrum of blues styles from down home to uptown.

Fig. 6: Combining Color Notes

Performance Notes

1. Bars 1–2: Use finger rolls (see Chapter 1) to execute the B–F♯ (9th–6th) combination; this is a favorite phrasing device of Freddie King.
2. Bars 5–6: Adding the 6th and 9th to the melodic flow creates linear, step-wise phrases with a somewhat jazzy quality.
3. Bar 9: This is a typical T-Bone Walker-style phrase including a half-step bend from the 6th to the ♭7th.
4. Bars 13–14: This stepwise run through the various tones is a strong idea for ending a solo (12-bar blues soloing will be covered beginning in Chapter 8).

With the addition of color notes to the core blue-note pentatonic, the melodic vocabulary used by mainstream blues soloists to play over a single dominant seventh chord is complete.

Chapter 6 Summary

1. **Blues Core:** The set of tones encompassed by the blue-note pentatonic scale that makes up the bulk of blues phrases.
2. **Blues Tonality:** Rather than dividing blues melodies into separate major and minor scales, blues tonality combines them into a single, distinct melodic family.
3. **Notes and Feelings:** Different notes evoke different emotional responses, and the art of blues soloing is to recognize and control those responses.
4. **Expanding the Blues Tonality (Color Notes):** The 6th and 9th add stylistic and emotional variety to the melody and also provide smooth melodic connections.

Practice

Overall concepts, such as blues tonality and connecting notes with feelings, aren't things to be practiced in the technical sense, but they provide a framework for the lifelong process of organizing and choosing the notes you play.

Color Notes

The best way to begin expanding your melodic vocabulary is by memorizing and repeating phrases like those presented in Figs. 3, 5, and 6 note-for-note. By playing them over time, the sounds will become familiar. You'll be able to fit them into your existing vocabulary and also recognize them in other players' styles.

1. Practice each phrase at a slow tempo until you can execute it perfectly and then play it with the track.
2. Go back to Chapter 3, Exercises 1–2 and experiment with substituting 6ths and/or 9ths within the phrases while keeping the same rhythmic framework. As this book goes forward, color notes will be demonstrated in a variety of different contexts.

Listen

Blues Tonality

When we describe a player as "bluesy," it means fundamentally that their phrasing draws from the blues core—technically, the blue-note pentatonic. When you listen to a player who has a bluesy quality, pinpoint where the "bluesiness" comes from, i.e., what specific notes and phrasing choices create that effect. At first, this might be difficult, but as you develop your ear for blues phrasing, it becomes much easier to identify the common ingredients that are shared by blues-influenced players regardless of the stylistic context.

Notes and Feelings

The best way to learn how feelings and notes are connected is to listen to great performances and analyze the parts that affect you the most to see how the player is making it happen. Feeling is not only about notes, of course—attack, touch, tone, and a number of other factors all play an important role in creating an emotional message—but note choices are critical. There are obviously countless great blues performances on record to choose from, but here are a couple of recommendations:

- **"The Freeze" (Albert Collins):** Very early in his career, Collins recorded this track, which consists of just four phrases repeated over and over with the riveting tone, attack, and utter commitment that became his trademark. When he hits a note, it simply feels like the truth.
- ***Live at the Regal* (B.B. King):** This 1964 album is universally regarded as one of the greatest recorded live performances of all time. King expresses a universe of emotion and has the crowd hanging on every note throughout.

Color Notes

How much a certain player uses color notes is a matter of personal style, but certain players use them consistently and have influenced countless others in the process.

- **6th:** "Sweet Little Angel" from B.B. King's *Live at the Regal* is a masterpiece of expression. King uses the 6th in combination with the major 3rd on the opening lick of each solo to establish a sweet, romantic vibe on which he builds through the rest of each chorus.
- **9th:** "Call It Stormy Monday" is T-Bone Walker's best-known composition and also showcases his hugely influential phrasing. He completes his solo with a trademark lick featuring the 9th that's similar to the example shown in bars 13–14 of Fig. 6. Decades later, Hendrix adapted T-Bone-style phrases including the 9th (similar to Fig. 5 bars 9–10) on his own slow-blues classic "Red House," and Stevie Ray Vaughan subsequently followed suit in a number of different solos.
- **6th and 9th:** Nearly all sophisticated players, B.B. and T-Bone included, routinely use both the 6th and the 9th in various combinations, but Freddie King combined them particularly effectively in the instrumental "Side Tracked." Check out the second chorus, where you'll hear a phrase similar to the one in bars 1–2 of Fig. 6. You can also hear similar phrases in King's "Lonesome Whistle Blues" as well as the horn section arrangement to B.B. King's classic "Every Day I Have the Blues."

7 Getting Around the Neck

Until now, our view of the fretboard has been limited to barely more than one octave of a single fingering pattern. In fact, many great blues guitarists have spent almost their entire careers playing within those boundaries, but there's a lot more territory to explore on the neck, and each new pattern offers unique phrasing opportunities.

In this chapter, you'll learn how to play along the entire length of the neck using the popular and easy-to-understand organizing system known as *CAGED*. Each pattern is illustrated with a series of two-bar phrases that will simultaneously expand your knowledge of the neck and your blues soloing vocabulary.

The CAGED System

CAGED is the acronym for the five open-position major chord fingerings that most players learn as soon as they take up the guitar.

Fig. 1: C, A, G, E, and D Open-Position Voicings

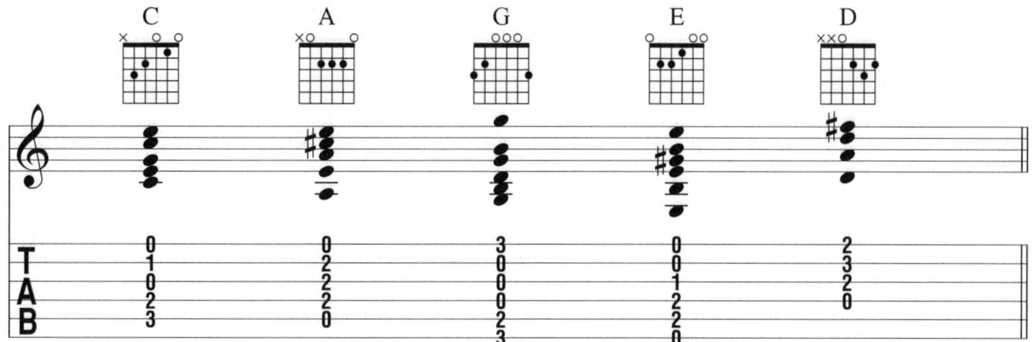

Each of these chord shapes can be transposed to different keys by moving the shape up the neck to the appropriate root and re-fingering it as a barre chord—i.e., laying your first finger across the strings to take the place of the nut. For example, here are the same chord voicings laid end-to-end to create five different versions of C major. (The fingering details are not significant, and some voicings are not even practical—what's important is to see how the shapes are arranged sequentially along the neck.)

Fig. 2: CAGED Voicings in C

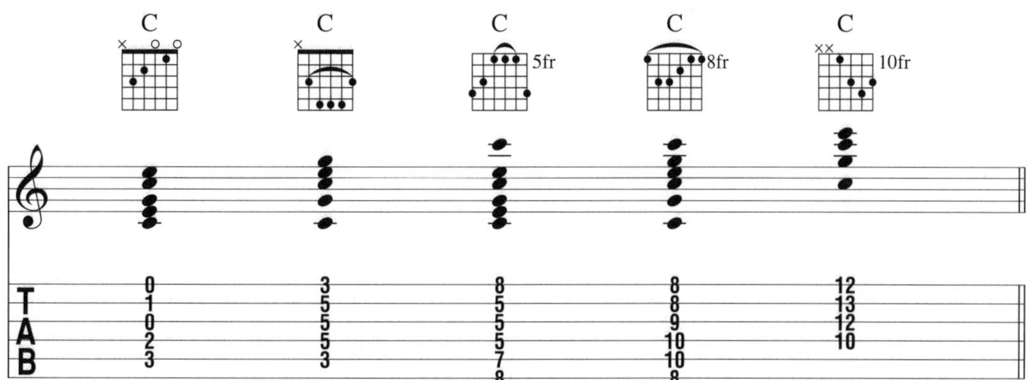

When the voicings are laid end-to-end in a single key, they form a set of overlapping shapes that divide the first 12 frets of the neck into five regions (past the 12th fret, the shapes repeat in the same order). These regions or patterns are numbered 1–5 in ascending order starting with the open C chord.

Fig. 3: The Five-Pattern System in C

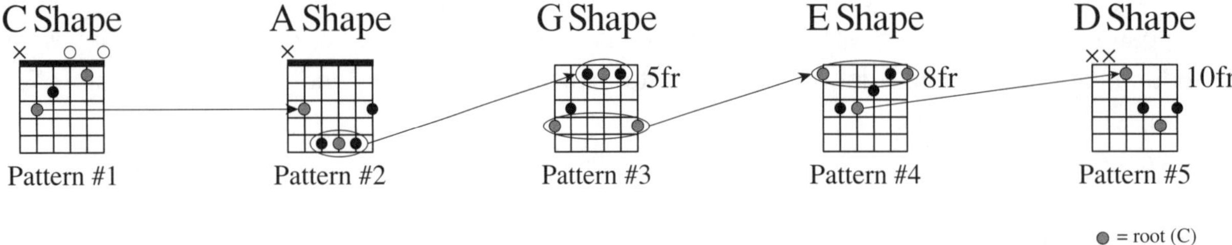

The same five patterns can be laid out in any key, beginning with the root closest to the nut and arranging the patterns along the neck using the same numbering system as for the key of C. In the key of A, for example, the A voicing closest to the nut is the open A chord, which corresponds to Pattern #2. Going up the neck, the next voicing is #3 (the "G shape"), then #4 (the "E shape," which is the only pattern we have used so far), then #5 (the "D shape"), and #1 (the "C shape"). After this, the same shapes repeat in the same order.

Fig. 4: The Five-Pattern System in A

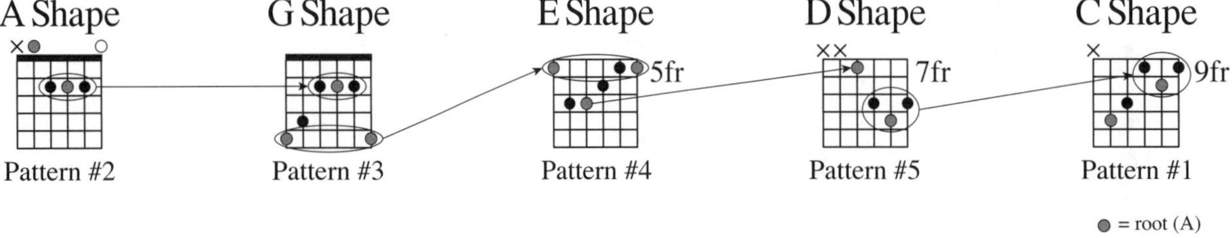

This pattern system is not limited to major triads; minor triads, dominant seventh chords, and their related scales can also be organized into five patterns using the same method.

It is essential to memorize the locations of the roots within each pattern. The roots are the foundation of each chord and scale and are the main focal points for blues phrasing. The string numbers where the roots are located in each pattern are shown below; compare them with the neck diagrams in Figs. 3 and 4 and with your own guitar neck to imprint these locations in your brain:

Pattern	Strings Where Roots are Located
#1	5, 2
#2	5, 3
#3	6, 3, 1
#4	6, 4, 1
#5	4, 2

For the sake of consistency and focus, we will continue to work only in the key of A. However, to learn songs and play with other musicians, you do need to be able to locate other keys quickly and play with confidence. As you learn phrases in each pattern, you are highly encouraged to transpose them to all keys using the cycle of fourths as described in Chapter 1. To play any fingering pattern in any key, locate the roots and then build the chord or scale around them. The positions change, but the patterns are identical in all keys. If you only know the names of the notes on the sixth, first, and fifth strings, you can use the octave shapes to find roots on the remaining strings.

So far, almost all of our attention has been focused on the upper octave of Pattern #4, so we'll expand first into the lower octave of the same pattern.

Pattern #4 Lower Octave

The lower octave of Pattern #4 (see Fig. 5) is an extension of the upper octave "box," but most standard phrases include a position shift that both helps the melodic flow and avoids using the weaker fourth finger (certain phrases work better when you stay in position, but this exception will be pointed out when it occurs).

- **Descending:** Slide down the fifth string from the seventh fret to the fifth fret with your third finger (placing your first finger on the third fret) and land on the low A with your third finger.
- **Ascending:** Slide back up the fifth string with your third finger.

Fig. 5: Pattern #4 Lower Octave – A Minor Pentatonic Scale

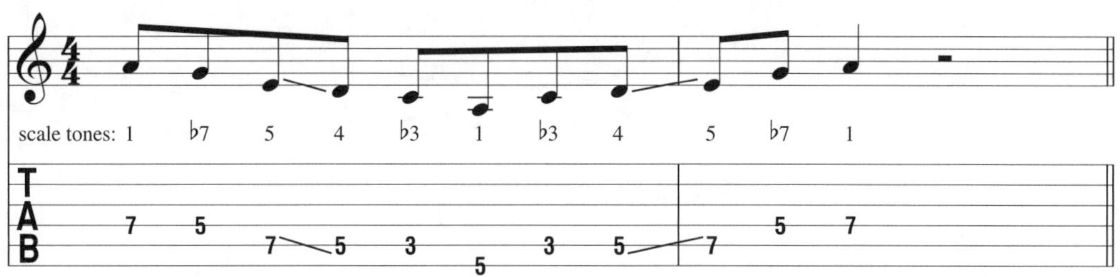

As a general rule, any phrase that fits within one octave can be replicated in any other octave within any pattern—with the exception of certain position-specific techniques like string-bends—so with just a few changes in fingering, most of the phrases that you have learned in the upper octave of Pattern #4 can be transposed to the lower octave.

An excellent way to learn the layout of this and every new pattern is to transpose familiar phrases using visualization, as follows:

Transposing Familiar Phrases to New Patterns

- Play the new pattern on the neck until you can visualize it clearly, including the numbering of the scale steps, and then put the guitar down.
- Hum a familiar phrase and visualize the normal fingering.
- Analyze the structure of the phrase by converting it to a series of scale steps—e.g., 1 – ♭3 – 1 – 4 – ♭3 – 1.
- Visualize your fingers playing the same sequence of steps in the new pattern, accounting for any necessary adjustments in fingering and technique.
- Pick up the guitar and play the phrase in the new pattern just as you visualized it.
- Compare the sound and fingering of the phrase in the new pattern to the original pattern. Repeat the process until your ability to visualize in the new pattern is consistently accurate.

To illustrate, the following figure shows how some typical one-bar phrases from the upper octave of Pattern #4 are transposed to the lower octave. Before you play it, visualize each phrase in both octaves; listen to the audio demonstration to hear phrasing details.

Fig. 6: Pattern #4 – Transposing Phrases to the Lower Octave

Performance Notes

1. Bars 1–2: In the lower octave, use your first finger to play the blue 7th.
2. Bars 3–4: In the lower octave, fret the first note with your third finger in preparation for the slide.
3. Bars 5–6: The fingering is identical in both octaves; execute the half-step slides with your third finger.
4. Bars 7–8: Rake into the first note in both octaves. In the lower octave, execute the quarter-tone D bend with your first finger and then shift quickly to your third finger to execute the whole-step bend; complete the phrase in third position.

The next example shows some two-bar phrases that are based mostly in the lower octave of Pattern #4. Even though the melodies are much like those in the upper octave, "low down" phrases like these have a fresh quality since most players use the lower octave much less frequently (see also Chapter 10: "Soloing in the Lower Register").

For extra dynamic range, use your picking-hand fingers to "pop" some of the low notes with a combination of skin and fingernail (hybrid technique). This sound was exploited by bare-finger stylists including Johnny "Guitar" Watson, Gatemouth Brown, and Albert Collins (all three players also used guitars with single-coil bridge pickups, like a Tele or Strat, that provide maximum bite and definition on the lower strings).

Fig. 7: Phrasing in Pattern #4 Lower Octave

Performance Notes

1. Bars 1–2: Fret this phrase with just your first and third finger; execute the final slide on the fourth string with your third finger.
2. Bars 5–6: a phrase that emphasizes the major sixth and major 3rd in a style similar to B.B. King.
3. Bars 9–10: Another classic riff requiring only the first and third fingers.
4. Bar 13–14: Begin this Freddie King-style phrase with a reverse rake (see Chapter 4), dragging an up-stroke of the pick across the muted high strings (King used both a thumb and finger pick).

Demo 7-1
(0:30)

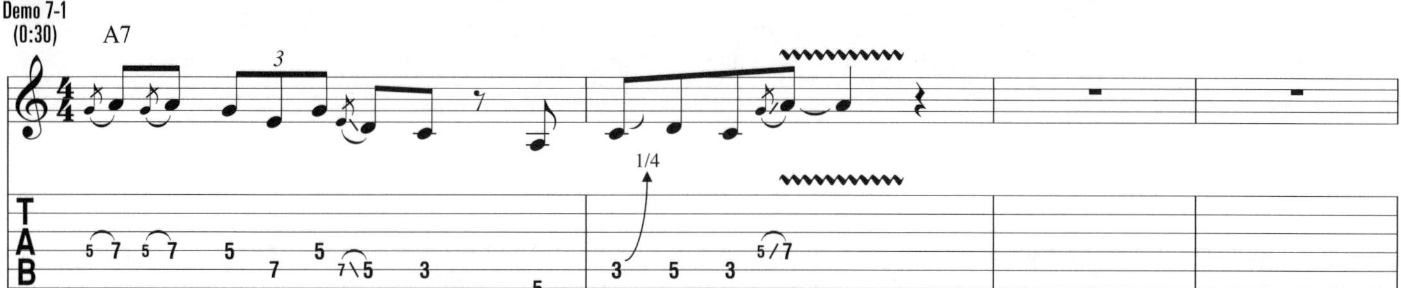

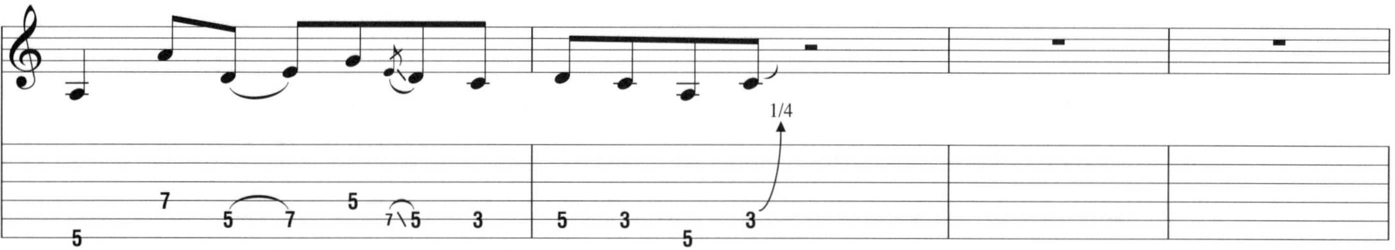

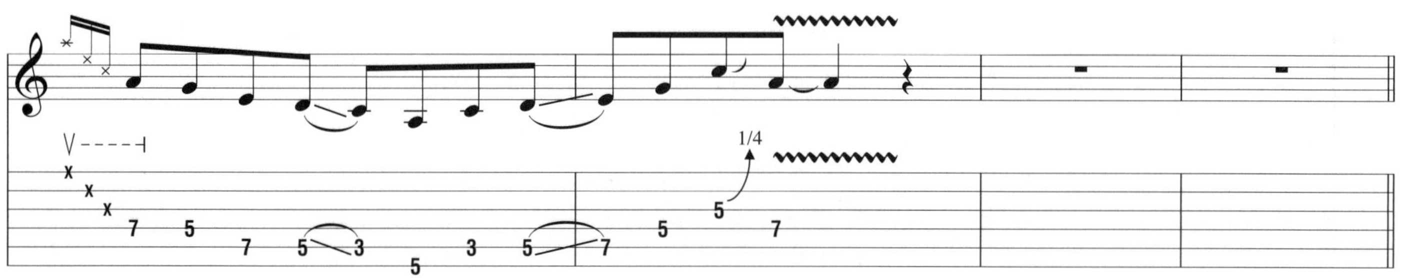

Pattern #5 Upper Octave: The "Albert King Spot"

Moving up the neck from Pattern #4, Pattern #5 corresponds to the open D chord shape that is centered on the second-string tonic fretted by the third finger. Most common phrases in this pattern are played on just the top three strings, reaching the highest note (E, the 5th) by bending the first string up a whole step.

Fig. 8: Pattern #5 – A Minor Pentatonic Scale

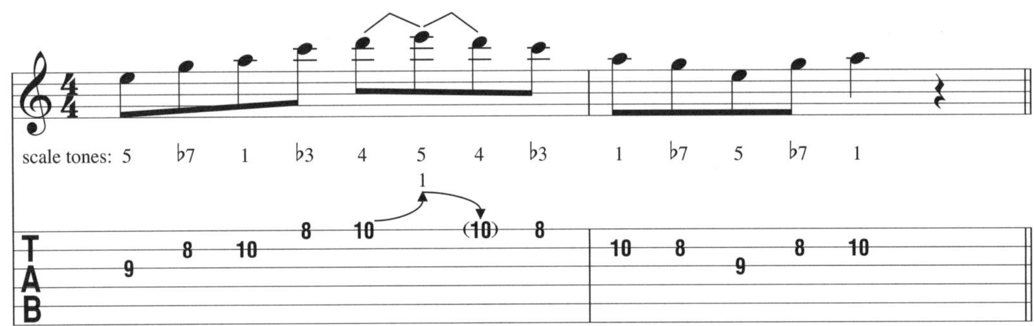

Despite its limited range, Pattern #5 is one of the most-used patterns for blues soloing in general and for Albert King-style phrasing in particular. (As discussed in Chapter 5, King's own guitar setup was unorthodox, but many of his trademark string bends can be approximated within this pattern.) The pattern's limitation is also its advantage, because with fewer note choices available, you can focus instead on timing and touch.

The following example illustrates some King-style phrases in Pattern #5; to get closer to Albert's sound, pluck the strings as he did, with just your bare fingers and thumb, or use hybrid technique (Stevie Ray Vaughan, for example, came extremely close to matching King's sound and touch using whole-step bends in Pattern #5 combined with hybrid picking). The phrases in bars 5–8 show how to "fake" some of Albert King's trademark bends by converting two-step bends into a seamless combination of whole-step bends (*compound bends*), a challenging technique that requires very careful attention to both hands.

Fig. 9: Albert King-Style Phrases in Pattern #5

Performance Notes

1. Bars 1–2: This classic King-style phrase uses mainly the first and third fingers.
2. Bars 5–6: Use a finger roll to fret the final two notes (D–A).
3. Bars 9–10: In bar 9, fret the first string with the first, second, and third fingers combined, bend to the high E, then mute the string with the bare third finger of your picking hand. Silently release the bend, quickly shift down two frets, and bend from C to D with the first and second fingers combined. In bar 10, execute the bend from D to E using a pre-bend.
4. Bar 14: Bend from C to D with the first and second fingers combined.

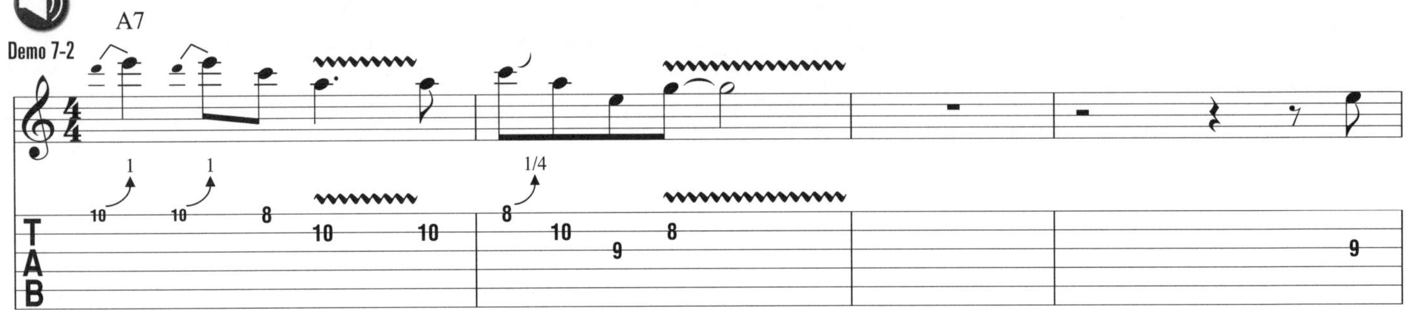

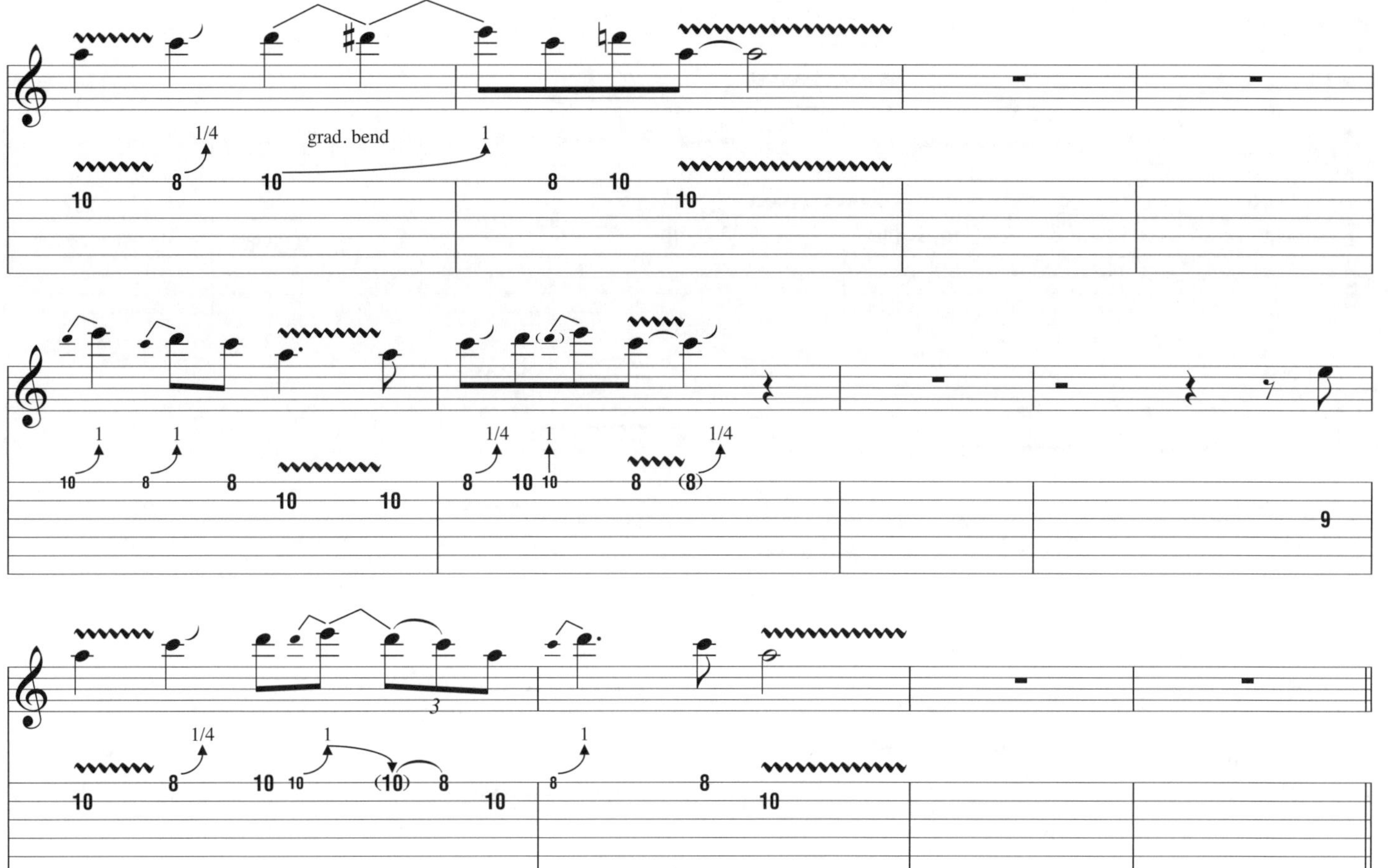

Another way to replicate King-style bends is to re-finger them on the second string as shown in Chapter 5, Fig. 7 ("Big Bends"); there is a sacrifice in tone, but it is offset by the advantage in playability. To compare the sound and feel of the two techniques, convert the phrases in Fig. 9 to two-step bends on the second string; likewise, convert the bends from Chapter 5, Fig. 7 to compound bends in Pattern #5. Generations of players have discovered just how challenging it is to attain King's level of string-bending skill, but whichever technique you choose, the payoff is well worth the effort.

Blues Tonality in Pattern #5

Pattern #5 is closely identified with Albert King's minor pentatonic-based vocabulary, but almost every mainstream blues guitar soloist has made extensive use of the same pattern. You can access all colors of the blues tonality—i.e., the major 3rd (key of A: C♯) is on the first string under your second finger, the 9th is down one fret from the minor 3rd, and the major 6th is one fret below the ♭7th. As illustrated in the next example, B.B. King-style phrases featuring the major 3rd and 6th fit very comfortably in this pattern.

Fig. 10: Blues Tonality in Pattern #5

Performance Notes

1. Bars 1–2: One of B.B. King's main stylistic trademarks is his emphasis on the major 3rd, as in this phrase.
2. Bars 5–6: Reach down an extra fret to play the 6th (F♯) and use your second finger to fret E on the third string. In bar 6, rake into the bend, release it, and pull off from D to C♯ without picking.
3. Bars 9–10: A stepwise phrase that incorporates both the 9th and the 6th, there are several fingering options that work equally well.
4. Bars 13–14: As in bars 5–6, stretch down a fret with your first finger to play the 6th and use your second finger to fret E on the third string.

Combining Patterns #4 and #5

Patterns #4 and #5 are the two most-used positions for blues guitar soloing, so phrases that link the two patterns are very common. The following figure shows some phrases that connect the patterns by sliding along one string.

Fig. 11: Connecting Patterns #4 and #5

Performance Notes

1. Bars 1–2: This is a trademark B.B. King phrase; slide up the second string with the third finger.
2. Bars 5–6: Here's a B.B. King-style downward slide. Pull off from your third to first finger and then slide quickly down the second string with your first finger.
3. Bars 9–10: The third-string slide between these two patterns is extremely common; slide up with the second finger and down with the third.
4. Bars 13–14: This is a series of slides up and down the first string; slide up with the third finger and down with the first.

Pattern #1 Upper Octave: The "B.B. King Spot"

Building on T-Bone Walker's foundation, B.B. King expanded and refined the use of techniques like string-bending and vibrato to create a style that has defined the sound of electric blues for generations and made his name synonymous with electric blues guitar. After first achieving success on the African-American "chitlin' circuit" in the early 1950s and iconic status among blues-rock guitarists during the 1960s, King finally became a household name among general white audiences in 1970 when he reached the pop charts with his smash hit, "The Thrill Is Gone."

Compared to the rough, down home sound of Delta and Chicago blues, King's style is sweeter and more romantic with emphasis on the major 3rd and major 6th melodic tones and a clean, smooth delivery. Pattern #1, the "C shape," is home to a number of B.B.'s trademark phrases. In fact, King exploited this pattern so consistently and successfully that it has become widely known as the "B.B. King Spot."

Pattern #1 is centered on the tonic of the key on the second string (key of A: 10th fret) fretted with your index finger. Without moving out of position, you can bend the second string with your third finger to reach the major 3rd (or 4th or onward) and bend the first string with the same finger to reach the sweet major 6th. (Like Pattern #5, most classic blues phrases in Pattern #1 are played on just the top three strings.)

Fig. 12: Pattern #1: The "B.B. King Spot"

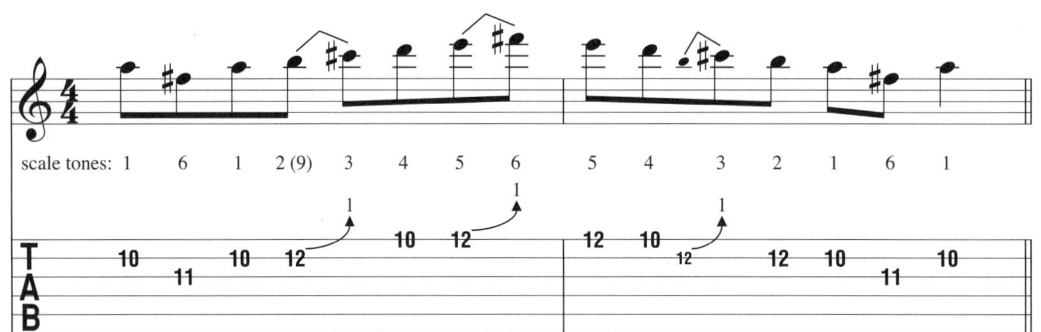

If you compare Pattern #1 to Pattern #5, you'll see that they share identical fingerings, but when you play the patterns in the same key, the melodies sound completely different because they have a different relationship to the tonic. When you learn any new pattern, it is essential to memorize not just the fingerings and physical shape but also the sound and scale degree associated with each finger and fret. You must always keep your fingers under the control of your ears—not your eyes.

Fig. 13: B.B. King-Style Phrases in Pattern #1

Performance Notes

1. Bars 1–8: This is a series of typical King-style one-bar phrases in which the last note receives the main emphasis (called *pickup phrases*—see Chapter 8). Each phrase is arranged so that the last note lands on the downbeat of the bar. Listen to the rhythm-section demo to hear the proper timing.
2. Bars 9–16: These two-bar phrases feature King's trademark rake (see Chapter 4), which adds dynamic intensity to string bends.

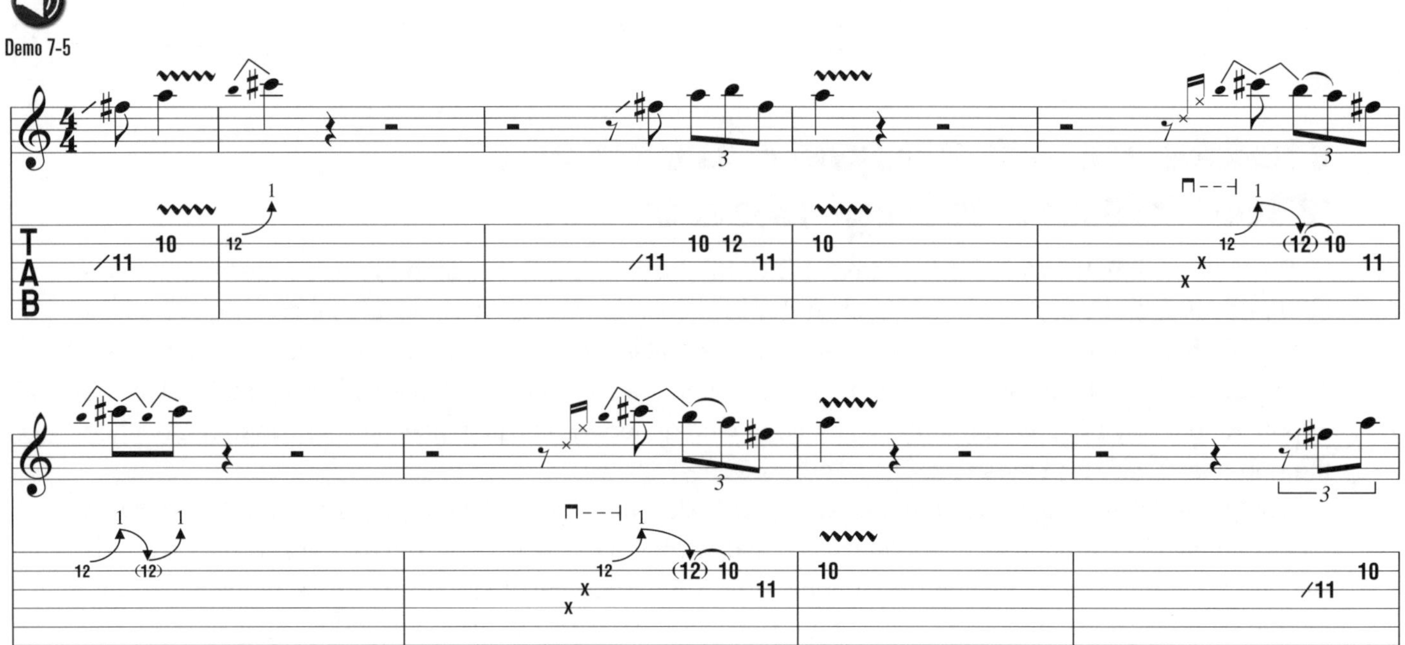

Blues Tonality in Pattern #1

An advantage of Pattern #1 is that it provides easy access to the "sweet" notes, but of course it also contains the complete blues tonality. For example, one of B.B.'s favorite moves in this pattern is to bend the 5th on the first string an additional half step from the 6th up to the ♭7th, instantly taking a phrase from sweet to edgy (see bars 9–10 below). The next figure demonstrates some of the variety of blues tonality in Pattern #1.

Fig. 14: Blues Tonality in Pattern #1

Performance Notes

1. Bars 1–2: As an optional fingering, use your second finger to bend the third string; this requires a small stretch, but it also allows you to use your third finger to execute the hammer-on/pull-off combination. Use palm muting on the lower strings and fret the notes very carefully to reduce unwanted open-string noise.
2. Bars 5–6: Use your second finger to fret G on the third string.
3. Bars 9–10: Fret with three fingers to execute the wide bend.
4. Bars 13–14: Again, use your third finger to fret C on the second string and second finger to fret G on the third string.

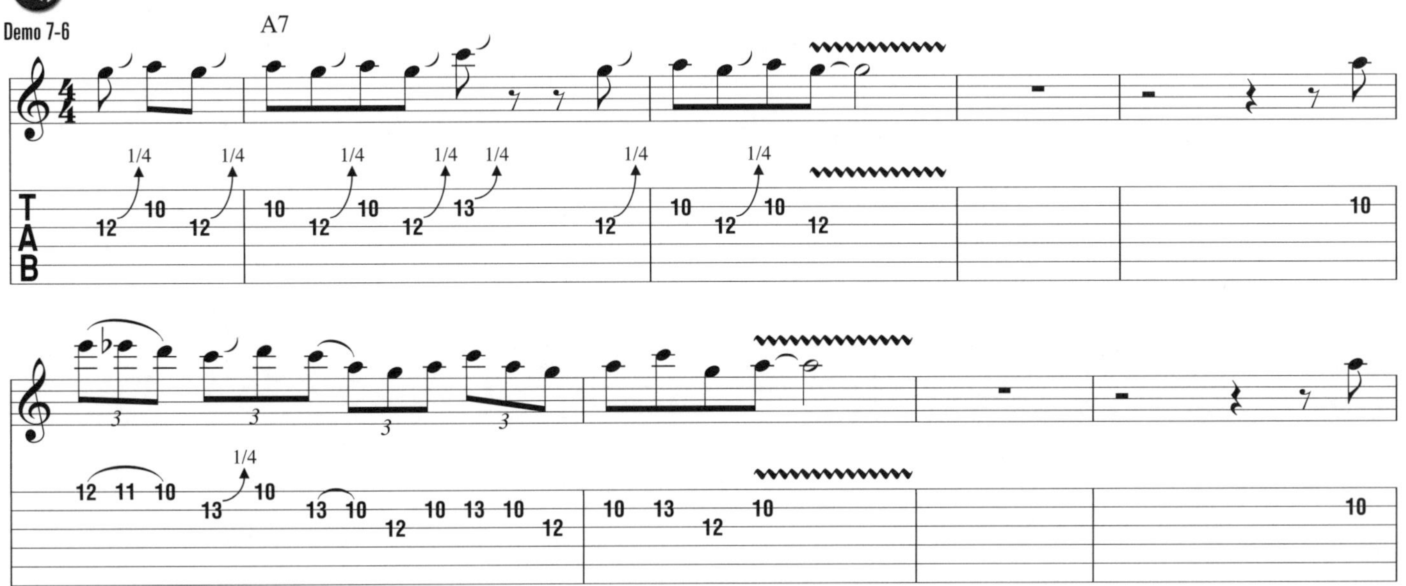

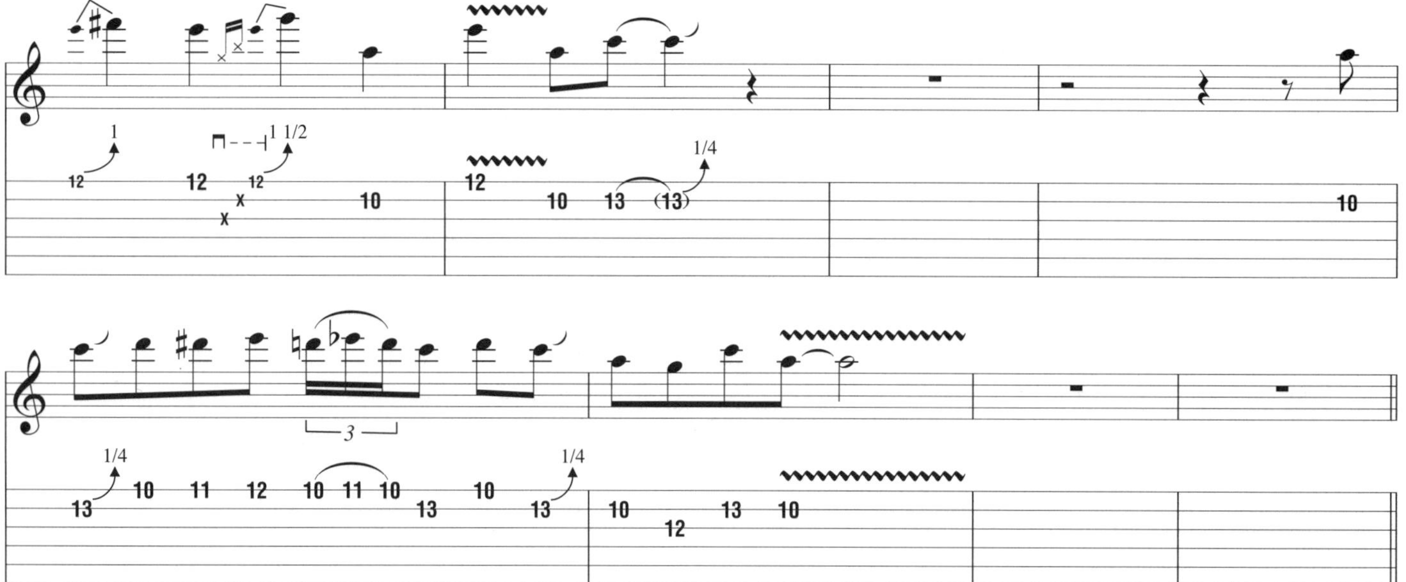

Combining Patterns #1, #5, and #4

Most common phrases in Patterns #5 and #1 are played on just the top three strings, so extending the range higher or lower typically involves shifting (a rapid, silent position change) or sliding (an audible position change) to adjacent patterns rather than moving across the neck within the same pattern. Here are a few phrases that expand on the position shifts shown in Fig. 11 to include techniques for connecting all three patterns.

Fig. 15: Connecting Patterns #1, #5, and #4

Performance Notes

1. Bars 1–2: In bar 1, shift your hand from 10th to eighth position between E and C♯ (hammer-on from C to C♯ with your first and second fingers); in bar 2, shift back to 10th position by moving your third finger one fret at a time from D up to E, shifting back down between E and C.
2. Bars 5–6: This move from the top of Pattern #1 to the lower octave of Pattern #4 uses a combination of shifting and sliding; ending a phrase on the lower-octave major 3rd is one of B.B. King's common moves.
3. Bars 9–10: This shift takes advantage of a two-note interval fingering that is the same in all three patterns, an idea that was explored by Stevie Ray Vaughan, for one. As you slide the interval shape up the third and second strings from fifth to eighth to 10th position, notice how the tonality changes from sweet to bluesy and back to sweet again.
4. Bars 13–14: This quick shift and slide through all three patterns is similar to a Freddie King move ("The Stumble") that was inspired in turn by one of his Chicago mentors, Jimmy Rogers. On beats 1–2, shift from D to C with your first finger, and on beat 3 slide down the third string with your third finger.

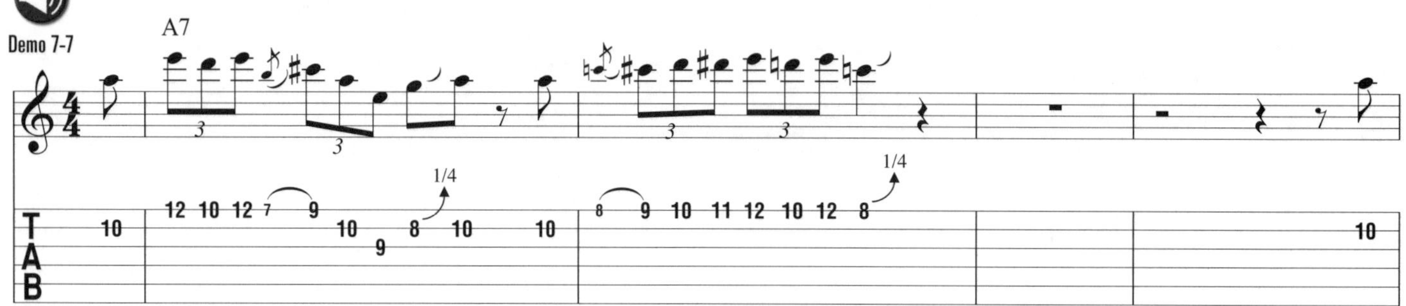

Pattern #2: The "A Shape"

Pattern #2, built around tonics on strings 5 and 3 (the "A shape"), is located halfway between Pattern #4 and its octave. The heart of the pattern covers the same range as Pattern #5, but it also provides access to higher and lower notes.

The following figure shows the layout of the minor pentatonic scale in Pattern #2 starting with the tonic on the third string. The position shifts on the fourth string allow you to use just your first and third fingers to play through most of the pattern as in the lower octave of Pattern #4. (Depending on how a certain phrase is arranged, it may make more sense to stay in 12th position and use your fourth finger to fret the low C or G, but the position shift is more common.)

Fig. 16: Minor Pentatonic Scale in Pattern #2

This pattern is the location for iconic "down home" phrases dating back to 1920s Texas blues star Blind Lemon Jefferson that were carried into the electric era by Lightnin' Hopkins in Texas, Jimmy Rogers and Eddie Taylor in Chicago, and their common disciple Freddie King. The next example shows how to get from one end of the pattern to the other based around this style of phrasing.

Fig. 17: Phrasing in Pattern #2

Performance Notes

1. Bars 1–2: The phrasing of the minor 3rd and 5th (C and E)—bending the second string a quarter tone without bending the first string—is one of the most down home sounds in blues.
2. Bars 5–6: Here's a Lightnin' Hopkins-style phrase; bend from D to E with your third finger and fret the high G with your fourth finger.
3. Bars 9–10: Accent the high G with a rake; the rest of the phrase shows how to move smoothly to the lower part of the pattern.
4. Bars 13–14: Execute the "reverse rake" on the low E by muting the higher strings and dragging the pick upward; from there, the same phrase is duplicated in two octaves before a Lightnin'-style finish.

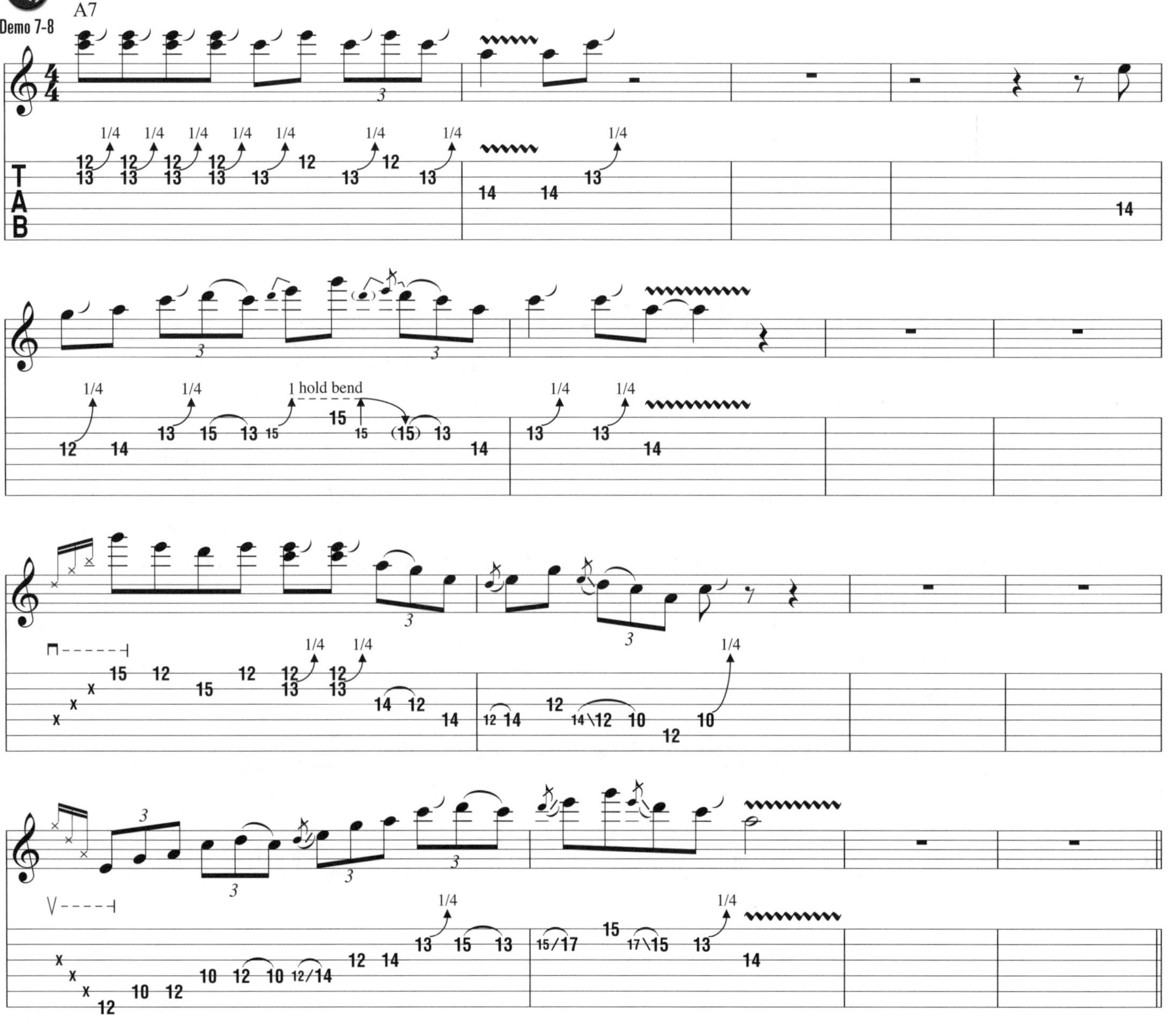

Blues Tonality in Pattern #2

Like all patterns, Pattern #2 encompasses both the salty and the sweet. The next example shows some phrases that combine core and color tones.

Fig. 18: Blues Tonality in Pattern #2

Performance Notes

1. Bars 1–2: This phrase expands on a Freddie King idea from "The Stumble" to include every color in the blues tonality.
2. Bars 5–6: Fret the first A with your second finger to put your hand in position for the next part of the phrase. The descending line at the end of the phrase is also inspired by "The Stumble."
3. Bars 9–10: Stretch with your first finger from G to F♯ and then shift position from D to C with your first finger at the end of bar 10.
4. Bars 13–14: In bar 13, shift from D to D♯ to E with your third finger and roll it onto the third string to fret A; then stretch an extra fret with your first finger to reach F♯.

Pattern #3: The "G Shape"

Many players first become acquainted with the part of the neck occupied by Pattern #3 (the "G shape"—tonic on strings 6, 3, and 1) through a simple fingering trick: if you move minor pentatonic scale Pattern #4 three frets closer to the nut and continue playing in the same key, the melody still fits the chord, but the sound changes from bluesy to sweet. In melodic terms, changing the position without changing the pattern puts your fingers on scale tones 1, 2, 3, 5, and 6, otherwise known as the *major pentatonic scale* (Chapter 6).

Fig. 19: Shifting Pattern #4 Minor to Pattern #3 Major

A minor pentatonic (Pattern #4)

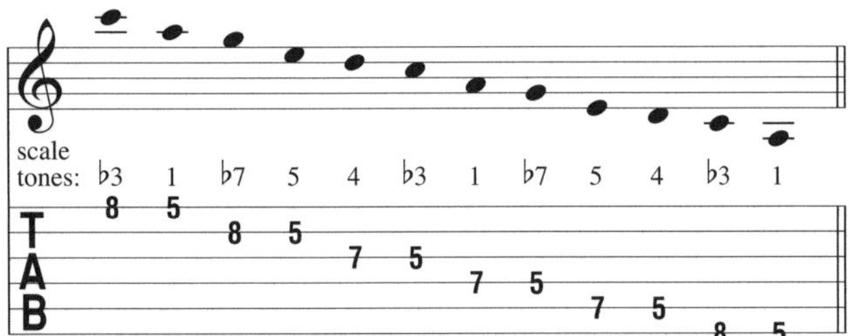

A major pentatonic (Pattern #3)

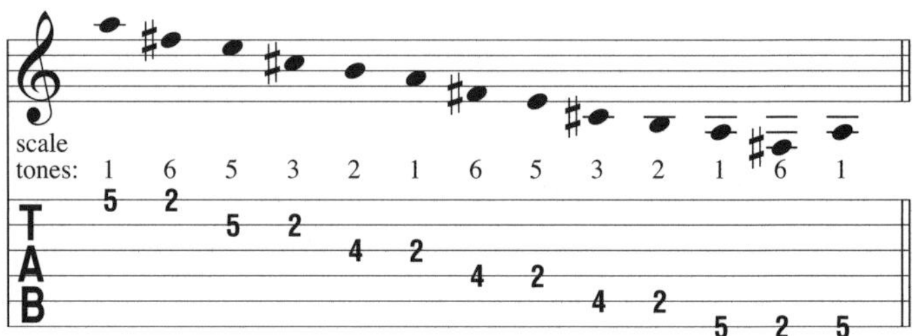

This "down three frets" trick is one of the oldest in the blues guitar soloing book and makes Pattern #3 one of the most popular spots on the neck for sweet-sounding phrases. However, while the patterns look the same, they obviously don't sound the same, and simply moving a given lick from one position to the other without adjusting for that difference can result in phrases that sound unresolved.

In order to get the most musical value out of Pattern #3, you need to connect the fingerings with the actual sounds. One of the best ways to do this is to copy phrases from Pattern #1, since the fourth, third, and second strings of Pattern #3 cover the same melodic range. Transfer the phrases from Fig. 13 into Pattern #3 (to keep the phrases in the same octave, play Pattern #3 in 14th position). Compare fingerings and identify where the chord tones are located; like Pattern #1, the tonic in Pattern #3 falls under the first finger, so most phrases are based around this rather than the third finger as in Pattern #4.

Going beyond the sweet side of Pattern #3, the next example demonstrates some phrases that cover a wider range of the blues tonality.

Fig. 20: Blues Tonality in Pattern #3

Performance Notes

In the key of A, Pattern #3 is playable in both second and 14th positions; the examples are notated in the lower position, but the fingering in the higher position is identical.

1. Bars 1–2: The major 3rd in bar 1 is answered with the blue 3rd in bar 2.
2. Bars 5–6: Use your fourth finger to fret A on the sixth string and D on the fifth string, shift down a fret with your first finger to fret the slide from D♯ to E on the fourth string, and use your fourth finger to fret C on the third string.
3. Bar 9–10: This phrase takes advantage of easy access to the series of half steps between the 9th (B) and the 5th (E); at the end, roll with your third finger between E and C.
4. Bars 13–14: Hold down the high A with your fourth finger while you use your other fingers to fret the notes below it; pick with hybrid technique. Playing a melody against a fixed note (*pedal point*) is a favorite trick of Buddy Guy, Lonnie Mack, and Stevie Ray Vaughan, among others (see Chapter 11).

Moving Around the Neck

If you analyze the styles of a variety of great blues soloists, you will find some, like T-Bone Walker, Gatemouth Brown, and Albert Collins, who work almost exclusively in just one or two patterns. Others, however, like B.B. King, Buddy Guy, Jimi Hendrix, and Stevie Ray Vaughan, move easily all over the neck. There is no relationship between the quality of your phrasing and how many patterns you use, but if you hear melodies that go beyond the confines of a single position, it's important to develop the means to follow them. The next few examples show some ways to move smoothly along the entire length of the neck.

Shifting and Sliding

We have already explored shifting and sliding as techniques for linking phrases between adjacent patterns. The next examples use the same techniques to link a series of phrases moving through all five patterns, both ascending and descending (the different patterns are indicated above the notation).

As such, these are intended as technical exercises rather than complete blues phrases, but each 8-bar example can also be broken into a series of two-bar phrases that can be played independently (on the audio demo, they are played back-to-back in order to demonstrate the overall flow along the neck).

Practice each example until you can play along with the audio demo in tempo; the rhythm track continues for an additional eight bars, so you can either repeat the example or experiment with your own ideas. Once you get the hang of it, you can also shift and slide between patterns at any number of different points. The only technical rule is to avoid two consecutive slides with the same finger, since that makes it more difficult to control your touch (of course, like every rule, there are exceptions—see "Soloing on One String" on the next page).

Fig. 21: Shifting and Sliding Through Patterns: Ascending

Performance Notes

1. Bar 1: Slide from B to C♯ with your second finger.
2. Bar 2: Slide from G to A with your third finger (this is a trademark move of B.B. King).
3. Bar 4: Slide from E to F♯ with your second finger.
4. Bar 6: Slide from B to C with your second finger.
5. Bar 7: Slide from C to C♯ with your first finger.

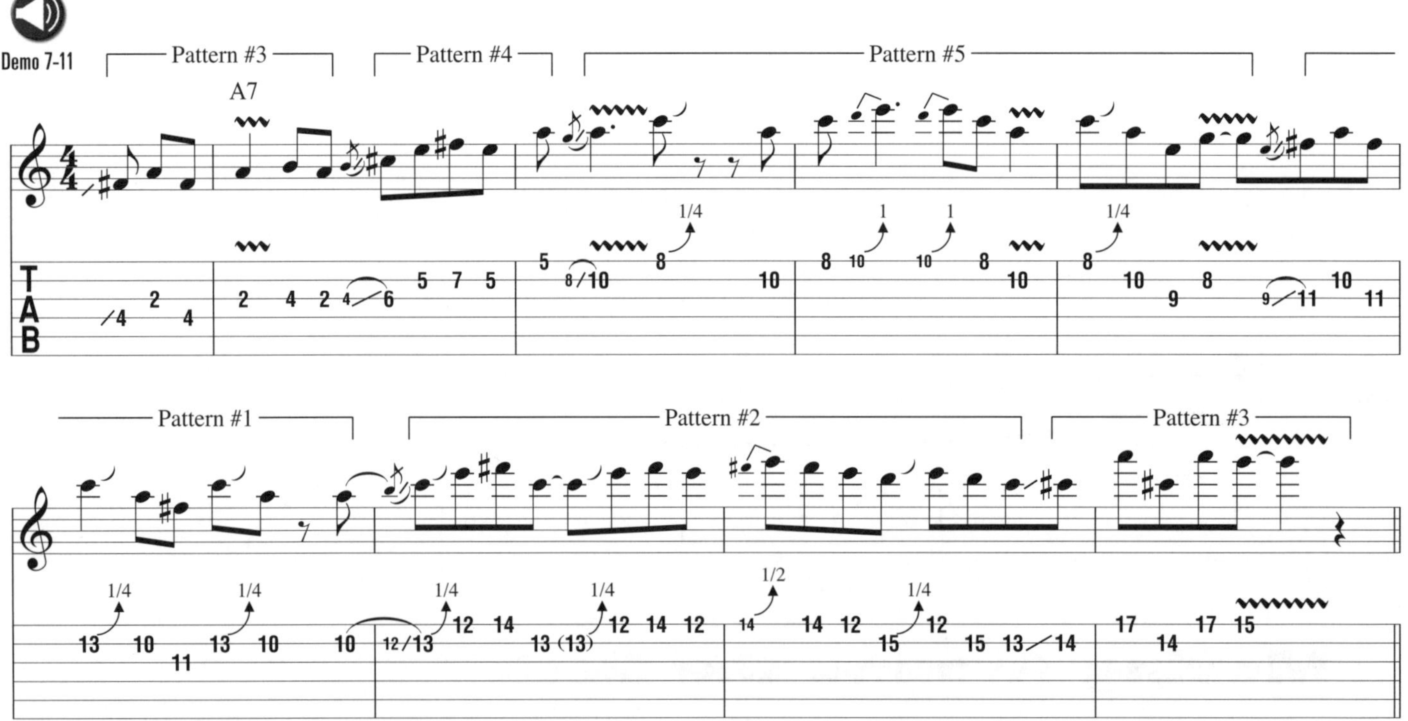

Fig. 22: Shifting and Sliding Through Patterns: Descending

Performance Notes

1. Bar 1: Slide from D to E and E back to D with your third finger.
2. Bar 3: Shift from 12th to 10th position with your first finger.
3. Bar 5: Shift from 10th to eighth position with your first finger.
4. Bar 7: Slide from G to E with your first finger (a favorite B.B. King move) and from E to D with your third finger.
5. Bar 8: Fret the first C with your first finger and the second C with your second finger to put your hand in position to fret the final A with your first finger.

Soloing on One String

The ultimate way to explore a linear approach to the guitar neck is to solo on just one string. Although this might seem extreme, it's actually a very traditional technique that was familiar to guitarists growing up in the rural South who played a home-made, one-string *diddley bow* (see Chapter 5 "Big Bends"). A one-string instrument forces a player to rely on just their ear and touch. On a six-string guitar, playing one-string melodies is an excellent way to break out of ruts and get back to basics. Hendrix, for example, frequently included one-string passages in his solos, and Clapton's solo on "I'm So Glad" from *Fresh Cream* (inspired by Delta guitarist Skip James) can be played entirely on the G string using a combination of slides, shifts, and bends. As shown in Chapter 5, Albert King built his style around large, one-string bends, and a classic version of imaginative one-string playing is Guitar Slim's solo on the slow blues epic "The Things That I Used to Do," which is largely confined to the high E string.

Whatever your style or background, putting normal patterns aside to play on one string forces you to concentrate on the *intervals*—the steps or leaps between any two notes—which are the basic building blocks of melody. One-string phrasing is a colorful addition to your repertoire in its own right, but one-string thinking also trains you to rely less on pre-arranged fingering patterns and more on your ear—even when you phrase in your normal style.

The following figure illustrates some bluesy phrases played exclusively on the high E string in the key of A. After you learn the phrases on one string, re-finger them within normal patterns and compare the sound. Likewise, converting pattern-based phrases to one string gives them a completely different character—you have to "think outside the box" in more ways than one.

Fig. 23: One-String Melody

Performance Notes

The audio example is picked with bare fingers to provide extra dynamic variety.

1. Bars 2–3: Fret the final A in bar 2 with your third finger, slide it up two frets, and bend up a half step without picking again; the slide-into-bend combination is especially slippery.
2. Bar 5: On beat 3, hammer on from your third to your fourth finger and then pull off from fourth to third to first fingers in a continuous motion.
3. Bars 7–8: Slide from D to C and then shift to B and A with your first finger. On beat 2, hammer on and pull off with your first and fourth finger and then pull off from your first finger to the open string in one continuous motion. When the pitch of the open string belongs to the key (E is the 5th of A), it can be incorporated into phrases played up the neck by using this pull-off technique.

Chapter 7 Summary

1. The CAGED system divides the neck into five patterns based around common open-position chord voicings:
   a. Pattern 1: The "C" pattern
   b. Pattern 2: The "A" pattern
   c. Pattern 3: The "G" pattern
   d. Pattern 4: The "E" pattern
   e. Pattern 5: The "D" pattern
2. Each pattern is home to certain classic blues phrases. When all are combined, the five patterns provide access to almost all of the standard blues soloing vocabulary.
3. Shifting and sliding between patterns allows you to play melodies along the entire length of the neck, freeing your fingers to go wherever your imagination takes them.

Practice

You don't need to be equally adept at all patterns or even go beyond one or two patterns to play effective blues solos, but the better you know the neck, the more freedom you have as a player. In addition to learning the specific examples shown in this chapter, the exercises described below explore more ways of tying together the different regions of the neck. Some are pattern-specific and others more general, but all will help you to become better acquainted with the neck and the relationship between melodies and feelings that is at the heart of the blues style.

1. **Pattern #4 Lower Octave:** Transpose each of the one- and two-bar phrases from Chapter 3, Exercises 1 and 2 to the lower octave of Pattern #4.
2. **Pattern #5:** Transpose the phrases in Fig. 9 to the second string and convert the combined whole-step bends to two-step bends. Likewise, transpose the two-step bends from Chapter 5, Fig. 7 to Pattern #5 and convert them to combined whole-step bends.
3. **Pattern #1:** Most typical phrases in Pattern #1 are played on the top three strings, but of course the pattern can be extended across the neck, and the extra range is very useful. To open up the lower octave of Pattern #1, transpose phrases from Pattern #3 (Fig. 20) up an octave and re-finger them in Pattern #1.
4. **Pattern #2:** Transpose phrases from Pattern #5 (Figs. 9–10) and phrases connecting Patterns #4 and #5 to Pattern #2, which covers the same overall range.
5. **Pattern #3:** Transpose phrases from Pattern #1 (Figs. 13–14) into Pattern #3 in 14th position to match octaves.

Pattern-Connecting Exercises

In addition to the examples shown in this chapter, here are some exercises that will help you to connect the patterns to each other and learn to use every part of the neck:

- **Shift between patterns in the same key**
  Start playing two-bar phrases in your most familiar pattern over a one-chord medium shuffle groove in any key. After four bars, shift to the next adjacent pattern in the same key and continue soloing in the new pattern. Repeat every four bars until you have covered all five patterns in that key. Repeat the exercise in different keys. For an additional challenge, shift patterns every two bars. By playing this exercise consistently over time, you'll develop a consistent vocabulary of phrases in all patterns and eliminate blind spots on the neck.

- **Shift between patterns in the same position**
  For this challenging exercise you need to pre-record a rhythm track. Play four bars of a basic shuffle rhythm at a slow-to-medium tempo for each chord in the cycle of fourths in the following order (do not pause between changes):

  A7 D7 G7 C7 F7 B♭7 E♭7 A♭7 D♭7 G♭7 ♭7 E7

  Pick any pattern for A7—for example, Pattern #4 in fifth position—and begin playing two-bar phrases. When the key changes, switch to the closest pattern for that key—e.g., D7 Pattern #2—and continue soloing. Continue in the same manner over all 12 chords, switching to the closest pattern for each new key (you can find all patterns within a six-fret span). This exercise teaches you how to find melodies over any chord anywhere on the neck—a skill that will become especially important when you begin to play over chord changes.

Phrase Analysis

A scale pattern is set of notes with a pre-determined melodic relationship, but to create effective phrases on your own, you also need to be aware of the internal relationships between the melody, tonality, and harmony (at this point, the latter two are identical: A7). Analyze each phrase from the examples in this chapter and identify the relationship between the notes and the emotional effects. Some phrases sound sweeter, some tougher; these specific choices ultimately form your musical personality.

Shifting/Sliding

A good non-technical exercise for expanding connections between patterns is to play non-stop blues phrases at a medium tempo while you force yourself to shift or slide into a new pattern every two bars. If you can't think of what note to play next, just repeat the same note until you do (repetition is an important blues phrasing tool in its own right). This exercise requires you to think quickly and develop connections "on the fly."

Listen

All blues guitarists (at least those with standard setups and tuning) use patterns similar to those shown in this chapter, so analyzing any blues guitar solo to figure out what position the player is using will help you to broaden and deepen your understanding of the neck. Often there is more than one possible choice, but when you listen in depth to any one player, you can usually develop a fairly accurate idea of how they arrange phrases on the neck (of course video is extremely helpful if it's available). When it's not clear what position a player might be using, the least technically-complicated option is usually the right one.

The tracks mentioned below all offer examples of pattern-specific phrases that you can use to enhance your own knowledge of the neck. The patterns match the ones explained in this chapter, but most of the recordings are not in the key of A, so you'll need to transpose.

- **Lower Octave Pattern #4:** Freddie King was fluent in the lower register; check out the instrumentals "Sen-Sa-Shun," "The Stumble," and "Side Tracked" for phrases that cover the width of the neck. Gatemouth Brown was a bare-finger picker who liked the low strings ("Boogie Uproar"), and his disciple Albert Collins also liked to pop the low strings ("Don't Lose Your Cool"). The versatile Chicago stylist Earl Hooker also liked to play in the lower octave; check out his version of the classic R&B hit "The Hucklebuck" and his instrumental "Frog Hop."
- **Pattern #5:** Albert King had his own unique pattern system, but the string bends on "Crosscut Saw," "Personal Manager," and "Oh Pretty Woman" have been copied by generations of players, usually re-fingered in Pattern #5. *In Session*, a live audio/video recording featuring King and Stevie Ray Vaughan playing side-by-side, offers an extremely helpful

picture of how Vaughan transferred King's phrases and essential qualities into a standard guitar configuration.

- **Pattern #1:** There are countless recorded examples of B.B. King that feature him soloing in Pattern #1. Among them, the various slow blues solos from *Live at the Regal*—particularly "Worry, Worry"—provide an especially good cross-section of his phrasing, including his trademark major-oriented phrases, dynamic range, touch, and flow between and through patterns.
- **Pattern #3:** Pedal-point phrasing like that shown in Fig. 20 was used by Buddy Guy ("Leave My Girl Alone") and Lonnie Mack ("Why"), both of whom were major influences on Stevie Ray Vaughan. Eric Clapton used Pattern #3 on his well-known version of Freddie King's "Hide Away"; King played the opening major melody in open position (key of E, Pattern #4), but Clapton transposed it up the neck. Allman Brothers' guitarists Duane Allman and Dickey Betts also favored Pattern #3 for major-oriented phrasing; check out Betts' solo on "Statesboro Blues."
- **Connecting Patterns:** Particularly influential and/or classic examples of players roaming up and down the neck include Guitar Slim's "The Things That I Used to Do" (mostly played on the first string) and Lightnin' Hopkins' "Hopkins Sky Hop" (Hopkins observed no limits in E, his favorite key). Buddy Guy also routinely jumps the length of the neck. Other examples include "Pride and Joy" by Stevie Ray Vaughan, which draws on "The Stumble" by Freddie King, which itself draws on "That's All Right" by Jimmy Rogers. Hendrix was exceptionally linear in his phrasing; any of the many versions of "Red House" show his total command of the neck. Clapton is also very fluid; check out his version of "Hide Away" with John Mayall and the Bluesbreakers and "Crossroads" or "I'm So Glad" with Cream.

Part 2
12-Bar Soloing

The first section of this book presented all of the fundamental technical skills of blues soloing plus a comprehensive method for creating one- and two-bar phrases over a single chord anywhere on the neck. In other words, it was a large collection of blues licks. However, a good blues solo is much more than a string of licks; it's a complete musical story that is told with melody, harmony, rhythm, form, and touch. The next section of this book will show you how to make the leap from playing individual licks to creating coherent solos over one of the most common progressions in music: the 12-bar blues.

8 12-Bar Blues

Of the various ways in which blues songs have been written over the past hundred years, the most popular by far is the *12-bar blues.* Several years before the first commercial recordings of blues appeared in 1920, the 12-bar progression began appearing in popular piano sheet-music arrangements such as W.C. Handy's classic "St. Louis Blues." It was an innovative songwriting form that was appealing both for its harmonic simplicity—three chords arranged in an intuitive, self-contained cycle—and its lyric structure, which was designed to encourage spontaneous composition and arrangement. 12-bar blues has been with us ever since, but in the hands of creative writers and performers, it remains as fresh as it was when it was first created.

The chord arrangement within the 12-bar progression is based on general principles of harmony that also apply to music ranging from classical to pop to folk songs, but blues harmony has some unique qualities that affect the melodies we play when we solo.

Blues Changes

Blues harmony combines African and European musical influences that were brought to America through both the slave trade and immigration. Africans brought an emphasis on rhythm, micro-tonal melodies, and an interactive, improvisational performing style. From Europe came a highly structured approach to harmony and form as well as instruments meticulously designed for ensemble performance. Together, they contributed to the the distinctive sound of blues changes.

Diatonic Harmony

The chord progressions that we hear in most styles of popular music are based on the European system of *diatonic harmony.* In this highly-organized system, chords are created by stacking the notes of diatonic (seven-note) major or minor scales on top of each other to create a *harmonized scale.* The figure below shows the harmonized A major scale with each scale step harmonized by the notes three and five steps above it, forming triads. (The same method applies to all keys, and the same principle also applies to diatonic minor scales.)

Fig. 1: Harmonized A Major Scale

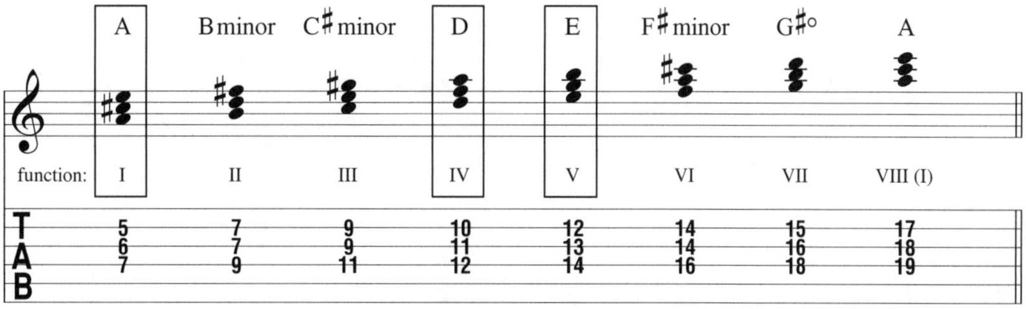

Of the seven different chords in the harmonized scale, the three that form the core of most progressions are those built on the first, fourth, and fifth scale steps. These are known formally as *tonic, subdominant,* and *dominant* but in "street" terms as the "one chord," "four chord," and "five chord" and are numbered I, IV, and V, respectively (chords are indicated by Roman numerals to distinguish them from melodies).

In harmonic terms, the one chord represents "home," or the place where the progression usually starts and ends. The four chord represents "going away" (a temporary departure from home), and the five chord represents "coming back" (the last stop before returning home). Each of the remaining chords in the harmonized scale is considered to be a variation on one of these three main chords, so the I–IV–V progression represents diatonic harmony stripped to its most basic elements. It's a perfect foundation for a no-frills style like blues, but before it can accommodate the unique sound of blues melody, it needs some blues-style modification.

Blues Harmony

In the tidy diatonic system, melody and harmony are in complete agreement with each other, but the non-diatonic, micro-tonal, shifting nature of blues melody means that devising the best chords for accompaniment is more an approximation than an exact science. As you know from the phrasing exercises so far, the chord quality that comes closest to matching the unique sound of blues is the dominant seventh, and this is also true for the other chords in the progression. The following example compares the minor pentatonic scale to the I7–IV7–V7 chord structures; while the scale and chords don't match exactly, they effectively approximate each other:

Fig. 2: Pentatonic Scale and Blues Harmony

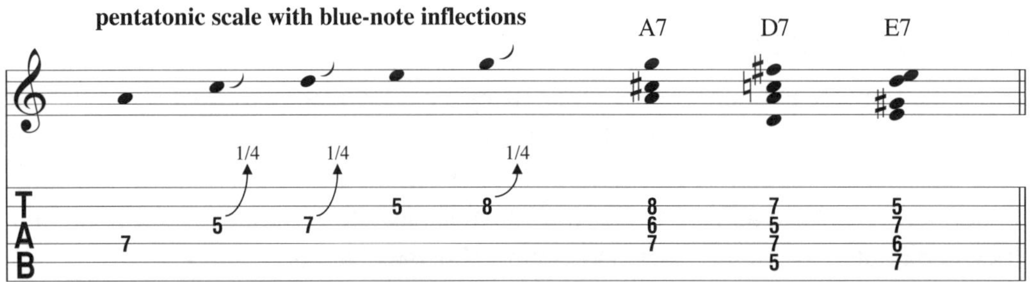

Compared to diatonic pop music, dominant seventh-based harmony contains a slight dissonance, a feeling of constant underlying tension. Like blues melody, there's always a little salt mixed in with the sweet, and together, the complementary sounds of dominant-based harmony and blue-note melody create the unique effect of blues tonality. The following example compares a diatonic I–IV–V progression to the dominant-seventh blues version; play the two back-to-back to hear the difference.

Fig. 3: Diatonic Harmony vs. Blues Harmony

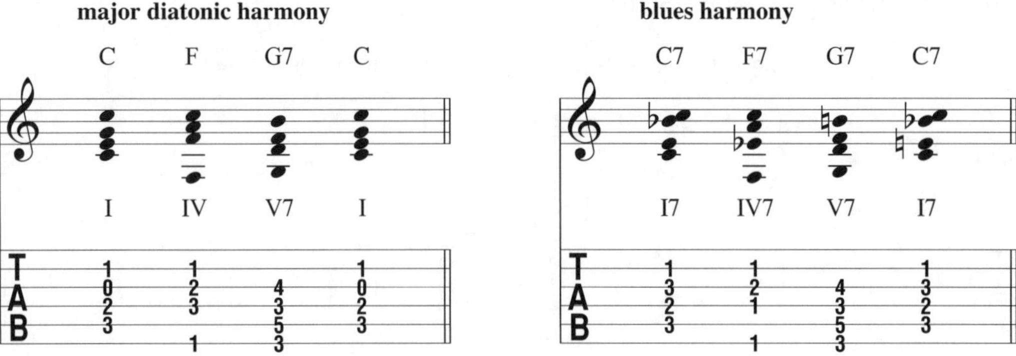

12-Bar Form

Popular song arrangements usually include different sections—intro, verse, chorus, bridge, etc.—each with different lyrics and chord changes, but 12-bar blues is based on a much simpler concept: three lines of lyrics accompanied by three dominant seventh chords arranged in an infinitely repeatable cycle.

The simplicity of the 12-bar form makes it easy to create or modify a blues song on the spot. You can invent melodies or change the key, tempo, or rhythmic style. You can add or subtract 12-bar repetitions (choruses), rearrange the number and order of vocals and solos, or change the lyrics, all without the need for charts or rehearsal.

Standard 12-bar form is illustrated below. The second bar shows an optional change to the IV7 chord called a *quick change* or *quick four* (conversely, staying on the I7 chord for the first four bars is known as a *slow change*). The last two bars in the progression are called the *turnaround* (the IV7 on the turnaround is also optional; turnarounds are examined in much more detail later in this chapter).

Fig. 4: 12-Bar Form

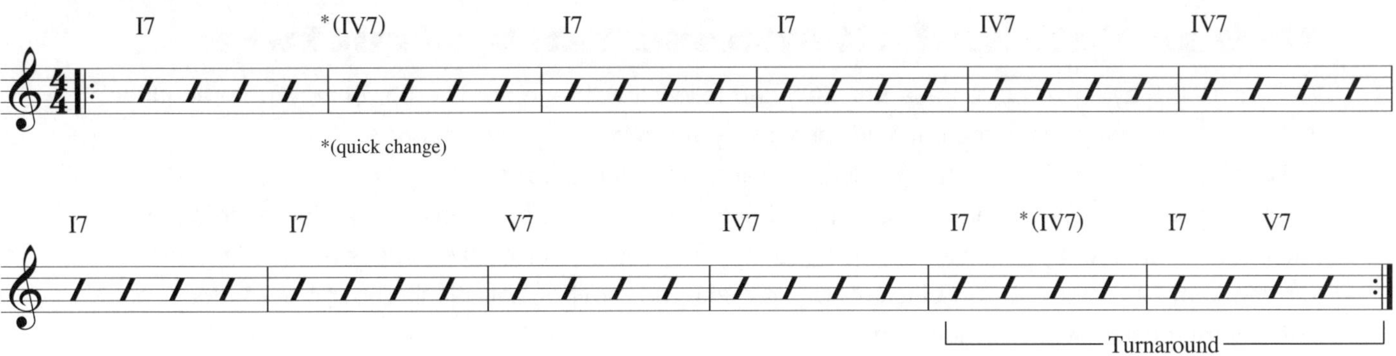

12-bar song form is divided internally into three four-bar sections. The first section consists of two bars of lyrics followed by a two-bar instrumental interlude. In the second section, the same words are repeated over different chord changes, and in the third section the idea concludes and is followed by an instrumental turnaround. The lyrics of a blues song are usually based around a central theme, but the 12-bar format allows a singer to create lyrics on the spot either by drawing ideas from the common well of blues tradition (known as *floating verses*) or making them up "freestyle."

The following example illustrates classic 12-bar form with one of the best-known blues songs of all time: "St. Louis Blues" by W.C. Handy (we'll look more closely at how the melody is arranged later in this chapter).

Fig. 5: 12-Bar AAB Lyric Structure

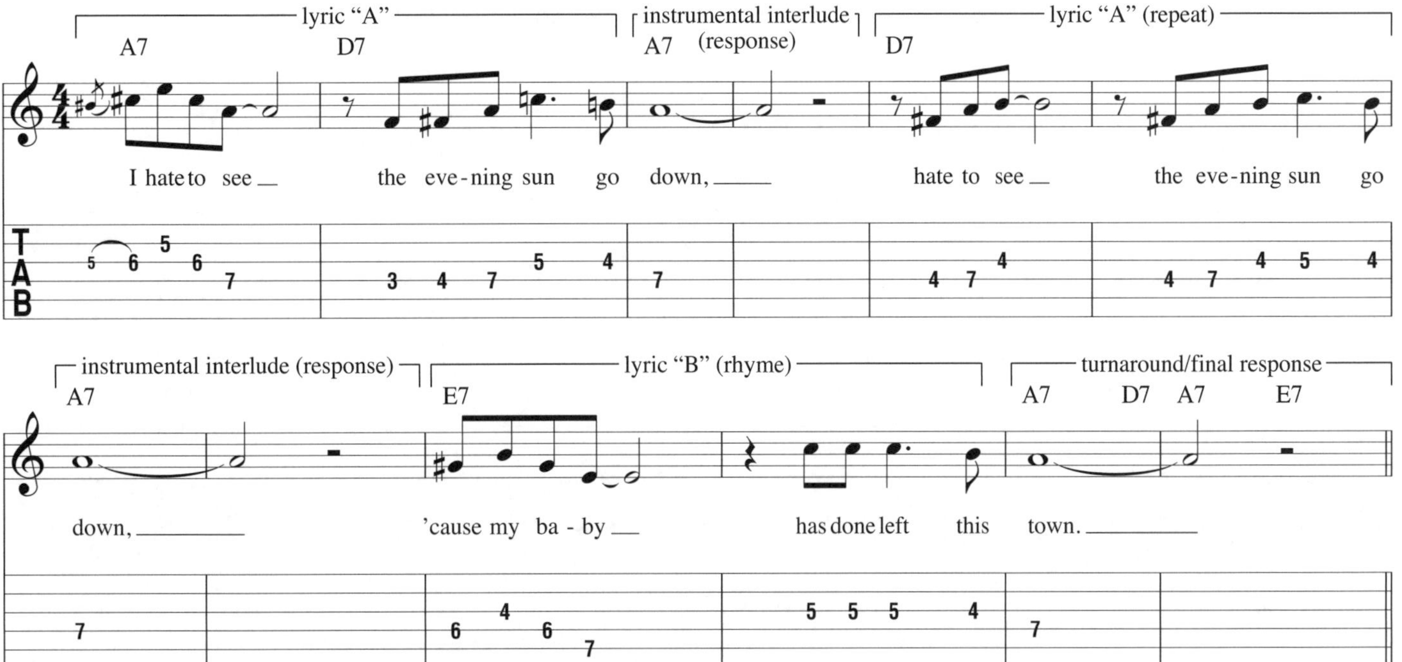

Call-and-Response Phrasing

From field hollers to gospel to jazz and blues, one of the common defining characteristics of African-American musical styles is the constant form of interaction known as *call-and-response.* Call-and-response takes place on a number of levels—within a two-bar phrase, between phrases, between singers and instruments, between a solo and the band, and even between the band and the audience.

12-bar structure is specifically designed for call-and-response interaction, with each two-bar vocal phrase followed by a two-bar instrumental break (or fill) intended to "answer" the vocal. When you play a guitar solo, the same call-and-response structure applies, but the guitar carries on both sides of the conversation, as follows:

12-Bar Call-and-Response Solo Structure

Bars 1–4: Play a two-bar phrase (the call) and follow it with another two-bar phrase (the response).

Bars 5–8: Repeat the same call-and-response pattern with slight variations.

Bars 9–12: Play a different two-bar "call" followed by a turnaround.

Using call-and-response phrasing, you can build a complete 12-bar solo out of as few as three phrases and a turnaround, and you can keep it going for any number of additional choruses by inserting new ideas into the same structure. It's an efficient way to make the most out of a limited number of ideas, but it's also a very musical way of organizing a solo no matter how many licks you know.

The following example illustrates a 12-bar solo arranged with call-and-response phrasing. Phrasing is like a three-legged stool resting on a combination of melody, rhythm, and touch, and the example shows how the three balance one another. The melody is minimal and repetitive, but strong rhythmic phrasing and touch complete the message. Albert Collins was a particular master of this style of phrasing, but all great blues guitar soloists know how to make a lot out of a little; it's a big part of what makes blues sound like blues.

> **NOTE:** Essential elements like picking style, dynamics, and tone can't be captured by notation, but you can hear them on the audio demo.

Fig. 6: 12-Bar Call-and-Response Solo

Performance Notes

1. Bars 1, 5, 9: Pluck the note very hard with a bare finger, instantly slide up two frets and add vibrato; this specific combination of techniques was a trademark of Albert Collins.

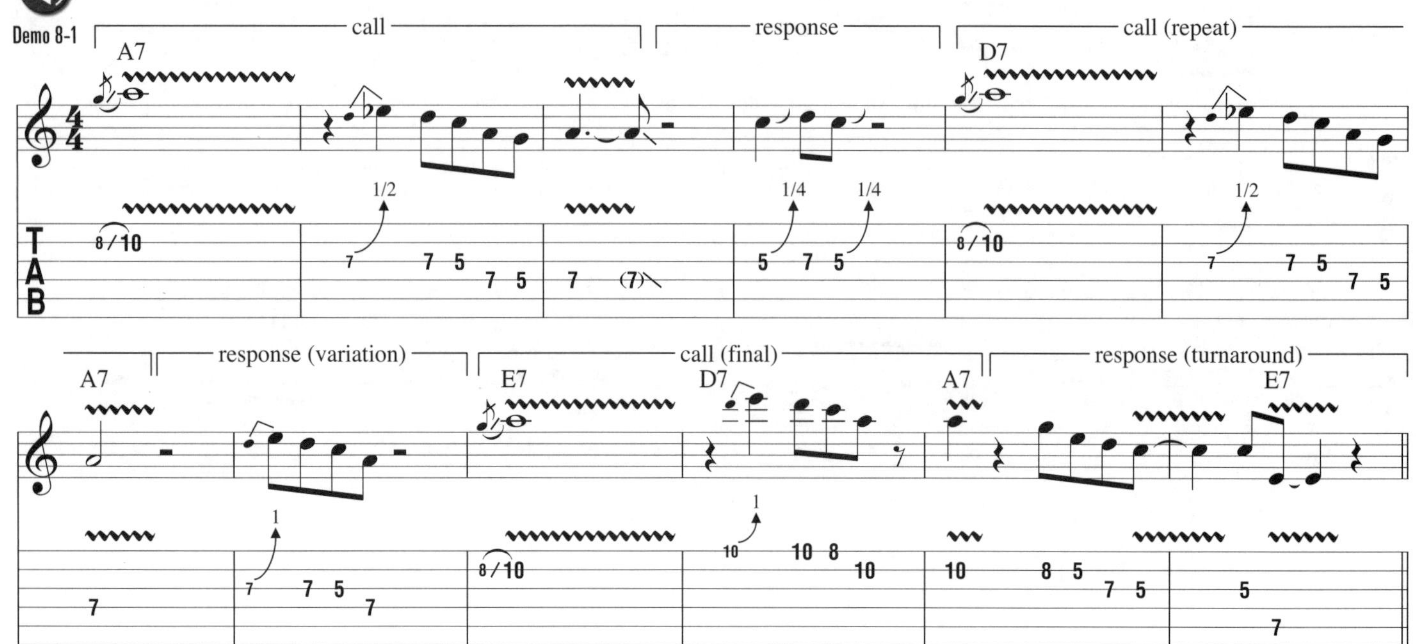

Making the Changes

The next step in learning how to solo over 12-bar form is to look closely at how the chord progression affects your phrasing. Changing the harmony behind a melody changes the emotional qualities of the notes, and playing a solo that takes this into account, known as *making the changes*, requires you to become aware of the relationship between the key and the chords.

Harmonic Awareness: Key and Chord

So far we have focused exclusively on learning how various note choices create different feelings over a single dominant seventh chord. Playing the major 3rd (C♯) over A7, for example, sounds "sweet," and as long as you solo over that chord, the emotional quality remains constant. But when the chords change, the feeling evoked by a note also changes. Over D7 (IV7), the relationship of C♯ to the harmony shifts from a major 3rd to a major 7th—an extremely dissonant interval—and what was sweet quickly turns sour.

The chords and the melody all belong to the same key, or underlying tonality, but the melody also has a unique relationship with each chord. To create effective melodies over a chord progression, you need to develop *harmonic awareness*—i.e., the ability to simultaneously hear the relationship of the melody to the central tonality, or *key center*, and to the specific harmony at the moment, or chord tones.

Key Center Phrasing

The *key center scale* is the scale that is most closely related to all of the chords in a given key; in blues, this is the blue-note pentatonic. The first step in developing harmonic awareness is to locate the roots of the I7, IV7, and V7 chords within the pentatonic scale and make them the focus of your phrasing over each respective chord. You don't need to add any new notes to your vocabulary; just adjust the timing of your phrases so that you hit the root of each chord on the downbeat. For example, in Fig. 6, replace A with D in bar 5 and with E in bar 9, and without making any other alterations to the notes or rhythms you'll "hear" the changes and the form even when you play it without accompaniment. This is the essence of harmonically-aware phrasing.

You can very quickly begin the transition from playing over one chord to playing harmonically-aware 12-bar solos by simply integrating the roots of the IV7 and V7 chords into the phrases presented so far in this book. The next example shows how to do it. This 12-bar solo consists entirely of familiar one- and two-bar blue-note pentatonic phrases; the only difference is that when the progression changes to IV7 and V7, the melody is adjusted to target the root of the new chord on the downbeat.

Fig. 7: Key-Center Phrasing

Performance Notes

1. Bars 1–4: The solo opens with a simple call-and-response melody; the rhythm "breathes" in the same way a vocalist sings.
2. Bars 5–6: The sustained D (root of IV7) allows the phrasing to rest briefly before the second "call" resumes.
3. Bars 7–8: The melody targets A on the downbeat followed by the rest of the response.
4. Bars 9–10: The melody targets E, the root of the V7 chord, and then D, the root of IV7.
5. Bars 11–12: The turnaround melody targets E (V7) in bar 12 before leading back to A to start the next chorus.

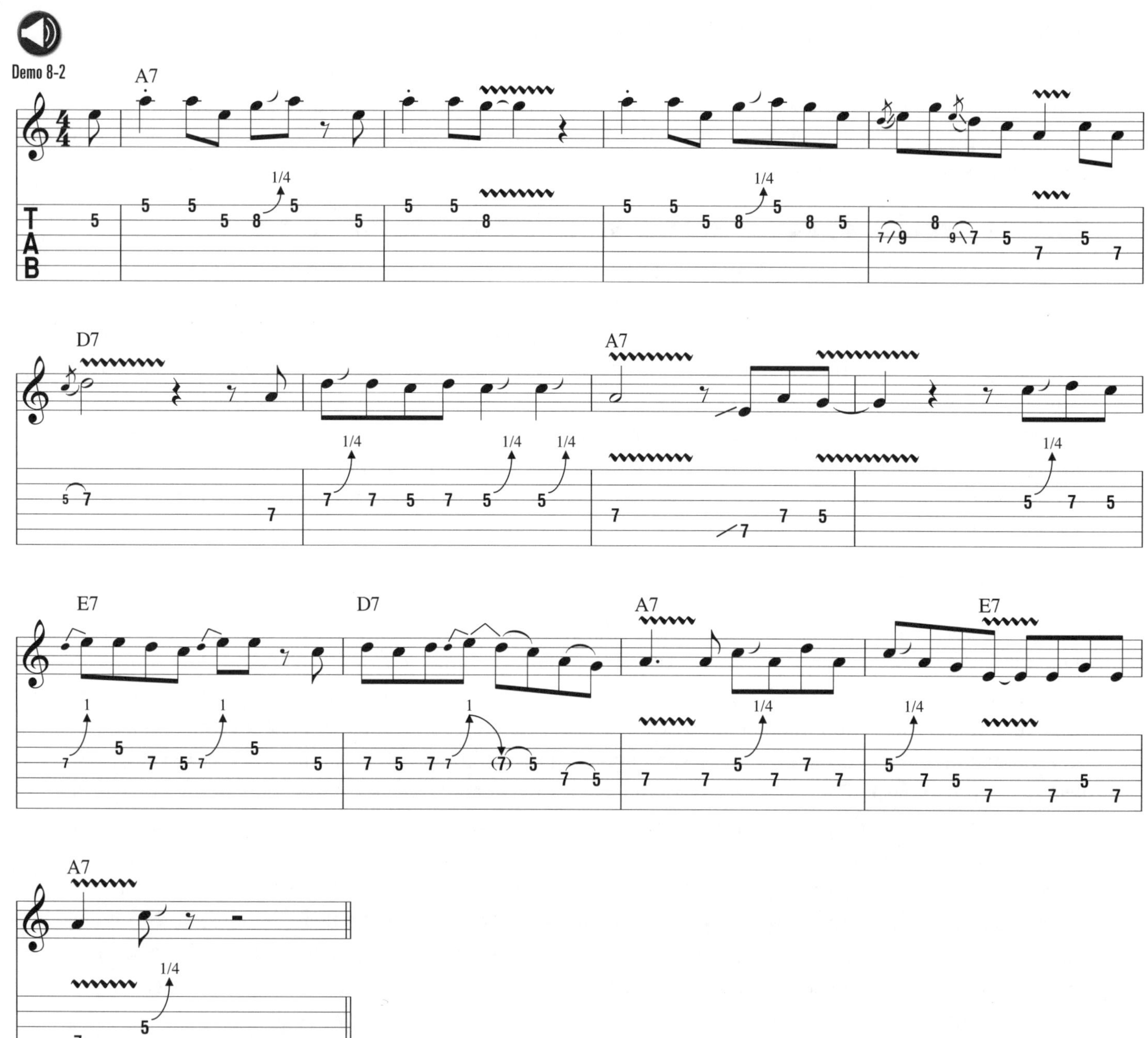

Chord Tones: 3rds and 7ths

The key center encompasses a huge variety of melodies, and some players rarely go beyond it, but songs like "St. Louis Blues" and solos by players like B.B. King display a level of harmonic awareness that isn't captured by key-center melodies alone; these reflect the sound of *chord tones*. In addition to the root, the two chord tones that together most clearly define the sound of a dominant seventh chord are the major 3rd and minor 7th. Learning to integrate these chord tones into your phrasing along with the root greatly increases your melodic range.

To practice targeting chord tones, we will divide the 12-bar progression into two pairs of changes: I7–IV7 and I7–V7. Fig. 8 demonstrates phrases that are based around the half-step connections between the 3rds and 7ths of I7 and IV7. These are not just exercises but actual phrases that have been used in blues songs and solos for decades; the concept of chord tones may seem theoretical, but when the phrases are played with a strong rhythm and touch, the results are pure blues.

Before you play the example, prepare by taking these steps:

- Compare the A7 and D7 chord voicings in fifth position (see the chord diagrams).
- Find the closest connection between the tones of A7 and D7:
  - » The major 3rd of A7 (C♯) is a half step above the 7th of D7 (C).
  - » The 7th of A7 (G) is a half step above the major 3rd of D7 (F♯).

Fig. 8: 3rds and 7ths: I7–IV7

Performance Notes

1. Bars 1–4: This is a standard phrase similar to the melody of the all-time T-Bone Walker classic "T-Bone Shuffle" that is built around the shift from C♯ (the major 3rd of A7) to C natural (the 7th degree of D7); this half-step shift is at the heart of countless blues phrases over the I7–IV7 change.
2. Bars 5–8: The A7 phrase emphasizes G (the 7th degree of A7); the final G sets up the change to F♯ (major 3rd of D7) at the beginning of bar 7. The rest of the phrase outlines the D7 chord before setting up the return to C♯ at the beginning of the next bar.

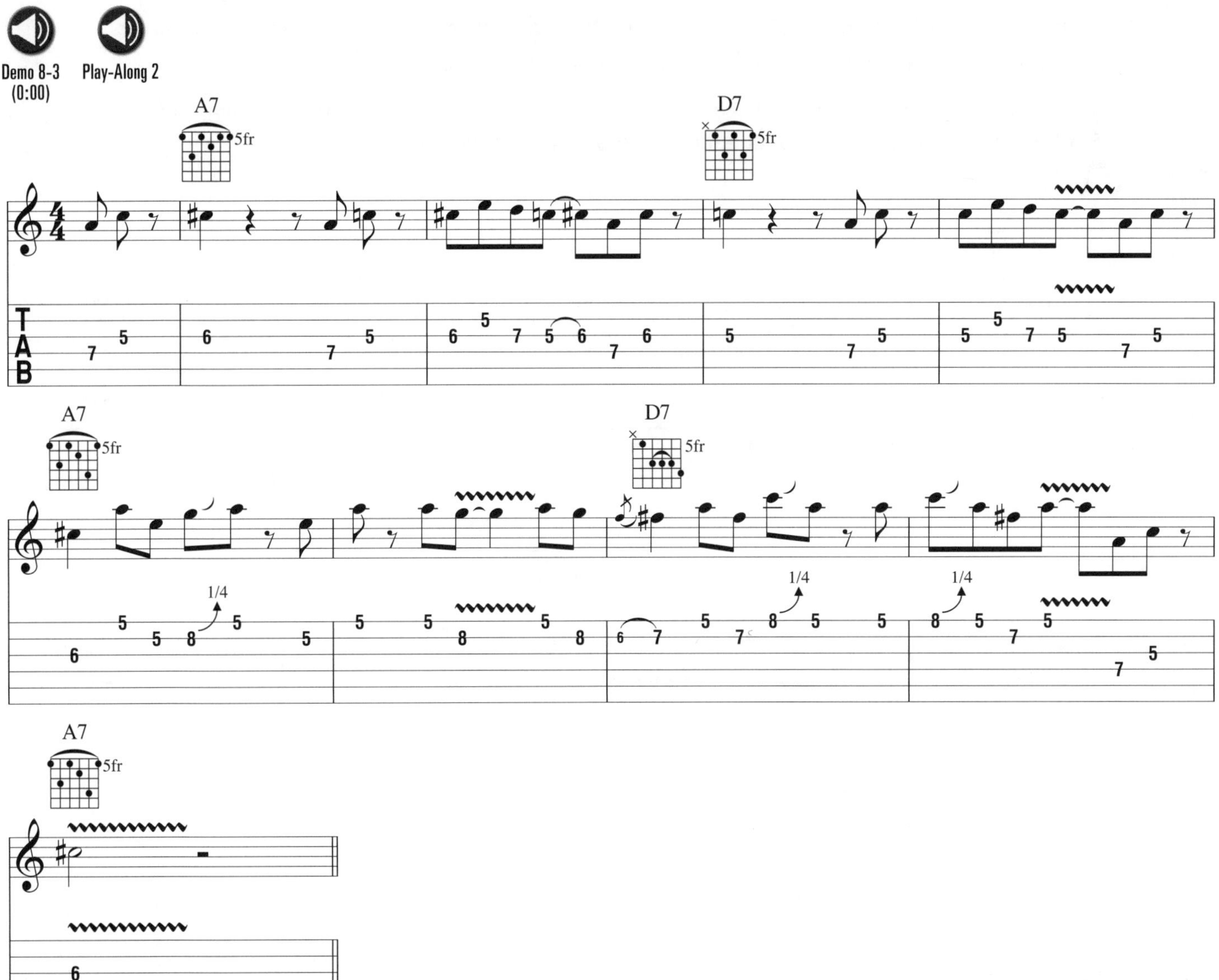

Memorize these phrases to jump-start your chord tone vocabulary. The same chord tones are everywhere on the neck; when you can comfortably see and hear the half-step connections in this position, you can extend the same idea to other positions by following the same procedure, but always balance every new melodic idea with equal parts timing and touch to keep the phrases convincing and not too "technical." Play over the changes again and again until you can consistently hear and feel the next chord coming before it gets there—that's the definition of harmonic awareness.

Next, we'll apply the same approach—targeting 3rds and 7ths—to the I7–V7 change. Again, play the chord voicings in fifth position (see the diagrams provided) and compare shapes:

- The major 3rd of A7 (C♯) is a half step below the 7th of E7 (D).
- The 7th of A7 (G) is a half step below the major 3rd of E7 (G♯); the root (A) is a half step above the same note.

Fig. 9: 3rds and 7ths: I7–V7

Performance Notes

1. Bars 1–4: This phrase reminiscent of the Louis Jordan/B.B. King classic "Caldonia" emphasizes C♯ (the major 3rd of A7); on E7, the melody shifts up a half step to the 7th of E7 (D) and goes on to outline the E7 chord shape. The final G gives a blue-note twist to the major 3rd of E (G♯) before resolving to A at the beginning of the next bar.
2. Bars 5–8: The A7 phrase emphasizes G (the 7th of A7), which slides up a half step to G♯ (the major 3rd) of E; the final blue-note G again sets up the return to A.

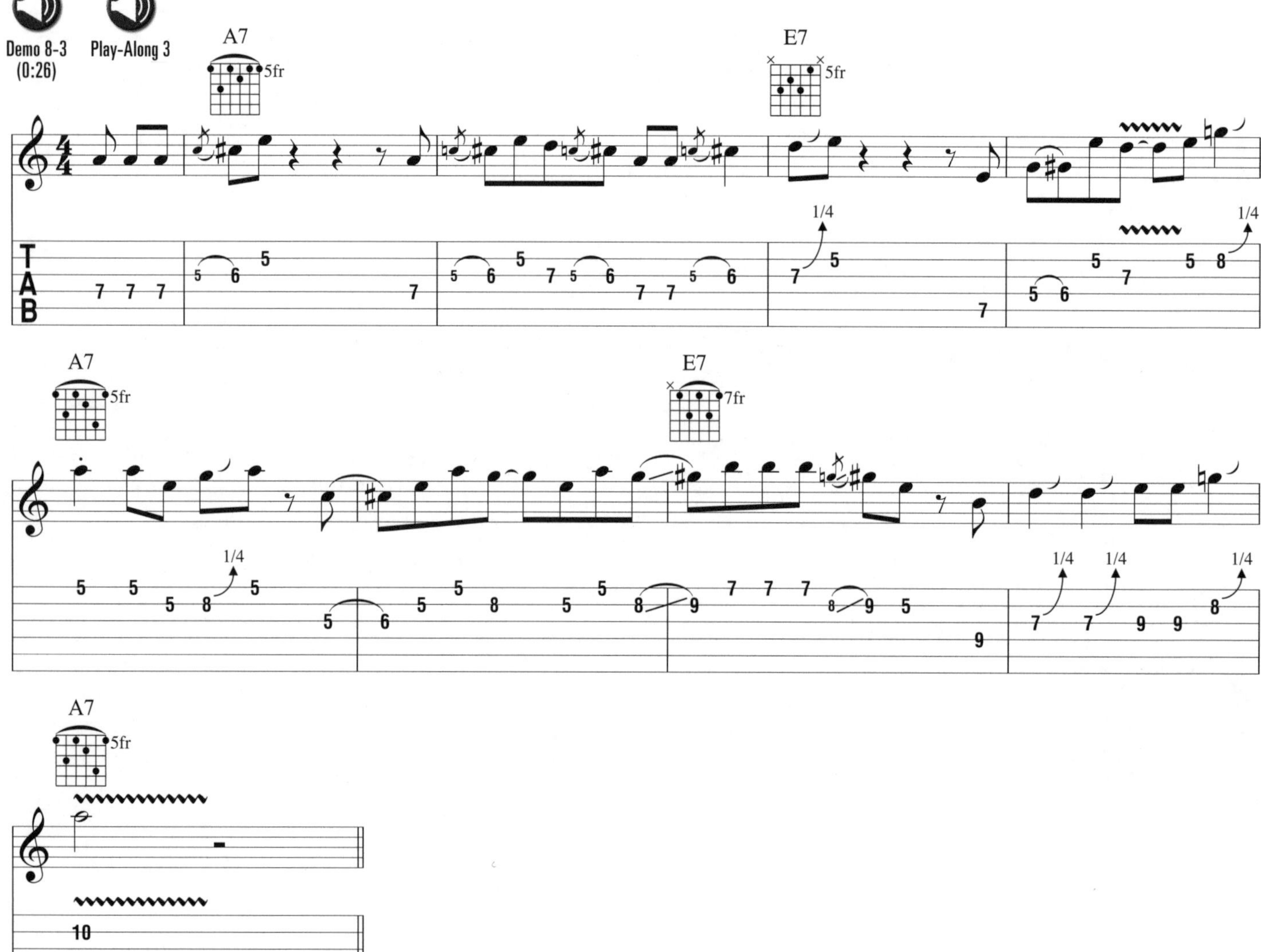

12-Bar Chord-Tone Phrasing

The next example assembles the I7–IV7 and I7–V7 changes into a 12-bar progression. The melody arranges the half-step shifts between 3rds and 7ths in a 12-bar call-and-response structure similar to blues classics like "T-Bone Shuffle" and "Caldonia." The sparse melodic phrasing leaves the "answers" open for the rhythm section to fill, like the classic horn-section arrangements of 1940s and 1950s blues.

Fig. 10: "Three-Seven Blues"

Performance Notes

1. Bars 1–4: The main theme centers around the major 3rd of I7 (C♯).
2. Bars 5–6: C♯ drops to C natural, the minor 7th of D7 (IV7), while the rest of phrase remains the same.
3. Bars 9–10: E7 is reflected with just one note, the 7th (D), followed by a variation on the main theme that includes the 3rd of D7 (F♯).
4. Bars 11–12: This standard turnaround phrase concludes with the root of V7.

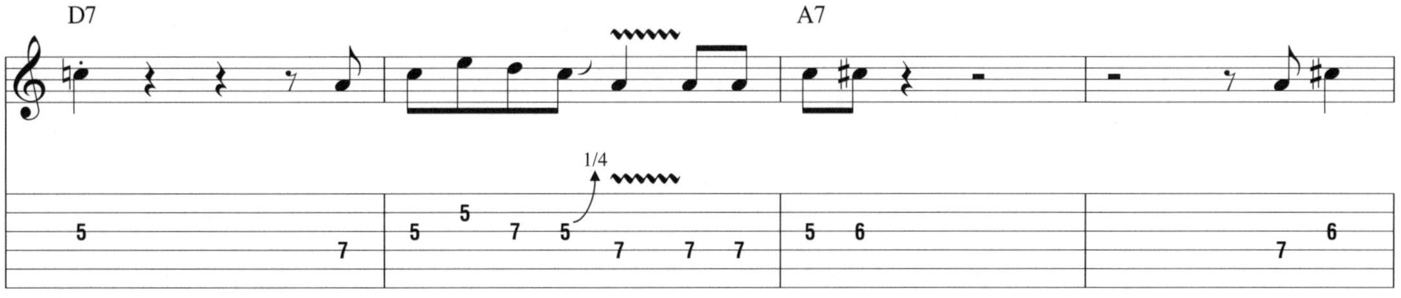

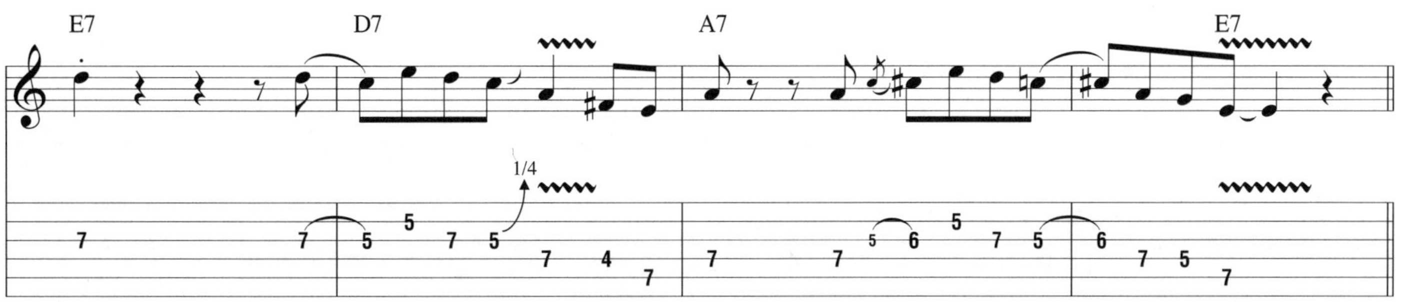

The next example is a 12-bar solo roughly based around the melody of "St. Louis Blues" that integrates chord tones and color tones (the 6th and 9th) as well as filled-in responses for more continuous flow. Greater harmonic awareness helps give the phrasing some of the natural melodic qualities of a vocal line, and in fact one of the best ways to develop and expand your use of chord tones is to imitate and analyze vocal melodies.

Fig. 11: "St. Louis Blues" Chord-Tone Solo

Performance Notes

1. Bars 1–2: The first "call" quotes the vocal melody of "St. Louis Blues" with a few embellishments. On the quick change in bar 2, the melody emphasizes the 3rd (F♯) and 7th (C) of D7, while the shift to Pattern #3 provides easier fingering.
2. Bars 3–4: The response is based around the A7 chord structure, filling in the melodic line with the 6th and then moving in half steps down to C (the 7th of D7).
3. Bars 5–6: The melody echoes "St. Louis Blues" again, emphasizing the 3rd and 7th of D7 as the fingering shifts again to Pattern #3.
4. Bars 7–8: The second response is a variation of the first.
5. Bars 9–10: The high point of a 12-bar blues solo usually comes over the V7 change—here, the melody emphasizes B and G♯ (the 5th and major 3rd, respectively, of E7) and outlines the D before returning to A.
6. Bars 11–12: This is a standard turnaround phrase based on chord tones; the added IV7 in the turnaround is a common variation in melodic blues.

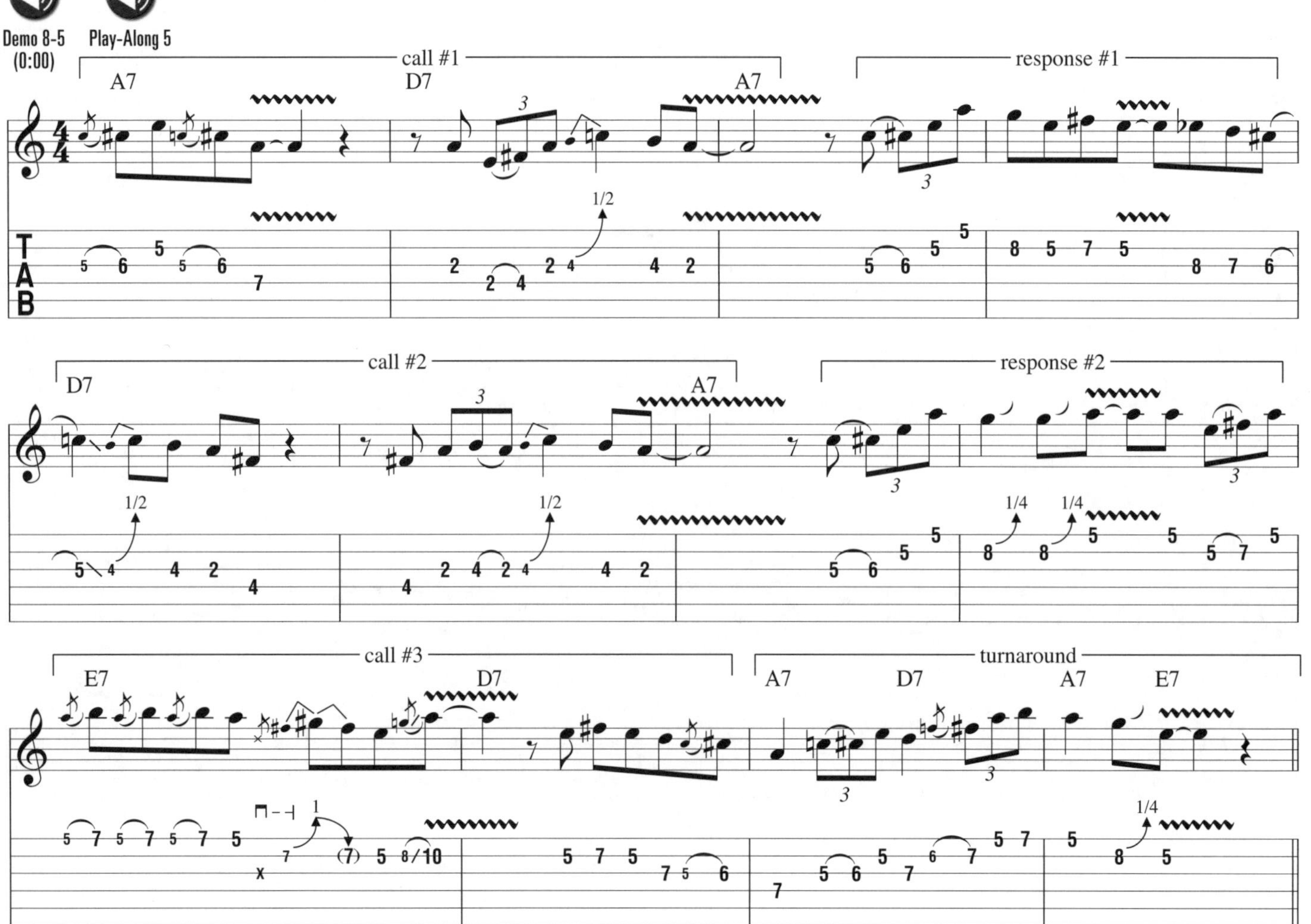

(**NOTE:** The examples in Figs. 11 and 12 are performed on the audio demo back-to-back.)

The next example demonstrates how drastically the attitude of a solo can be affected by making different melodic choices. It is based on the same rhythmic phrasing as "St. Louis Blues," but in this case the melody stays mainly within the key center, and in place of an emphasis on chord tones, awareness of the form and changes is suggested mainly through the rhythm. Where the previous example is smooth and sophisticated (uptown), this example is somewhat more down home.

Fig. 12: "St. Louis Blues" Key-Center Solo

Performance Notes

1. Bars 1–2: The opening phrase roughly follows the rhythm of "St. Louis Blues," but the melody uses the key-center minor pentatonic in a style similar to Albert King (on the audio demo, the picking technique also shifts from flatpicking to bare fingers).
2. Bars 3–4: The response is a classic down home blues lick.
3. Bars 5–6: The second "call" varies the rhythm and hints at the D7 chord with the quick slide down to F♯ (the major 3rd). The continuation in bar 6 uses two consecutive finger rolls in the style of Freddie King.
4. Bars 7–8: The second response is another straight-ahead blues lick.
5. Bars 9–10: The G quarter-tone bend creates a blue 3rd over E7, a classic down home effect. The D7 phrase moves down the neck through three different patterns, again reminiscent of Freddie King.
6. Bars 11–12: The turnaround is similar to the phrase in bar 6. The solo concludes with a classic half-step move into the I7 chord (see more on turnarounds and endings later in this chapter).

Comparing Key Centers and Chord Tones

We have approached key centers and chord tones separately in order to focus attention on the details of each concept, but they are really two sides of the same coin. The important question is not which technical or theoretical approach to take, but rather how you want the melody to *feel*: gritty and down home, sweet and romantic, or any other shade of emotion that suits the song. Key centers and chord tones are just different tools for organizing the notes you play and translating feelings into melodies, and with practice the concepts merge into a single, comprehensive approach to soloing.

Pickup Phrases

The examples of 12-bar solos shown so far consist almost entirely of familiar two-bar phrases arranged in a call-and-response format. However, these examples also display an essential phrasing technique that we have not yet examined in detail: *pickup phrases*, or short phrases that conclude on the downbeat of a bar. Pickup phrases (or simply *pickups*) are an essential ingredient in harmonically-aware phrasing because they help to emphasize important points in the solo, draw listeners in, and carry them along with the flow of ideas.

In Fig. 11, for example, pickups lead into bars 4, 8, 9, and 12. And in Fig. 12, they lead into bars 4, 5, 8, and 9. In each case, the pickup is specifically arranged to set up a chord tone on the downbeat, and like the cymbal splash at the end of a drum fill, it's the last note that has the greatest effect. Pickups sound so intuitive that they're easy to overlook, but like most "natural" techniques, learning to use them effectively takes thought and practice.

Pickups can start on various beats, but the most common starting point is the third upbeat of the bar (the "and" of beat 3). The following example shows an all-time classic sweet-sounding blues pickup phrase used by B.B. King and many others followed by a somewhat saltier version based on the same rhythm; like all blues phrases, the melody of a pickup can draw on any part of the emotional spectrum.

Fig. 13: "And of Three" Pickup Phrases

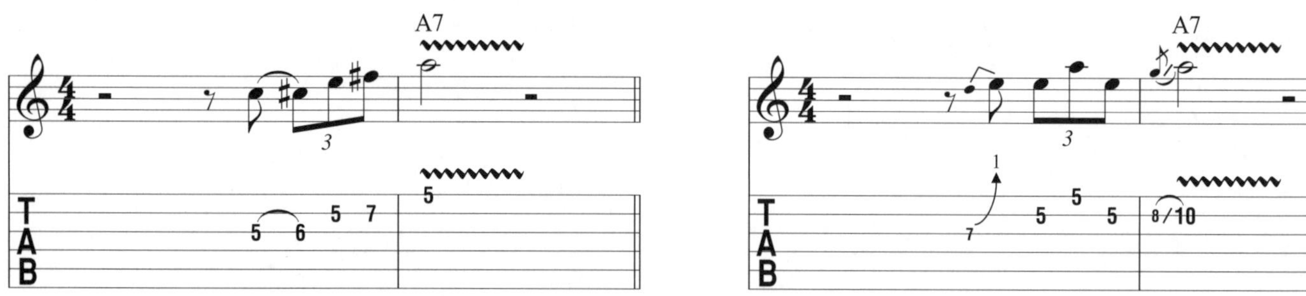

The following 12-bar pickup exercise employs the same rhythm to lead into every bar of a 12-bar progression, always concluding on a chord tone. This constant repetition is designed to reinforce the concept, but of course in practice it's best to avoid such overly predictable phrasing and instead reserve pickups for key points in the solo (see Fig. 15).

Fig. 14: Pickup Blues

Performance Notes

1. Bar 1: A classic B.B.-style intro lands on the root of I7 (A); the pickups in bars 3, 8, 11, and 12 also land on the root of I7.
2. Bar 2: The pickup lands on the 7th degree of IV7 (the quick change).
3. Bar 4: The pickup lands on the 7th degree of I7, which creates a feeling of anticipation for the change to IV7 in the next bar.
4. Bar 5: The pickup lands on the major 3rd of IV7.

5. Bar 6: The pickup lands on the 5th degree of IV7.
6. Bar 7: The pickup lands on the blue 3rd of I7.
7. Bars 9–10: The pickup lands on the 5th degree of V7 and IV7, respectively.

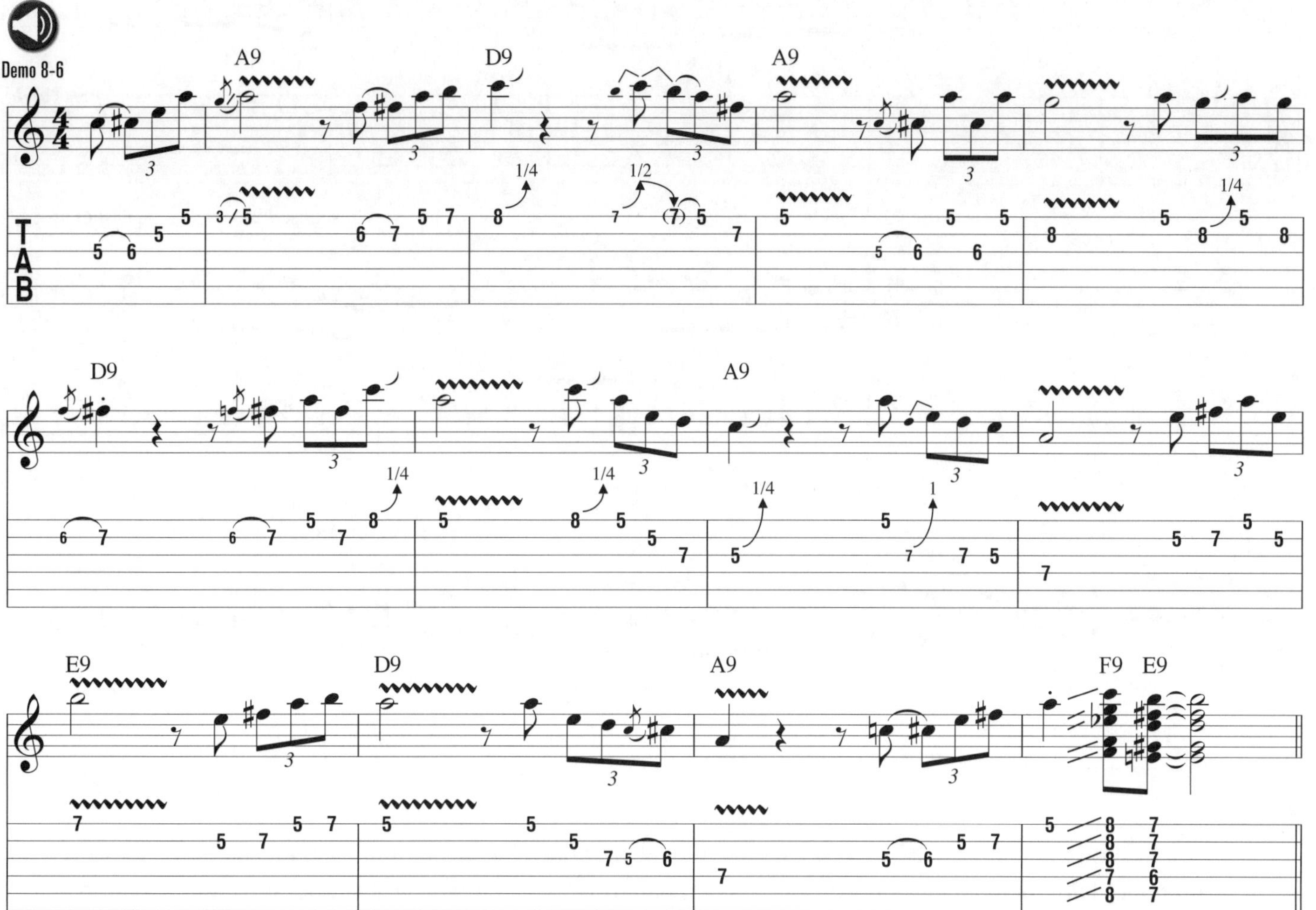

Combining 12-Bar Phrasing Skills

The following example combines three of the 12-bar soloing concepts presented so far: call-and-response phrasing, chord-tone melodies, and pickup phrases. The individual phrases themselves are nothing new, but the emphasis is on creating a coherent, harmonically-aware 12-bar solo. Like all good phrasing skills, when these techniques are used properly, a listener will not even be aware of them—despite the amount of practice and thought that goes into creating a good 12-bar story, it should sound effortless.

Fig. 15: Combining Phrasing Skills

Performance Notes

1. Bars 1–4: A pickup phrase introduces the main "theme" of the solo, which is extremely simple: two eighth notes on the downbeat (similar to B.B. King's solo on "Rock Me Baby"). The answer in bars 3–4 is followed by a pickup into IV7.
2. Bars 5–8: The second call uses the same rhythm as the first and emphasizes the 7th of IV7. In bar 6, use either your third or fourth finger to execute the rapid hammer-on/pull-off (if you use your third finger, then use your second finger to fret F♯ on the second string). Note that the rhythm in bar 8 matches the rhythm in bar 4, another subliminal repetition that helps to tie the solo together. At the end of bar 8, a pickup leads into V7.
3. Bars 8–12: The melody emphasizes chord tones on V7 and IV7 before concluding with a standard Freddie King-style melodic turnaround phrase.

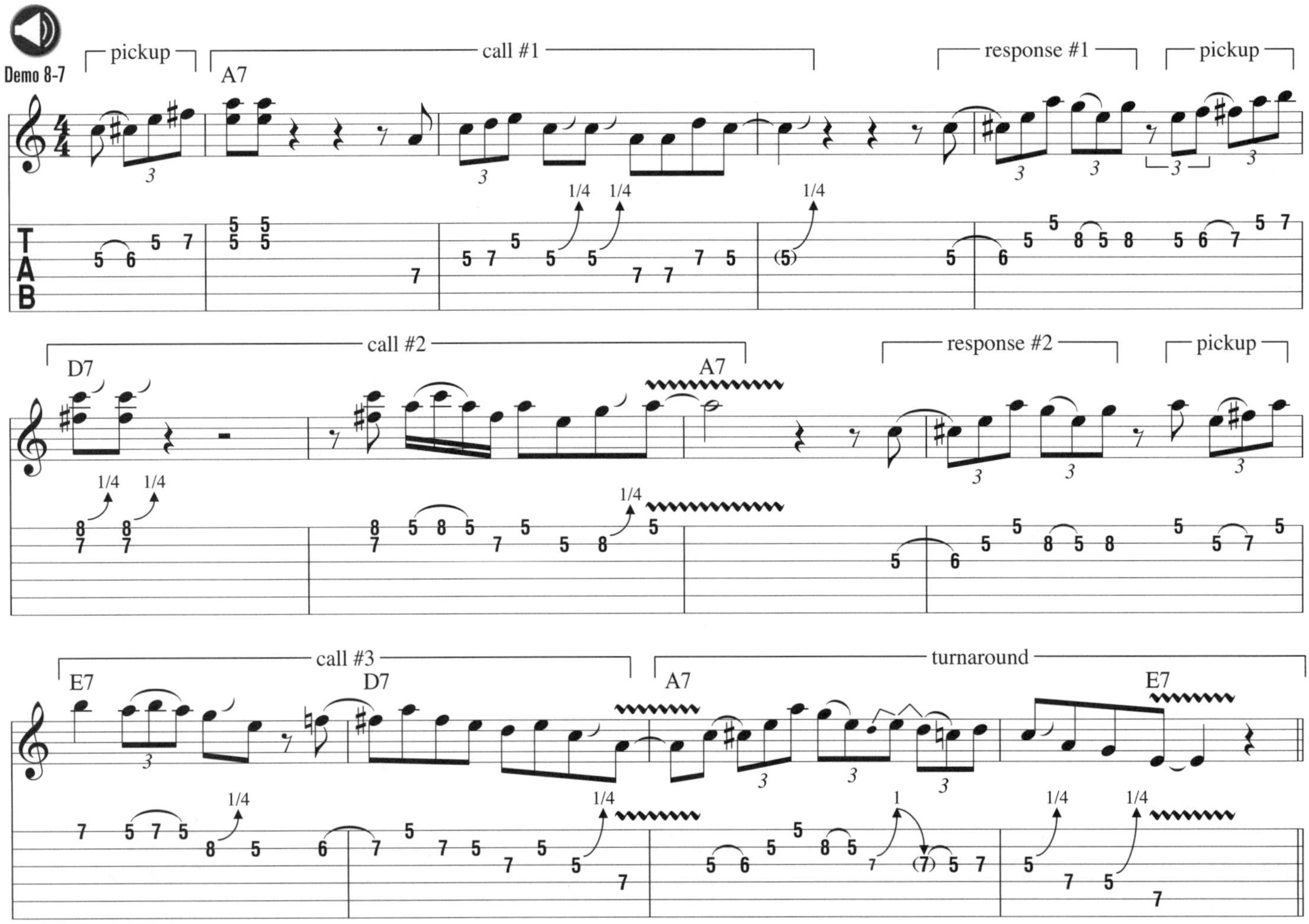

Demo 8-7

All of these soloing concepts have been derived by analyzing a number of great blues solos and comparing different techniques and approaches. Learning these concepts will strengthen the foundations of your own playing, but there is no substitute for doing the same thing on your own. All good blues players must go through the process of microscopically studying the players who preceded them and using what they learn to inspire their own creativity.

Turnarounds

The difference between a series of blues licks and a good 12-bar blues solo lies in how you combine the individual phrases into a complete story. Every story needs a good ending, so we need to pay particular attention to how we handle the final two bars of the progression, or *turnaround*. The turnaround can function either as the transition into the next chorus or as the final statement of a song, and to be effective in either role, it needs clear ideas and strong delivery.

Classic Turnarounds

The type of turnaround that was common in blues arrangements of the 1920s and 1930s was derived from even older popular music styles—*ragtime* and *barbershop quartets*—which characteristically featured a certain chord pattern in the final two bars of the progression.

Fig. 16: Classic Turnaround Harmony

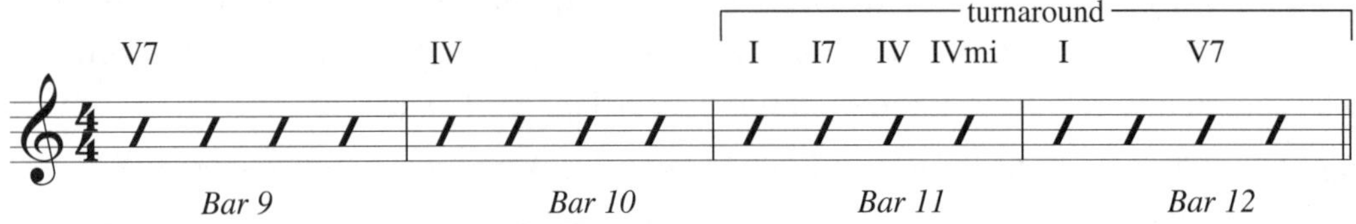

The piano was the main harmonic instrument in early pop music styles, and piano players devised an assortment of stock turnaround phrases to fit the changes in bar 11. These melodies were designed to connect the tonic chord on the downbeat of bar 11 to the tonic chord on the downbeat of bar 12 by moving *chromatically* (in half steps) from one chord tone to the next, as shown in the following example adapted for guitar (the lines can be played either descending or ascending):

Fig. 17: Source Melodies for Classic Turnarounds

A A7 D7 Dmi6 A

maj 3rd → root

A A7 D7 Dmi A

♭7th → 5th

A A7 D7(♭9) Dmi6 A

5th → maj 3rd

As bare-bones melodies, these lines don't sound like much, but with a little rhythmic and melodic shaping, they emerge as very familiar phrases. Classic turnarounds almost all follow the basic format shown here, and once you know how it works, they're fairly easy to learn and modify:

Classic Turnaround Structure

1. Begin the turnaround phrase on the second beat of bar 11.
2. Play a melody consisting of either a single line moving against the tonic or any combination of the melodic lines from Fig. 17 played in harmony.
3. Phrase the melody in shuffled eighth notes or triplets.
4. End the melody on the downbeat of bar 12, followed by the V7 chord on the second upbeat ("and" of beat 2).
5. After the V7 chord, fill the rest of bar 12 with a transitional phrase leading into the downbeat of the next chorus.

The following examples show some classic turnaround phrases based on this format. To practice these turnarounds in the context of a solo, plug each of the examples into the last two bars of the solo in Fig. 15 in place of the existing turnaround (the audio demonstration for each turnaround begins with the same melody from bars 9–10 of Fig. 15). When you play your own solos, pick a specific turnaround ahead of time and practice making a seamless transition from your solo into the turnaround.

Classic turnarounds were particularly common among guitarists in the Mississippi Delta region who directly influenced the first generation of electrified Chicago musicians, including Muddy Waters, Elmore James, Jimmy Reed, and many others. These turnarounds remain essential when you perform down home styles—particularly Chicago and Delta blues. It's important to point out that, particularly in medium to up-tempo electric blues, the harmony of the turnaround usually does not match the changes shown in Fig. 16—the IV and IV minor chords in bar 11 are nearly always eliminated, but the melodic phrasing remains the same either way.

The first example was a favorite of Chicago blues great Jimmy Reed.

Fig. 18: Jimmy Reed-Style Turnaround

Performance Notes

1. Melodically, the turnaround consists of two lines descending in harmony: the 3rd down to the root and the 5th down to the 3rd.
2. Pick the notes with a flatpick or use hybrid picking; either way, hybrid picking is recommended for the double stop on the downbeat of bar 12.
3. After the conclusion of the turnaround figure, the rest of the bar shows a typical Chicago-style phrase used to connect the turnaround to the beginning of the next chorus. Add stylistic flavor by using an up-stroke rake with the pick before the low B.

The next turnaround, a favorite of Chicago icon Muddy Waters, is based on two lines ascending in harmony (3rd up to the 5th, 5th up to the 7th); the same phrase is also often played descending.

Fig. 19: Muddy Waters-Style Turnaround

Performance Notes

1. Bar 12: The phrase that connects the turnaround to the beginning of the next chorus is slightly different from that shown in Fig. 18; these transitional phrases are fairly interchangeable, and as you become familiar with the sound and structure, you can invent your own. When you practice turnarounds, it's very important to include the transitional phrases—a 12-bar solo is not complete until you can account for every note from the opening pickup until the downbeat of the next chorus.

The next example is an effective and easy-to-execute generic turnaround phrase consisting of a single line descending against the tonic of the key.

Fig. 20: Moving Line Against Tonic

Performance Notes

1. Bar 12: The turnaround figure concludes with chords (♭VI9–V9) rather than single notes. Similar chords can be substituted for single notes on beat 2 of bar 12 in every turnaround example, although a rhythm guitarist will often play the same chords in the same place, so playing a melody provides some contrast. Choices for ending a turnaround are affected by the musical background as well as style. For example, dominant seventh chords are usually preferred for turnarounds on down home blues, while dominant ninth chords are slightly more uptown.

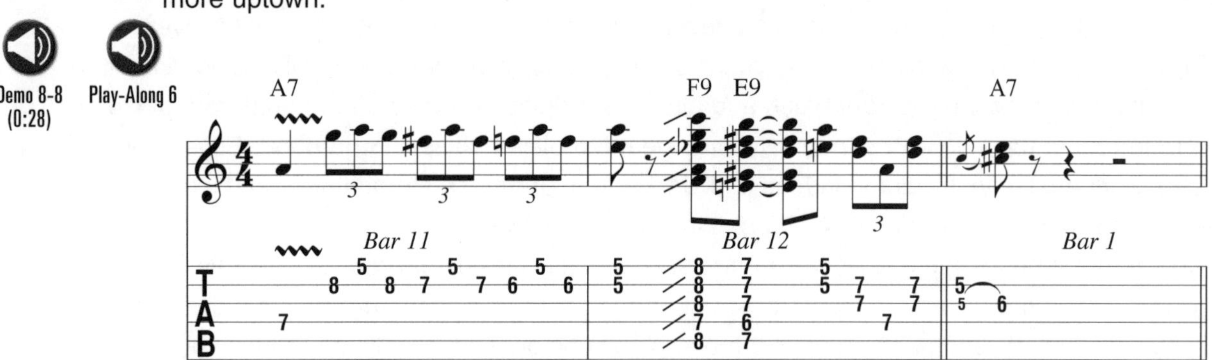

The next example is almost the same as the previous turnaround, but the descending line is transposed down an octave. This was Robert Johnson's signature turnaround, and he also used it as an introduction for many of his arrangements, transposed it to different keys and octaves, and played it with different rhythmic patterns. The same phrase turns up repeatedly in recordings by Johnson disciples Elmore James and Muddy Waters, often adapted for open-tuned slide guitar.

Fig. 21: Robert Johnson-Style Turnaround

Performance Notes

1. Due to the separation between strings, this turnaround is best picked with bare thumb and fingers or hybrid picking (Johnson used a thumb-pick and bare fingers). Fret the high A with your fourth (little) finger and use your first (index) finger on the G. Although the fingering at the start of the phrase is somewhat cramped, it's easy to move your index finger down the neck one fret at a time while leaving your fourth finger in position.
2. The final transitional phrase is an electric guitar adaptation of the Robert Johnson style.

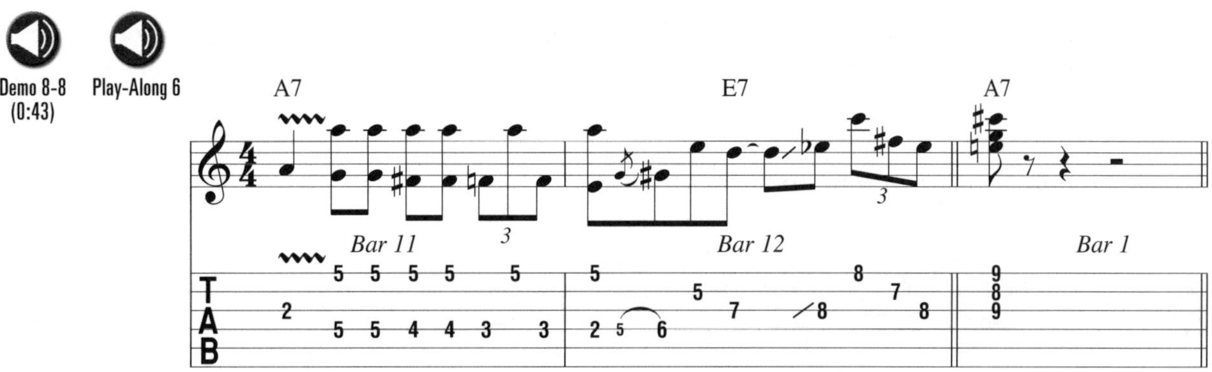

While there are many variations on classic turnarounds, these four examples are enough to cover most practical requirements unless you play a lot of Delta or Chicago-style blues. However, once you know how classic turnarounds work, it's fairly easy to pick up new variations or invent your own.

Transposing Turnarounds

After you memorize the fingering of a turnaround and understand how the notes are related to the key, transposing it to other keys or fingerings is relatively easy because the relationships remain the same regardless of key signature or location on the neck.

To transpose classic turnarounds to other keys, analyze how each phrase is related to the I7 chord and then duplicate that same relationship in the new key. For example, to play the Robert Johnson turnaround in the key of C, place your fourth finger on C (first string, eighth fret) and duplicate the fingering that you used in the key of A—the relationships of the notes to the chord and the fingering are both identical; only the position on the neck is different.

Single-String Turnarounds

Classic turnarounds are common in Chicago blues and down home styles, but they don't fit every style of blues. Players who follow the single-string guitar soloing tradition pioneered by T-Bone Walker—the nearly universal model for contemporary blues and blues-rock guitar—tend to phrase turnarounds as an extension of the rest of the solo rather than switching gears to play a classic turnaround. Either way, it's always best to work out some turnaround ideas in advance to guarantee a strong finish, and experienced players develop a repertoire of turnaround phrases for every occasion.

Single-note turnarounds fit into exactly the same framework as classic turnarounds, the only difference being the way in which the melody in bar 11 is structured. As with traditional turnarounds, the best way to expand your vocabulary is to learn ideas like those shown below and then listen to how your favorite players handle turnarounds (and steal a few of their ideas as well).

The following single-note turnaround is in the style of influential Chicago guitarist Eddie Taylor, who was both a solo artist and Jimmy Reed's long-time accompanist. It is common for two guitarists in the same band to play different turnarounds simultaneously, and Reed and Taylor would often combine traditional and single-note turnarounds between them to create their own blues-style counterpoint.

Fig. 22: Chicago-Style Single-String Turnaround

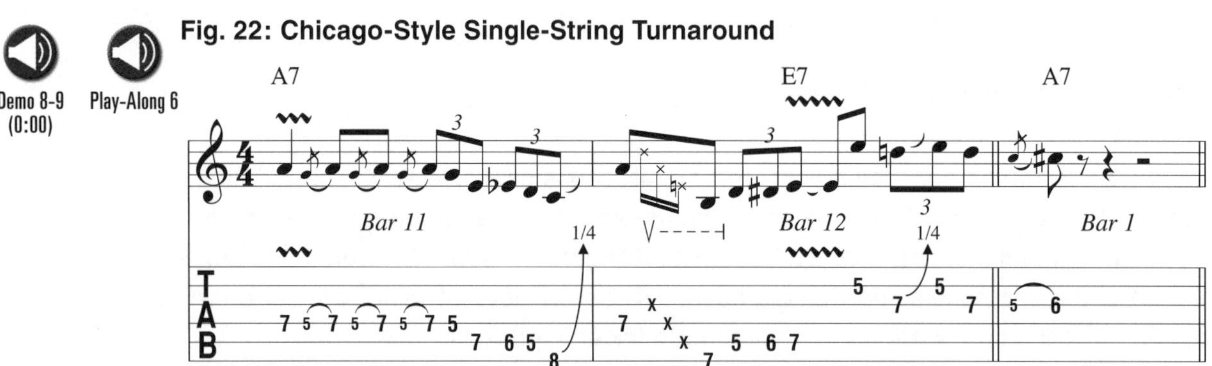

The next phrase is typical of the driving style of Freddie King, who directly influenced the entire generation of 1960s blues-rock guitarists—notably Eric Clapton (virtually the same turnaround is used in the solo in Fig. 15).

Fig. 23: Freddie King-Style Turnaround

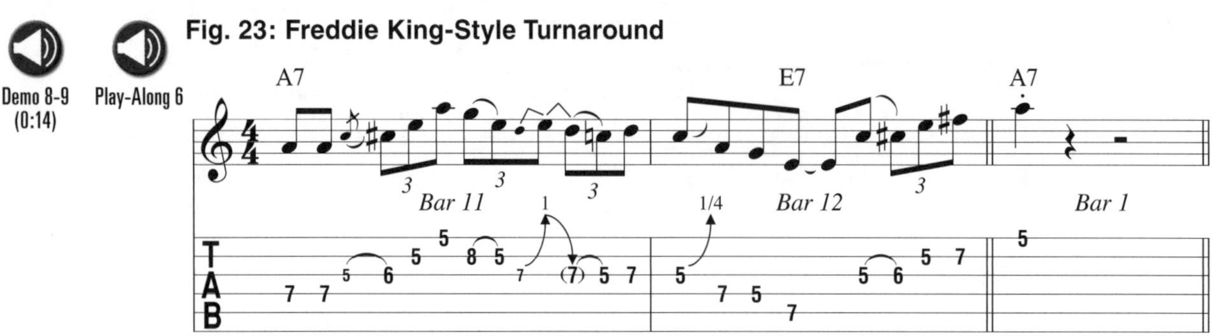

The following example outlines the turnaround changes in a style similar to the master of melodic phrasing, B.B. King.

Fig. 24: B.B. King-Style Turnaround

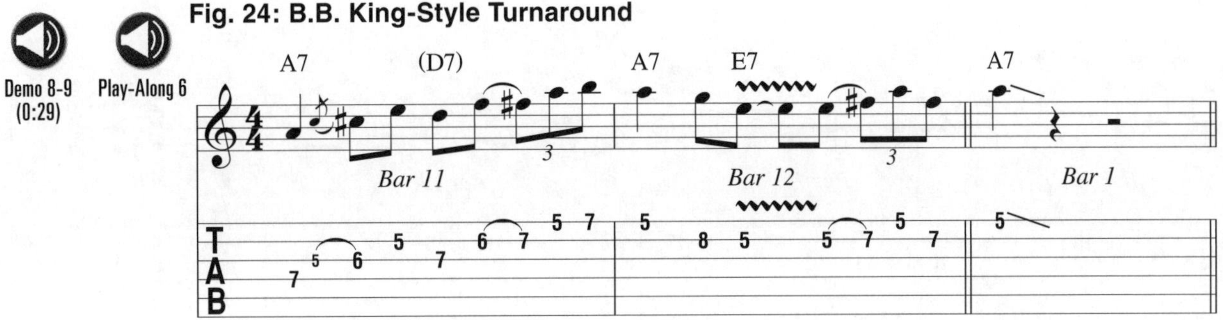

The last example is in the minimalist style of Albert King, hitting the strong beats with strong notes and a well-defined touch.

Fig. 25: Albert King-Style Turnaround

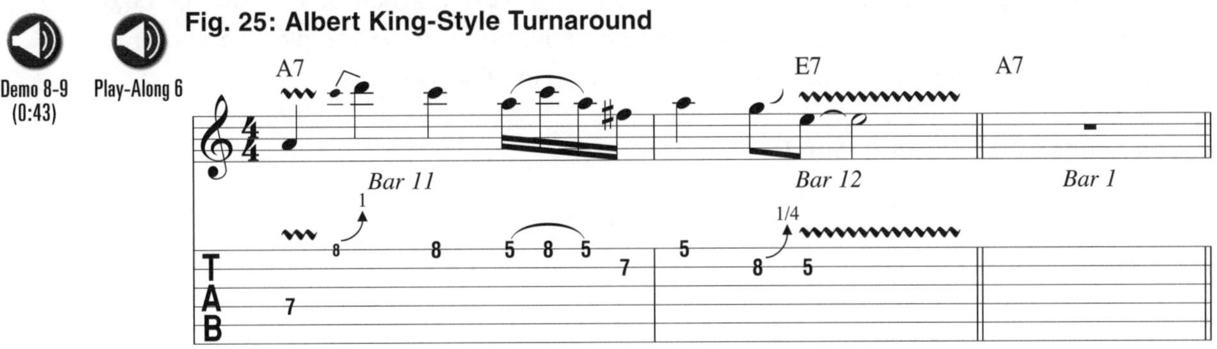

"No Turnaround"

As important as turnarounds are, it is also common in 12-bar blues arrangements to dispense with the V7 chord in bar 12 and remain on the I7 chord throughout the last two bars—a variation known simply as *no turnaround*. In this case, avoid playing a turnaround lick at the end of your solo and end the chorus instead with a normal two-bar phrase. Even though the final V7 chord is missing, the call-and-response structure is unaffected.

When you play in an unrehearsed setting like a jam session, the details of a progression—e.g., quick or slow change, turnaround or not, etc.—may not be clear before you start a song. When this happens, the number-one rule of blues performance survival for guitar players is to keep your eyes and ears focused on the bass player and follow whatever he or she does.

Endings

When you arrive at the end of a blues song, the final turnaround differs from all of the previous turnarounds in one very important way: rather than concluding the phrase in bar 12 with the V7 chord, the final turnaround must end on the I7 chord. During the rest of the tune, the purpose of the turnaround is to prepare for the next chorus, but when the tune ends, it means you are coming home––i.e. to the I chord––to stay.

Whether you're playing rhythm or soloing, the most common way to conclude the final turnaround phrase is with chords rather than single notes. In the next example, the Freddie King-style turnaround from Fig. 23 is modified to fit the end of the tune by substituting chord accents for the single notes in bar 12. The most common final chord figure is a descending half step from ♭II9 to I9 (B♭9–A9).

Fig. 26: Final "Freddie King"-Style Turnaround

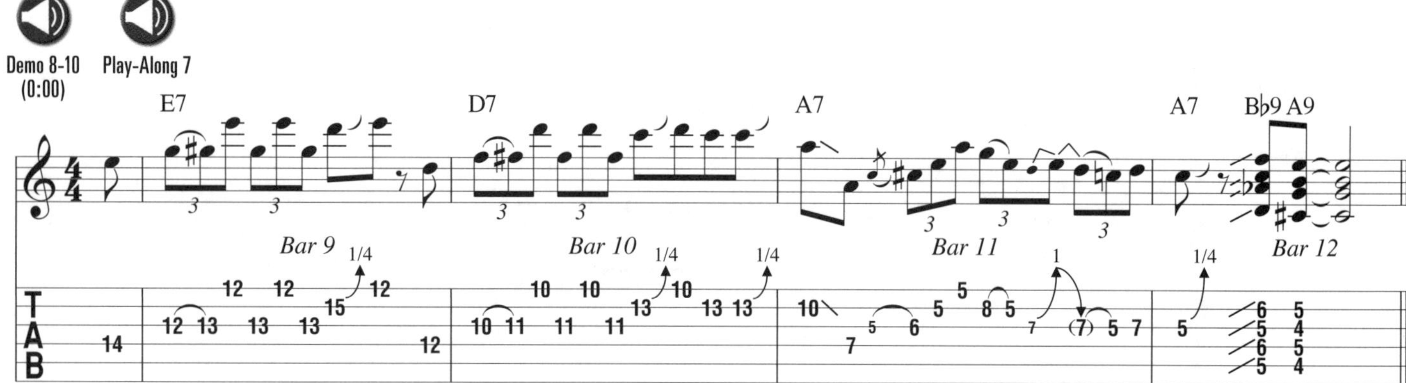

Down-home and Chicago-style blues endings typically use dominant seventh chords rather than the more uptown ninth chords. The next example shows the "Robert Johnson" turnaround (Fig. 21) with a seventh-chord ending; you can resolve into the final chord from either a half step above or below. Johnson, like most Delta guitarists, favored open-position chords, but in this example, the chords are voiced in fifth position so the fingerings can be easily transposed to other keys.

Fig. 27: Final "Robert Johnson"-Style Turnaround

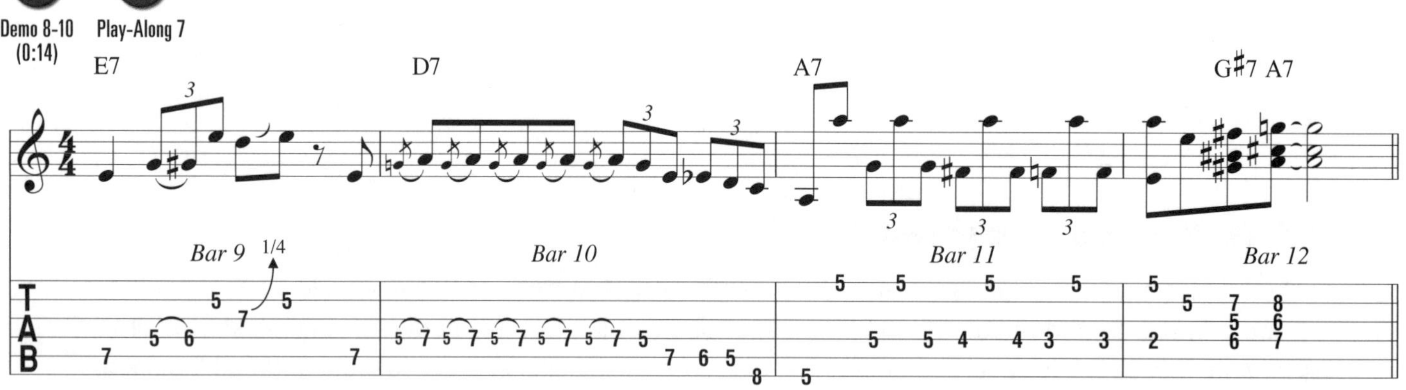

Breaks

As illustrated by the demo tracks for Figs. 26–27, blues endings also often include *breaks* where the band stops for a bar just before the final ending. These endings are often cued by hand motions from the singer or bandleader just a few bars before they happen, so it's essential to keep your eyes open.

The usual place for a break is between the downbeat of bar 11 and the final chord accents on beat 2 of Bar 12. Often the guitar has the job of filling this hole, which simply requires playing a standard turnaround/ending lick and concluding with the tonic chord—the lick works the same whether the band is accompanying the guitar or not. The number-one priority during this kind of break is to keep your phrasing rhythmically steady so the band can easily rejoin the guitar on the final chords.

Another version of the break ending occurs when a singer is singing the final chorus of the tune. To highlight the last line of the vocal, the band breaks for four beats starting on the downbeat of Bar 10 (this is how Hendrix ends "Red House"). After the vocalist fills the break, the guitar completes the ending with a standard lick.

When you listen to blues, pay attention to how the arrangements end and what the guitarist does in each case. Break endings are very intuitive, and the guitar phrasing is usually the same whether there is a break or not, so there's nothing special to practice—just be prepared to throw in a solid lick when the ending comes around.

Tags

Another common blues arranging feature is the "tag" or "repeat" ending. In this case, the last four bars of the final 12-bar chorus are repeated once or twice before the ending chords are struck. A tag ending is usually signaled when the singer wants to emphasize the final line of the lyrics, and like many blues arrangement details, it may be indicated on the spot by a vocal cue ("Let me say it again...") or hand signals (e.g., three fingers indicating "take it around three times" or five fingers indicating "take it back to the five chord"). The most important thing to remember about this ending is to not play a turnaround lick until the final repetition. Since each repetition of the tag begins on the V7 chord rather than I7, standard turnaround phrases send the wrong musical signal.

Intros

Pickup phrases and turnarounds are used not only during solos; they often also serve as introductions (*intros*) to the song itself. There are three basic no-rehearsal ways to begin a 12-bar blues, each of which usually involves a pickup phrase, turnaround lick, or both.

"From the One"

The most common way to start a blues is *from the one* (or "from the top"). This means just what it says: count off and start the song on the first chord of the 12-bar progression. If the guitar player is also taking a solo over the first chorus, this means that the guitarist is also normally expected to lead the band in with a strong pickup phrase. Almost any "and" of beat 3 pickup (Figs. 13–14) will serve the purpose, but the three pickups shown below are among the most common in the electric blues repertoire.

Fig. 28: Standard Intro Pickup Phrases

"From the Five"

The next most common blues intro, *from the five*, begins directly on the V7 chord of the key (bar 9 of the 12-bar structure) and continues through the last four bars of the 12-bar progression before launching into the standard cycle. If you're soloing over this intro, lead into the V7 chord with a pickup, play the same sort of phrases you would normally play during the last four bars, and conclude with a strong turnaround.

The following example illustrates a chord tone-based "from the five" intro line that includes a single-line turnaround (the last four bars of any 12-bar example in this book could also function as a "from the five" intro). If the vocalist starts singing right away, you would shift into the rhythm part, but if the guitar solo continues into the first chorus, play another pickup phrase during the transition out of the turnaround as shown here:

Fig. 29: "From the Five" Intro Line

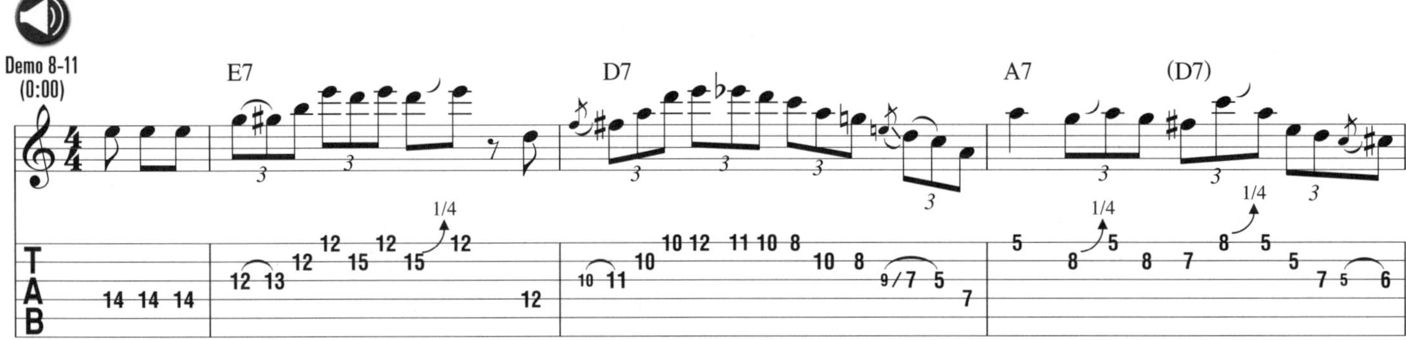

"From the Turnaround"

This means just what it says: start the song directly on the turnaround (bar 11). One option is to have the entire band hit the downbeat together and then have the guitar play the turnaround lick alone with the band joining back in on the chord accents (beat 2 of the next bar). Classic turnaround licks work well in this context because they give the band a clear rhythmic structure to follow.

Fig. 30: "From the Turnaround" Intro

Demo 8-11
(0:16)

Chapter 8 Summary

1. **Blues Changes:** Dominant seventh chord-based harmony (I7, IV7, and V7) gives blues a unique sound.
2. **12-Bar Form:** The most common blues song form is the 12-bar progression, which is arranged in three four-bar sections each consisting of a two-bar vocal phrase followed by a two-bar musical interlude.
3. **Call-and-Response:** Classic 12-bar blues solos use the same form as the vocals—i.e., a series of two-bar call-and-response phrases concluding with a final two-bar phrase called the turnaround.
4. **Playing Changes:** Harmonic awareness—i.e., keeping track of the harmony and form while soloing—is one of the key factors in creating a strong 12-bar solo. Two basic ways to organize melodies are:
   a. **Key Center:** This means centering on the fundamental scale of the key (the blue-note pentatonic).
   b. **Chord Tones:** This refers to reflecting the specific structure of each chord.
5. **Pickup Phrases:** These are short melodic phrases that rhythmically anticipate the beginning of the solo and other key points in the form.
6. **Turnarounds:** This is the last two bars of a 12-bar solo, ending one chorus and preparing to start the next. Depending on the style of blues and the preference of the soloist, turnaround phrases can be either classic "barbershop-style" or improvised single-note phrases.
7. **Endings:** The final chorus of a blues song ends on the I7 chord rather than V7; the final turnaround often also includes a rhythmic break that features a guitar fill.
8. **Intros:** There are three standard, no-rehearsal intros: from the one, from the five, and from the turnaround.

Practice

Call-and-Response

Call-and-response interaction has been at the very heart of the blues style since the beginning, and effective 12-bar solos are almost invariably organized around two-bar call-and-response phrasing. To instill the concept of call-and-response into your playing, learn vocal melodies on the guitar (e.g., "St. Louis Blues") and when you solo, alternate between playing the melody and answering with your own phrases. Aside from the built-in call-and-response structure, this also creates a solo that is tailored specifically to the song (see Chapter 9 for more on this approach).

When you play over a generic progression like "shuffle in A," you need to create your own identity for the solo. Start with a two-bar phrase as the main idea (almost any phrase presented so far in this book will work, but the more distinctive the better) and develop it using the call-and-response format. In the next chorus, pick another idea and follow the same process. While this may sound formulaic, the number of variations is almost infinite—after all, musicians have been exploring this structure for more than a hundred years.

The most important thing to learn from studying call-and-response interaction is an awareness of structure; call-and-response provides the sense of direction that a successful solo needs. Listen to your favorite players and analyze how they structure their solos. The call-and-response concept is highly flexible and can be applied in many different ways. Some may be more obvious than others, but it is a fundamental principle of blues soloing.

Key-Center Phrasing

All of the examples presented in the first seven chapters are key-center melodies, and 12-bar solos like those in Figs. 6 and 7 are also made up of one- and two-bar key-center phrases. When you learn a solo, practice each phrase at a tempo where you can play it perfectly and then work it up to the tempo of the demonstration, connecting it to the phrases that come before and after. Play each solo along with the audio demo as well as with the rhythm track alone; you don't really know it until you can play it accurately on your own, and it's even better if you can play it in tempo by yourself without the rhythm track. Record yourself and compare your timing and touch to the demo. Use your ear and musical judgment to determine when the phrasing sounds right.

Chord-Tone Phrasing

Begin by isolating the I7–IV7 and I7–V7 changes as in Figs. 8 and 9. When you can play these accurately, expand the concept to other parts of the neck as follows:

1. Choose any pattern in the key of A and locate the 3rd and 7th degrees of A7.
2. Locate the D7 pattern in the same position and find its 3rd and 7th.
3. Solo over the A7–D7 rhythm track and connect the chord tones in tempo using the same style of phrasing presented in the examples.
4. Repeat the process with A7 and E7.
5. Apply the same concepts in keys other than A.

From Fig. 11 on, most of the solo examples in this book are based on a combination of key-center and chord-tone phrasing. As you learn each example, analyze how chord tones and key centers are integrated. Phrasing is not a question of choosing one approach or the other, but rather of simultaneously hearing them both.

Practicing Without Accompaniment

It takes time and repetition to develop the ability to keep track of the rhythm, harmony, and form simultaneously while you're soloing. One part of the process is to practice along with rhythm tracks, but it's also essential to practice soloing without any accompaniment at all. After you learn each solo in this book, practice playing it with only your foot for accompaniment in order to train yourself to keep steady time. When you play your own ideas, follow these steps:

- Pick a tempo, feel, and key.
- Record yourself soloing for several 12-bar choruses in a row without a backing track, keeping time just by tapping your foot.
- Listen back and see how accurately you maintained the tempo and form.

Whether you're playing rhythm or soloing, the goal is to be self-contained—in other words, to tap your foot and feel the rhythm as accurately as a drummer and hear the changes as accurately as a bass player. When you are capable of keeping track of all of the musical elements by yourself, your phrasing will be much more coherent when you play with a band.

Pickup Phrases

Playing the exercise in Fig. 14 will train you to hear and feel standard "and" of beat 3 pickup phrasing, and all of the other solo examples throughout this book include pickups as part of the phrasing structure. In addition to these examples, when you transcribe solos by other players, focus on where they use pickups. Like all elements of phrasing, the best way to build your vocabulary is to steal from those who do it well and then harness their inspiration to develop your own ideas.

Turnarounds

Whether you play traditional or improvised turnarounds, the concept is not complete until you know how to transition smoothly from your solo into the turnaround and then out of the turnaround into the beginning of the next chorus (or on the final chorus of the song, from the turnaround to the I7 chord as described below).

To practice turnaround phrasing, loop the final four bars of the 12-bar progression and concentrate on making a seamless transition from your final "call" into the turnaround phrase and then through bar 12 to the beginning of the next chorus (the rhythm track provided with this book loops the final four bars four times in a row). For any turnaround to be useable, you must practice it in tempo and in context of the progression until your finger movements are accurate and you can get in and out smoothly.

It's also essential to practice turnarounds (along with everything else) in different keys. In any sort of jam or when learning different tunes, you will definitely find yourself playing blues in keys other than A; practice turnarounds in different keys using the cycle of fourths as described in Chapter 1.

For classic turnarounds, fingerings that work well in the key of A are impractical in certain other keys where you have to play too high or low on the neck, but in every case the turnaround can be re-fingered in a more practical location by moving to a different string set. For example, to play the "Robert Johnson" turnaround in the key of F, fret the tonic on the second string, sixth fret and move the melody down the fifth string from the sixth fret to the third fret. The relationship between the notes, key, and fingering is identical; the only difference is the strings on which you fret the notes.

Endings and Intros

Endings often include turnarounds, so when you practice turnarounds, whether classic or single-note, it is very important that you practice each turnaround in two versions: either continuing to the next chorus or ending the song. Nothing ruins an otherwise good performance more than hitting the wrong chord at the end (this also includes ending with stylistically inappropriate chord types such as major triads or power chords instead of dominant chords—always use blues-appropriate chords).

To practice endings, follow the same practice method as for turnarounds, but end each phrase with the I7 chord instead of V7. You must practice until you can handle endings with the same level of consistency as regular turnarounds (a rhythm track is provided that loops the last four bars of a standard ending).

When you listen to classic blues records, focus on how the guitar players and other musicians handle the ending; you'll hear all of the arrangement variations described here at one point or another. Ultimately, the best way to learn and practice arrangements is simply to play live with other musicians, whether in a rehearsal, jam session, party, or club.

Listen

Call-and-Response

Call-and-response is a basic element of songwriting, blues phrasing, and solo arrangement. When you listen to recordings by singers/guitarists such as B.B. King, learn both the vocal line and the answering guitar fills; these concise phrases provide a ready-made repertoire of responses and show you the player's call-and-response thinking. A few great examples of fills include:

Bobby Bland (Pat Hare, guitar)	"Farther Up the Road"
Freddie King	"Lonesome Whistle Blues"
Albert King	"The Sky Is Crying"
B.B. King	"Ten Long Years"

When you listen to a recorded solo, analyze how the player uses call-and-response phrasing; often a solo will differ considerably from the melody or rhythmic structure of the vocal, but on one level or another, call-and-response is always present.

Key Centers

The blue-note pentatonic contains the essence of the traditional blues melodic vocabulary, and all players use it, but Albert King is probably the best-known mainstream blues soloist who soloed almost entirely within the key center. What King lacked in melodic variety, however, he made up for with incredibly sophisticated rhythmic phrasing and touch, and he left no doubt as to his awareness of form and harmony. Check out "Overall Junction" along with practically any other track by King.

Chord Tones

Two classic examples of composed bluesy chord-tone melodies are:

- "T-Bone Shuffle" by T-Bone Walker (also covered countless times by other artists)
- "Caldonia" by Louis Jordan (also with countless cover versions, notably by B.B. King)

Among single-note soloists, every player mixes chord tones and key centers to varying degrees, and the way a player blends melodic ingredients is a basic component of personal style. Using the "three Kings" as an example, Albert favors key-center phrasing, B.B. uses considerably more chord tones in his melodies, and Freddie is somewhere in the middle—when he wanted a raw, muscular sound, he favored a key-center approach ("Going Down"), but he could also be quite lyrical ("Remington Ride").

Self-accompanied blues guitarists tend to favor chord-based solos since the guitar has to express the melody, harmony, and form simultaneously; this approach is discussed in more detail in Chapter 10. For examples of high-level self-contained performances, check out Stevie Ray Vaughan's tour-de-force solo acoustic version of "Rude Mood," Albert King's "Night Stomp" (*Live Wire/Blues Power*), where he keeps the crowd fully involved with just his guitar, or any solo acoustic performance by New Orleans guitarist Snooks Eaglin (collected as *Snooks Eaglin—New Orleans Street Singer*), a true, self-contained master musician.

Pickup Phrases

Pickups are so fundamental to blues phrasing that it's nearly impossible to find a solo that doesn't include them. You usually hear them most clearly at the beginning of a solo when the player wants to make a strong opening statement; here are just a few classic examples:

Albert King	"Don't Throw Your Love on Me So Strong"
B.B. King	"Sweet Little Angel"
Buddy Guy	"A Man and the Blues"
Freddie King	"You've Got to Love Her with a Feeling"
Stevie Ray Vaughan	"Texas Flood" (copied from the Larry Davis original)

Turnarounds

A few examples of the turnarounds described in this chapter include:

Jimmy Reed turnaround:	"Bright Lights, Big City," "Good Lover"
Muddy Waters turnaround:	"She Moves Me," "Stuff You Gotta Watch"
with Little Walter:	"Blues with a Feeling," "Key to the Highway"
Robert Johnson turnaround:	"Sweet Home Chicago" plus practically every other recording by Johnson
"Chicago-style" turnaround:	Jimmy Reed with Eddie Taylor: "Good Lover" and "Baby What You Want Me To Do;" Little Walter with Louis & David Myers: "Can't Hold Out Much Longer"
Freddie King turnaround:	"I'm Tore Down," "Side Tracked," "Sen-Sa-Shun"
B.B. King turnaround:	"How Blue Can You Get," "Rock Me Baby"
Albert King turnaround:	"Overall Junction," "Crosscut Saw"

Endings and Intros

- Bar 11 break: This is the default choice for a blues ending, so there are countless examples.
- Bar 10 break: This is usually used in order to highlight the last line of the vocal; a prime example is "Red House" by Hendrix.
- Tag ending: Check out "Next Time You See Me" by Junior Parker (the record fades out on the tag).
- "From the Five" intro: Again, check out "Next Time You See Me," plus Freddie King's original King Records versions of "I'm Tore Down" and "Sidetracked."
- "From the Turnaround" intro: Check out the later version of "I'm Tore Down" by Freddie King on the Shelter label; also his early King Records instrumental, "Manhole," is a prime example.

9 Soloing Strategies

Anyone with a moderate amount of skill can play a competent solo over a 12-bar blues progression, but of all the thousands upon thousands of 12-bar choruses that have been recorded over the years, only a relative handful are considered truly great. What takes a solo from good to great is on some level a mystery that defies technical analysis, but we can identify certain strategies that good soloists use in order to create the conditions for greatness to emerge.

Match the Solo to the Song

A common syndrome among guitarists is to think of blues not as actual songs with melodies and lyrics that express a certain point of view, but as generic "blues progressions." Stripped of melody and lyrics, one shuffle in A becomes the same as the next, and unfortunately for the listener, the solos are also likely to be interchangeable.

A fairly simple way to avoid this syndrome is to tailor the solo to fit the song. It is a fact that all 12-bar blues songs have a lot in common (and like any other kind of music, many are mediocre), but the good ones have something unique in the melody, lyrics, rhythm, or performance that makes them memorable. You can draw on these elements to create a solo that has equally memorable qualities. Even a jam over a nameless progression can become something special if you think of it in song-like terms.

When you get ready to solo on a blues song, do two things first:

- Learn the vocal melody on the guitar and use it as the foundation of your solo; i.e., it becomes the "call," with your own ideas as the responses.
- Listen to the lyrics and keep the general attitude—salty, sweet, vengeful, regretful, etc.—in mind as you play to help guide your choices.

Basing your solo on the song has two immediate benefits. First, it makes each solo sound a little different, which is much more interesting for the listener than when solos are all based around scale patterns or random licks. Second, if your technical skills are limited, vocal melodies generally don't require a lot of speed or range, so you can still create a musically interesting solo with the skills you have and add to it as you continue to improve.

Matching a solo to a song does not necessarily mean copying the vocal melody note-for-note; the idea is to find features of the song that inspire you to think more creatively and less technically. For example, the solos in Chapter 8 based on "St. Louis Blues" showed two approaches to song-based soloing: one staying fairly close to the vocal melody and the other based on the same melodic rhythm without using the same notes.

The next example is patterned loosely on another all-time blues classic, Jimmy Reed's "Bright Lights, Big City." In this case, the solo is inspired by bits of the melody and rhythmic phrasing with some pickup phrases added to fill in the blanks (few of Reed's recordings include guitar solos, but his iconic harmonica solos are prime examples of how to say a lot with just a few notes).

Fig. 1: Jimmy Reed-Inspired Solo

Performance Notes

1. Bars 1–2: The opening phrases are similar to the vocal melody.
2. Bars 3–4: The answer adds rhythmic and melodic embellishments to the melody; in bar 4, a two-beat pickup phrase sets up the next call.
3. Bars 5–6: The opening melody is repeated up an octave.

4. Bars 7–8: The second response builds on the melodic rhythm but with a straight-up guitar lick replacing the original melody.
5. Bars 9–10: The third phrase again builds on the rhythmic phrasing of the melody rather than the specific notes, with chord tone-based phrases over V7 and IV7.
6. Bars 11–12: This is a Jimmy Reed-style turnaround with some melodic variations.

Demo 9-1

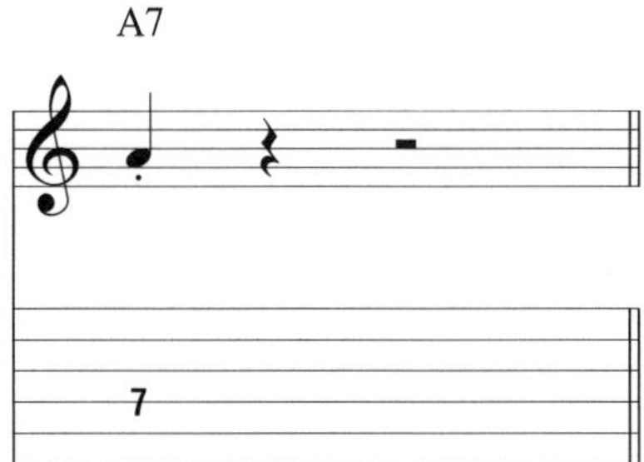

Every Solo Tells a Story

One of the best ways to learn how to arrange and play great blues solos is to tear apart some classics and see what makes them work. By analyzing how master blues guitarists organize and perform 12-bar solos, we gain invaluable perspectives on how to turn our own licks into coherent stories.

Each of the following examples shows one chorus of a 12-bar medium shuffle solo in the style of an influential player. For ease of comparison, all are demonstrated in the same key (A), but on the original recordings, the key, tempo, rhythm section feel, and instrumentation all vary. Each analysis focuses not just on the licks and techniques but also on how the ideas capture and hold our attention throughout the chorus. While each solo has different features, they all share a similar three-part structure:

- **Opening Idea:** The first phrase captures the listener's attention and establishes the tone for the rest of the solo. Whether you base a solo on an existing song or create something on your own, build each 12-bar chorus around a single main idea or theme to make it more cohesive and interesting. The best way to build a repertoire of strong opening ideas is to steal them from every source you can. This includes not only guitar solos, but vocal melodies, saxophone solos, harp solos—anything with a memorable quality.
- **Middle Section:** Each player handles the middle four bars somewhat differently, either repeating, varying, or contrasting with the opening idea.
- **Final Four:** The last four bars include the harmonic peak of the progression (V7) and the turnaround. Most players rely on pre-arranged turnaround phrases to guarantee that the solo ends strongly, and each of these examples includes an effective turnaround phrase.

Solo #1: Freddie King Style

Freddie King earned national recognition in 1961 with "Hide Away," which was the first in a series of outstanding guitar instrumentals that comprise a virtual encyclopedia of blues phrasing. Among the up-and-coming generation of blues-rock guitarists, his solos were studied and re-recorded by countless players, including Eric Clapton and Peter Green.

This example alternates a strong main theme similar to King's 1961 instrumental "Side Tracked" with classic answering phrases; the relentlessly driving melodic rhythm is a hallmark of King's high-energy style (King's recording is in the key of G; to transpose it to that key, simply move the notated fingerings down two frets).

Fig. 2: Freddie King Style

Performance Notes

1. Bars 1–2: The unbroken triplet theme reflects the quick-change chord structure (A7–D7).
2. Bars 3–4: The first response is a standard A7 blues phrase.
3. Bars 5–6: The middle section recaps the opening idea with the melody adapted to IV7 (C♯, the major 3rd of A, is lowered to C natural, the minor 7th of D).
4. Bars 7–8: The second response is a favorite Freddie King lick; roll your third finger to connect B to F♯ between bars 7–8.
5. Bars 9–10: The final call features another Freddie King trademark: a quick flurry of notes in bar 9 that punctuates the end of the phrase. Use consecutive up-strokes as indicated (see Chapter 12: "Conversational Phrasing" for more on this technique).
6. Bars 11–12: The turnaround, like the first response, is a staple of the electric blues soloing vocabulary (Clapton, for example, used very similar phrases during his epic solo on Cream's "Crossroads").

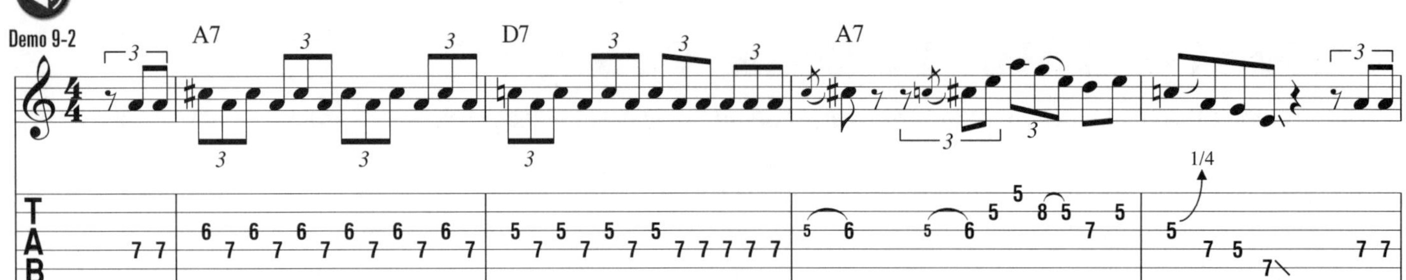

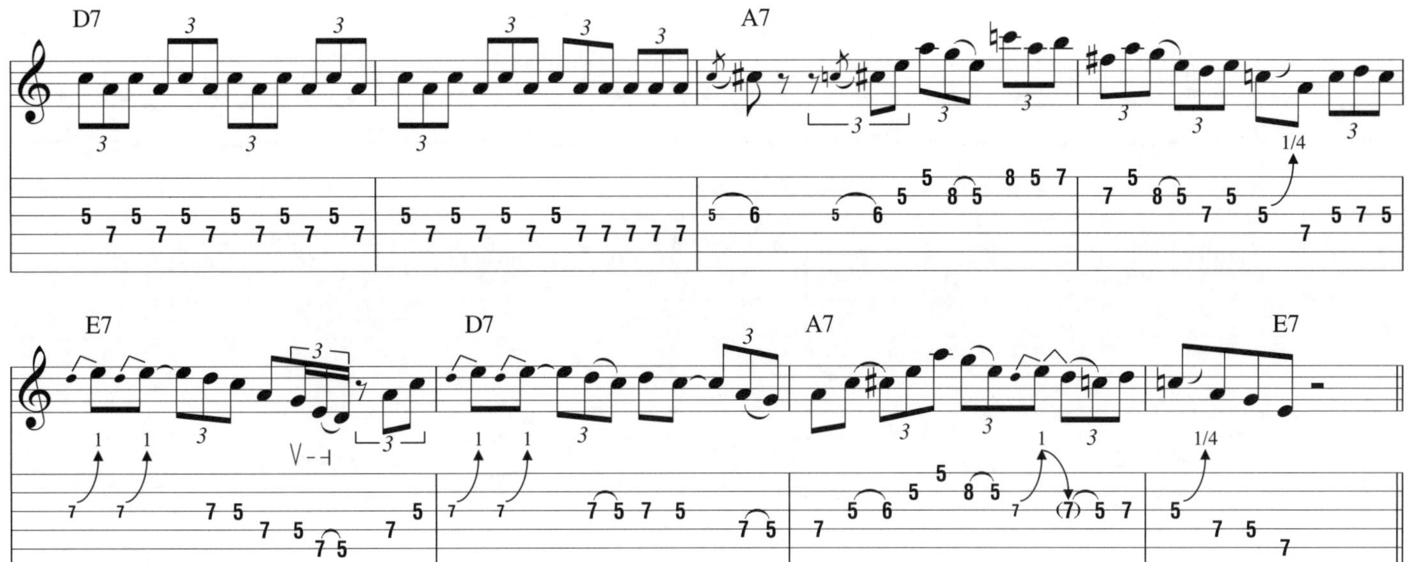

Solo #2: Billy Butler Style

In 1956, guitarist Billy Butler played a three-chorus solo on the blues instrumental, "Honky Tonk" (released under the name of organist/bandleader Bill Doggett) that quickly wound up on every guitarist's must-know list and even today remains one of the most-quoted solos in blues guitar history. Each chorus of "Honky Tonk" consists of a simple-but-catchy opening melody followed by classic call-and-response phrasing that succeeds on every level—from individual licks to overall composition.

In the following example, the opening theme is rhythmically identical to the Freddie King-style solo but based around different chord tones; both build energy while reflecting the harmony with subtle melodic changes. The emphasis in the middle section shifts to more traditional melodic phrasing with plenty of breathing room, and the last four bars have been quoted in countless solos over the decades (the original recording is in the key of F; to transpose, move the same fingerings down four frets).

Fig. 3: Billy Butler Style
Performance Notes

1. Bars 1–2: The opening phrase outlines an A6 chord; in bar 2, lowering C♯ to C converts it to D7 (compare to the opening phrase of the Freddie King-style solo). Keep your fingers pressed down on the chord shapes to sustain the notes as you pick; a recommended picking pattern is shown, but this can be varied as long as you remain in tempo. You can also vary the tone by picking the arpeggios close to the bridge.
2. Bars 3–4: The opening idea continues through bar 3; bar 4 is an extended pickup into the IV7 chord. Slide up to F♯ on the first string with your fourth finger and barre the top three strings with your index finger; use either alternate picking or consecutive up-strokes to outline the A9 chord before switching to a D7-based phrase before the actual chord change. Basing a melody on the next chord before it arrives is a sophisticated version of the setup phrase.
3. Bars 5–6: Repeat the phrase with slightly different timing and then move the same phrase to A, Pattern #4 to anticipate the return to A7.
4. Bars 7–8: The second response is a standard major-oriented blues phrase.
5. Bars 9–10: The melody outlines the E7 and D7 changes with 6th intervals (see Chapter 10).
6. Bars 11–12: This is a melodic turnaround phrase that clearly outlines the I7–IV7–I7–V7 changes.

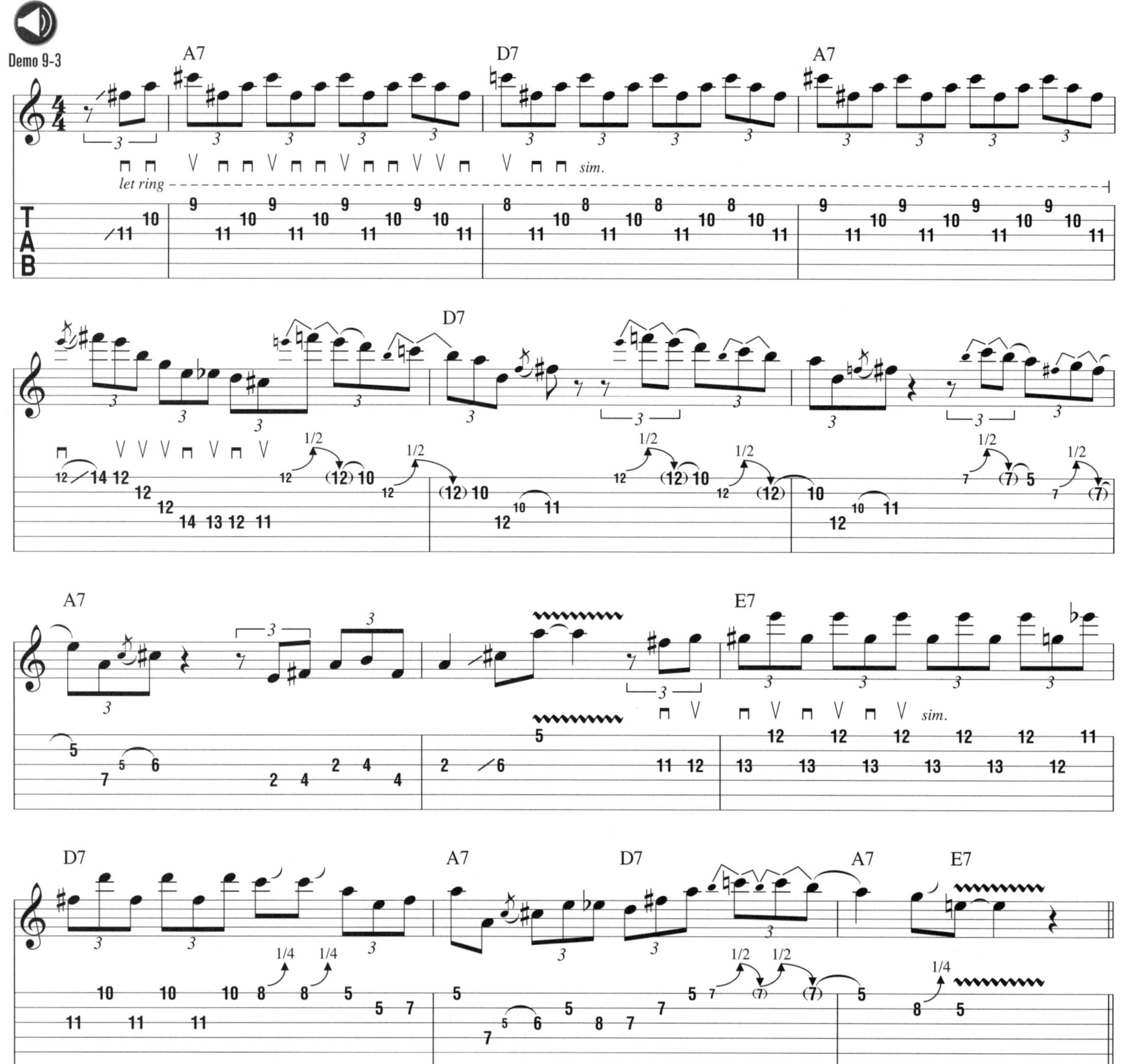

Solo #3: Albert King Style

Albert King is, along with his fellow Kings B.B. and Freddie, one of the most influential electric blues guitarists in history. His mid-1960s recordings on the Stax label had an immediate and profound influence on the sound of blues, and his licks were also quickly adapted by the emerging generation of blues-rock guitar heroes. King distilled blues phrasing to its essence, showing with every solo just how few notes it takes to tell a story when you support them with impeccable timing and touch.

The following example is in a style similar to one chorus of King's solo on the instrumental "Overall Junction." (The original recording is in the key of E; to transpose, move the same fingerings up to 12th position.) This example does not showcase King's radical string-bending technique; instead, it shows how timing and touch can transform a few notes into a fully-formed 12-bar statement. To understand the power of King's timing, hum the rhythms of his phrases separate from the notes—even without the melody, they are still complete musical ideas with an intuitive, conversational quality.

As noted elsewhere in this book, King's guitar setup was very different—upside-down with an unorthodox tuning and bare thumb-and-finger picking—and when we translate his phrases into a normal setup, some details change. But as this example shows, we can make adjustments without losing the essence of his style. The audio demo is played with bare fingers, but hybrid technique or straight flatpicking are also good options depending on what sounds and feels best to you.

Fig. 4: Albert King Style

Performance Notes

1. Bars 1–4: In contrast with the driving opening phrases in each of the other solo examples included here, King opens his solo as simply as possible by hitting the root on the downbeat followed a bar later by a trademark minor-pentatonic phrase; use finger rolls between A and E in both octaves. The melody remains entirely within the box pattern throughout, but inventive timing and interval skips provide depth and variety.
2. Bars 5–8: A series of short phrases separated by "breathing points" maintain an intuitive flow through the IV7 change (note the emphasis on D) back to I7. In bar 7, the pull-off/slide combination is another King trademark.
3. Bars 9–10: By emphasizing B (the 5th of E7) over the change to V7, King reflects the harmony with a subtle chord-tone emphasis rather than a more elaborate arpeggio-based approach. Notice the staccato attack on B; King gave his full attention to every note, and details like this add further dimension to simple phrases.
4. Bars 11–12: The turnaround is characteristically simple and direct; the band plays a "no turnaround" arrangement, but it's normal for the solo to hint at the V7 chord anyway. King almost never played classic turnarounds, rather treating the turnaround as an extension of his overall solo phrasing.

Solo #4: Pat Hare Style

In 1957, vocalist Bobby "Blue" Bland scored his first national hit record with "Farther Up the Road," a classic Texas blues shuffle that featured a blistering solo by Auburn "Pat" Hare, a Memphis-based guitarist who also played on influential recordings by Junior Parker, James Cotton, and Muddy Waters as well as under his own name. The following example demonstrates a solo in similar style. (The original recording is in F; to transpose, move the same fingerings down four frets.)

Hare combined an intense, dynamic attack with a strong sense of composition to make a few notes go a long way. Like Freddie King and Billy Butler, he immediately captures attention with driving triplets, but like Albert King, he uses breaks to control the energy over the length of the chorus.

Fig. 5: Pat Hare Style

Performance Notes

1. Bars 1–2: The solo opens with an extended pickup phrase leading into a strong opening lick, followed by a gap that builds anticipation for the next phrase. Silence is as important as the notes in shaping the overall effect of a solo; holding something back at the beginning makes the eventual climax that much more exciting.
2. Bars 3–4: The opening lick repeats before another extended high-energy pickup similar to the opening sets up the transition into the IV7 chord.
3. Bars 5–6: The middle section features a distinctive step-wise melody highlighted by intense attack and repetition.
4. Bars 7–8: The response releases the tension somewhat with a more typical pentatonic blues phrase.
5. Bars 9–10: The final section features key-center minor pentatonic phrases with a driving triplet rhythm similar to the fills that Hare plays between Bland's vocals, stylistically tying the solo and the song together.
6. Bars 11–12: A simple but clever turnaround phrase resolves to the root of V7.

Demo 9-5

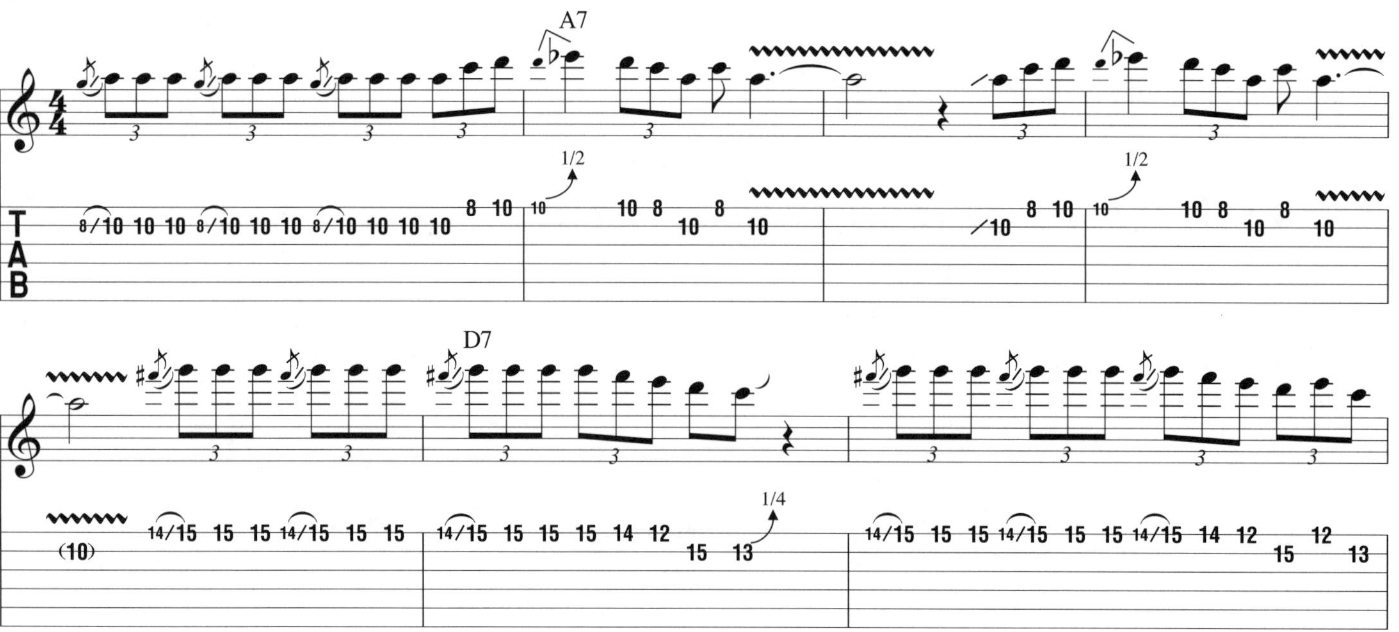

Once you know the essential techniques of blues phrasing and 12-bar soloing, the best way to expand your style is to apply the same process of listening and analysis used on these four solos to unlock the styles of the players who inspire you. Take any solo you like and analyze how it's put together—not just for the individual licks, but for the way in which the phrases are arranged within the 12-bar structure. Without exception, every great blues guitarist has undertaken this process and used the lessons learned as the basis for developing their personal style within the larger blues tradition. Method books can save you considerable time by providing organization, ideas, techniques, and perspectives, but they are no replacement for the lifelong process of listening and playing.

In this context, it's important to point out that even the greatest blues guitarists rarely "improvise" in the sense of inventing brand-new ideas on the spot; a more accurate term is *spontaneous arrangement.* A good blues solo balances familiarity and freshness; when B.B. King takes a solo, he almost certainly has played every phrase countless times before (and B.B., like everyone else, has stolen many ideas from his inspirations), but the freshness comes from slight variations in rhythmic placement, tone, touch, or other details of the performance. When we recognize the personal style of someone like B.B., it's precisely because we have become familiar with their phrasing and touch through repetition. For experienced blues stylists, improvisation doesn't mean inventing ideas on stage every night for the first time; rather, it's about performing familiar ideas as if it's the first time.

Stretching Out: Playing Multiple Choruses

Playing a strong one-chorus solo is a challenge due to the limited amount of time, but playing a solo that holds up consistently for two or more choruses presents a different kind of challenge. A coherent multi-chorus solo is more than just a series of one-chorus solos played back-to-back; for a longer solo to make sense, the "'story" also has to expand to fill the time allotted. Here are a few strategies for developing effective longer solos (see Fig. 6 for an example of a longer solo that incorporates these ideas):

Recycle Themes

One reason for the enduring popularity of Billy Butler's three-chorus solo on "Honky Tonk" is his use of *recurring themes.* Each chorus begins with a fresh idea, but some phrases are recycled from one chorus to the next (e.g. the 6th-interval phrase in bars 9–10), creating an effective balance between the new and the familiar. Likewise, Freddie King built instrumentals like "Side Tracked" around a handful of repeated ideas with slight variations. Learning and analyzing extended solos like these teaches you more than licks; it teaches you how to arrange your ideas for maximum impact.

Vary the Texture

Texture is a broad term that describes the different ways in which you shape the energy of a solo, including the pitch range, the balance of notes and rests, and the intensity of your attack. Analyze good multi-chorus solos like those mentioned above in order to see how players manage these elements:

- **Range:** Higher-pitched sounds create a greater sense of excitement, so a classic soloing strategy is to start in a lower range and save the highest notes for the end. Starting a solo high on the neck can be like painting yourself into a corner, but at the same time, a noticeable shift in either direction draws attention, so occasionally diverting a solo from high to low octave is also refreshing (check out Freddie King's "Just Pickin'," which features several octave shifts). Listen to how different soloists exploit the range of the instrument. Some players like Buddy Guy and Jimi Hendrix use the entire neck, while others like T-Bone Walker and Albert King stay within a fairly limited range.

- **Rhythm:** A standard bit of blues wisdom is "take your time"—coming in strong is a good strategy for a short solo, but in a longer solo it's a good idea to gradually build energy so it doesn't peak too early. Experienced players typically leave more open space (i.e., rests) between phrases at the beginning of a solo and fill them in as the solo progresses. *Repetition* is also an extremely valuable energy-building tool. Repeating a short, rhythmic phrase (like the triplets in the Pat Hare-style example) is a particularly effective way to transition from one chorus into the next or to finish the solo off at a high level of intensity.

- **Dynamics:** Playing at the same level of volume and intensity all of the time eventually wears listeners out and causes their attention to drift. Typically, experienced players increase the intensity of a long solo over time, but like shifts in range, noticeable dynamic shifts in either direction are exciting. Check out the live recording of B.B. King (one of the absolute masters of dynamic control) playing "Gambler's Blues" or "Worry, Worry" to hear what happens when he suddenly and drastically alters the dynamics mid-solo; the screams of the audience tell you everything you need to know about the power of dynamics.

Bridge Choruses

A common way to build energy in a multi-chorus solo is to bridge the last few bars of one chorus into the next; i.e., begin a short, repetitive phrase in bars 11–12 of the first chorus and continue it directly into the next chorus, bypassing the usual turnaround phrase and launching the next chorus at a higher energy level. When you listen to a longer solo, focus on how the player transitions from one chorus to the next. It's very helpful to have a few different strategies available when you need them.

Putting It Together

The following two-chorus solo illustrates several of the strategies described above:

- **Theme:** The first chorus is based around a two-part bluesy lick that is repeated with slight variations; the second chorus is based around string-bends with lots of breathing room until the energy peaks over the V7 chord.

- **Range:** The first chorus is played in Pattern #4, moving up to Pattern #5 during the turnaround/transition and remaining mainly in the higher register before returning to Pattern #4 for the final turnaround.

- **Rhythm and Dynamics:** The first chorus is built around short, conversational phrases with long rests in between; in the second chorus, the solo engages in call-and-response interplay with the rhythm section to create greater dynamic intensity without relying on speed.

- **Connecting Choruses:** A repetitive transitional phrase bridges the first turnaround and sets up the high note that starts the second chorus.

Fig. 6: Two-Chorus Solo

Performance Notes

First Chorus:

1. Bars 1–4: The opening idea is based around a series of short, classic blues licks with breathing space in between.
2. Bars 5–8: The middle section repeats the same ideas with slight variations.
3. Bars 9–12: The final section begins with a bluesy V7 lick, moves up the neck to a IV7 chord-tone phrase, then evolves into a repetitive, syncopated phrase over the turnaround that builds up energy to launch the second chorus.

Second Chorus:

1. Bars 1–4: The main idea is an Albert King-style bend with lots of breathing room; on the audio demo, the rhythm guitar plays a "horn-section" figure that provides the perfect setting for call-and-response between the solo and the rhythm section. Although there is more silence than notes, the energy is still elevated above the first chorus by the intensity of the attack, higher-pitched note choices, and a more driving rhythm section. In bar 4, bend up from C in a series of steps over a quarter-note triplet rhythm, a phrase based directly on Albert King ("Overall Junction").
2. Bars 5–8: A continuation of the Albert King style in bars 5–6 emphasizes IV7 chord tones; in bars 7–8, the phrase echoes the opening idea of the solo.
3. Bars 9–12: The solo peaks by outlining the V7 chord, which sets up the slide up to high A in bar 10. In bars 11–12, the melody drops back into fifth position (Pattern #4) and lowers the energy through the turnaround. A solo in the middle of a song is typically followed by a vocal, so it's normal to relax the energy of the solo during the final bars in order to create a smoother, more musical transition.

Like all aspects of blues soloing, the number of different ways in which you can manipulate the energy and emotion of a blues solo over two choruses or longer is practically infinite. When you hear a multi-chorus solo that captures your attention, analyze how the player manages the flow of ideas and energy. By the same token, if a long solo doesn't seem to be working, ask yourself why—often, it's a matter of just knowing when to quit.

Chapter 9 Summary

1. **Match the Solo to the Song:** Learn the vocal melody, rhythms, and lyrics and use them to help guide and inspire your solo.
2. **Repeat Yourself:** Establish a strong opening idea in the first four bars, repeat it in the middle, and vary it in the final four bars.
3. **Listen and Analyze:** The best way to build a repertoire of ideas and the foundation for a personal style is through listening, copying, and analyzing great solos.
4. **Multi-Chorus Solos:** To play effective longer solos, pace yourself and build the energy over time by varying the range, rhythm, dynamics, and transitions between choruses.

Practice

The concepts and techniques covered in this chapter aren't developed through specific exercises. The best way to learn how to organize your ideas and control the flow of a solo is through a combination of careful listening to other players and continuously working on your own ideas in the context of blues arrangements.

Creating a solo, whether it's based on a specific song or not, is a form of songwriting, and a number of highly-quoted blues solos either combine composed and improvised sections or are fixed compositions in their own right. "Honky Tonk" evolved out of an instrumental jam, but the guitar figures have a strong, compositional quality, and the solo is often performed note-for-note. Albert King essentially used the same set of core phrases on every solo throughout his career. Many of Freddie King's early instrumentals were based on existing vocal melodies or instrumentals by other artists. "Hide Away," for example, is basically a medley of themes from various tunes that were well-known at the time.

Whenever you come up with a good phrase, record it or notate it and then arrange a 12-bar chorus around it. As we have seen, you can create a good solo out of no more than three ideas and a turnaround, and if your ideas are good, no one minds hearing them over and over again—what we call "style" is essentially artful repetition.

Listen

Matching the Solo to the Song

- "St. Louis Blues" by Bessie Smith (1925 version): Smith's vocal alternates with classic fills by trumpeter Louis Armstrong in this highly influential recording.
- "I'm Going Down," "I'm Ready" by Freddie King (Shelter Records): King's hard-hitting solos are based on the same rhythmic structure as his tough, aggressive vocals.
- "Bright Lights, Big City" by Jimmy Reed: Compare the melody to the example shown in Fig. 1. Reed's harmonica solos, while not always based on the melody, are also very "vocal."

Every Solo Tells a Story

- "Side Tracked" by Freddie King: Almost all of King's instrumental recordings from his early-1960s period on King Records (no relation) are classic examples of melodic arrangement and solo phrasing.
- "Honky Tonk" by Bill Doggett (Billy Butler, guitar): An all-time classic blues instrumental, each of Butler's three solo choruses is a classic in its own right.
- "Overall Junction" by Albert King: This was cut during his most influential period at Stax Records; it's a relatively rare example of a traditional medium shuffle during a time when King was breaking stylistic ground by fusing blues with other styles (see Chapter 12).
- "Further Up the Road" by Bobby "Blue" Bland (Pat Hare, guitar): This is a classic on every level. Also check out Bland's other Duke label recordings: "It's My Life Baby," featuring guitarist Roy Gaines, and "I Woke Up Screaming," featuring guitarist Clarence Holloman; all were recorded around the same time period and feature similar phrasing.

Other Classic One-Chorus Medium Shuffle Solos

- "Rock Me Baby" by B.B. King includes a moody, restrained solo that perfectly extends the mood of the lyrics.
- "Little by Little" by Junior Wells (Earl Hooker, guitar) is a classic example of strong rhythmic phrasing and classic 12-bar solo structure. Hooker was considered by many of his peers to be the greatest guitar player in Chicago (and was even better known for his slide guitar work).

Multi-Chorus Solos

- "The Sky Is Crying" by Albert King (Stax Records, studio version): This is a two-chorus solo with a classic transitional phrase connecting the choruses.
- "Overall Junction" by Albert King (Stax): A medium-shuffle instrumental, it features several smooth shifts in dynamics and texture.
- "Gambler's Blues" by B.B. King (MCA Records, live version): King masterfully manipulates the crowd with dynamics.
- "Worry, Worry" by B.B. King (from *Live at the Regal*): This is more crowd-pleasing dynamics.
- "The Thrill Is Gone" by B.B. King (MCA): A masterpiece of emotional control, it develops themes over multiple choruses.
- "Okie Dokie Stomp" by Gatemouth Brown (Peacock): This is an arranged solo composition that Brown performs with a completely spontaneous feel.
- "Frosty" by Albert Collins (MCA; original studio version): An extended up-tempo instrumental, like "Okie Dokie Stomp," it features multiple changes in texture and dynamics.
- "Pride and Joy" by Stevie Ray Vaughan (Epic, studio version): Vaughan reverses the usual flow by starting higher on the neck and then reducing the intensity somewhat at the start of the second chorus.

10 Flavors and Textures

Up to this point, we have focused almost exclusively on one facet of blues guitar soloing: single-note melodies on the upper strings. This approach has dominated the sound of contemporary blues and blues-rock guitar since the beginning of the electric era, but as popular as they are, high-pitched single-note licks are just one way to play a great blues solo. In this chapter, we'll look at some other techniques and concepts that will add range and depth to your soloing vocabulary.

Double Stops

Double stop is the term for two notes fretted simultaneously. In terms of texture, double stops are halfway between single notes and chords, producing a bigger sound than the former but easier to move around the neck than the latter, and they have been a standard feature of the blues guitar vocabulary since the earliest acoustic days.

The two most common double stops used in blues solos are 3rds and 6ths; we'll look at techniques and applications for each.

3rd Intervals

An *interval* is the distance between two notes measured by the number of consecutive scale steps they include. For example, the interval C to E includes three scale steps (C–D–E), as does the interval D to F (D–E–F), so they are both called 3rd intervals. These 3rd-interval double stops (technically, *harmonic intervals*) provide a very effective way to "fatten" melodies. This sound is familiar from Spanish-style acoustic guitar melodies, but in blues, the best-known example of 3rds is probably the signature guitar lick on the all-time classic "Sweet Home Chicago."

To arrange 3rd intervals (or any other double stops) on the guitar, begin with a diatonic (i.e., seven-note) scale. Since blues harmony is based on dominant seventh chords, the corresponding diatonic scale is the *dominant scale* (also known as *Mixolydian* mode), which is equivalent to a major scale with a lowered seventh degree. To harmonize the dominant scale in 3rds, play the scale on the first string and harmonize each note with the note on the second string a diatonic 3rd below it—that is, two steps down the scale. The same principle applies to any two adjacent strings, but most classic blues 3rd-interval phrases can be arranged on just the top two strings.

Fig. 1: Dominant Scale Harmonized in 3rds

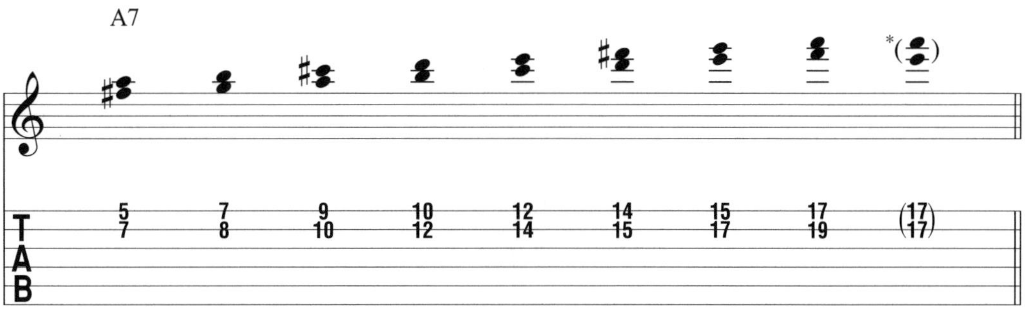

A7

T (string 1)	5	7	9	10	12	14	15	17	(17)
A (string 2)	7	8	10	12	14	15	17	19	(17)

*When the root is in the melody, it is typically harmonized with a 4th interval rather than a 3rd to provide a stronger feeling of resolution.

The irregular whole step/half step pattern of the scale creates two different 3rd-interval sizes, or *qualities*. These are technically known as *major 3rds* (two whole steps) and *minor 3rds* (one and a half steps).

For playing purposes, it's more practical to think of them simply as two different fingering shapes and to memorize the order in which they occur as you move up and down the neck.

Once you become familiar with the concept and fingering, you can harmonize almost any melody in 3rds. For example, the following 3rd-interval phrase running the length of the scale is designed to fit over the first four bars of a 12-bar solo. At a medium tempo, pick it using all down-strokes; when you dig in hard, 3rd intervals have an aggressive energy that carries directly from blues into rock 'n' roll.

Fig. 2: 3rd-Interval Opening Phrase

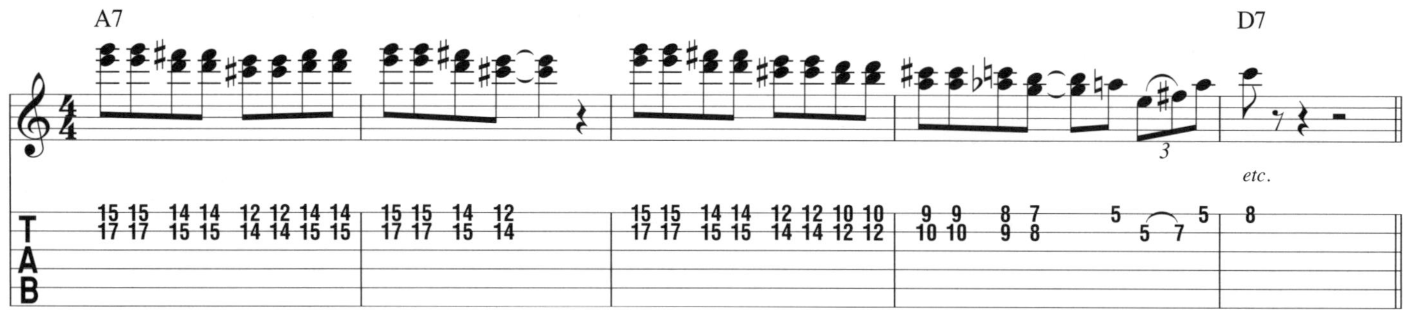

When you extend 3rd intervals over an entire 12-bar progression, blues harmony presents a challenge: the dominant scale only matches the chord built from the same note (e.g., the A dominant scale only matches A7). So to use 3rd intervals over all three chords, you need to adjust for the differences between the three dominant scales.

The figure below shows 3rd-interval patterns for D7 and E7 on the first two strings along the same part of the neck as the A dominant scale. Before you play each pattern, play the root of the chord on an open string so you clearly hear the relationship between the harmony and melody. Also, note the locations of the chord tones (root, 3rd, 5th, 7th) for each chord within the pattern. When you use double-stop patterns within a progression, these tones are the strongest melodic targets to hit when the chords change.

Fig. 3: D and E Dominant Scales Harmonized in 3rds

Given the technical challenge of organizing and fingering the various interval patterns up and down the neck, it's best to first memorize some 3rd-interval phrases that you can plug directly into a solo rather than trying to arrange on the spot. The next example is a 12-bar solo demonstrating 3rd-interval phrases that have been used by players from Lonnie Johnson (1920s) to Robert Johnson (1930s), Chuck Berry (1950s), Freddie King (1960s), and Stevie Ray Vaughan (1980s).

Fig. 4: 12-Bar Solo with 3rd Intervals

Performance Notes

Throughout the example, use your first (index) finger to fret all notes on the first string and either your second or third finger to fret the harmony note on the second string. Pick using either all down-strokes or alternate down-and-up depending on which technique you can execute accurately at a given tempo (both techniques are common).

1. Bars 1–4: The opening phrase is similar to "Sweet Home Chicago." Sliding into the first beat of a double-stop triplet from a half step below (as shown on the first triplet) is a common phrasing embellishment. Use the same technique throughout the example. On beat 1 of bar 2 and beats 1 and 2 of bar 4, bend the second string a quarter tone while holding the first string steady. You can also substitute the 3rd-interval lick from Fig. 2 as an alternate four-bar opening phrase; the transition to D7 is the same for both.
2. Bars 5–6: The intervals are based on the D dominant scale with the melody beginning on the 7th of D7 (C). At the end of bar 6, the melody moves up in half steps in order to arrive at the 3rd of A7 (C♯) on the downbeat of bar 7.
3. Bars 7–8: More half-step connections tie the phrases together; in bar 7, beat 4, add the F♯ with your fourth finger (the melody moves but the harmony doesn't). In bar 8, pick the notes separately to create a different 3rd-interval texture.
4. Bars 9–10: The E7 phrase is repeated down two frets over D7.
5. Bars 11–12: We go out with a standard turnaround melody harmonized in 3rds.

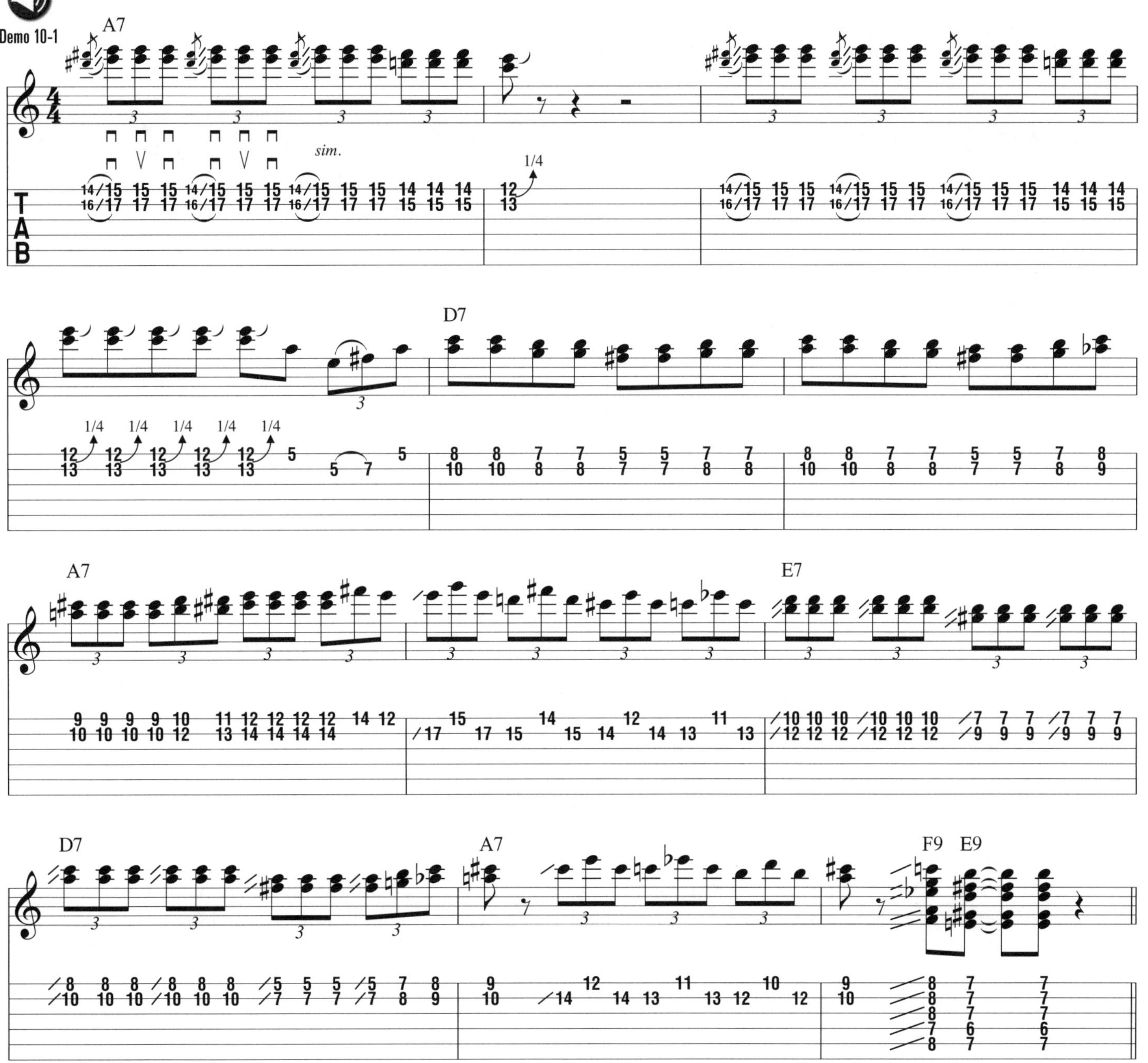

6th Intervals

Compared to the dense texture of 3rd intervals, 6th intervals have a lighter, more open sound. Well-known examples of 6th intervals in blues include "Honky Tonk" (Chapter 9) as well as Freddie King's early-1960s classics "Hide Away" and "The Stumble," the latter two each featuring a fast 6th-interval phrase that runs the length of the neck. The sweetness of 6th intervals also makes them a staple technique in gospel and R&B (the more commercial cousin of blues)—especially the work of Memphis-based guitarist Steve Cropper (Otis Redding, Sam & Dave).

6th intervals contain six consecutive scale steps (e.g., the interval C to A contains C–D–E–F–G–A). Like 3rds, they are derived by harmonizing the dominant scale of each chord, resulting in two qualities (major and minor) that form a series of interval shapes when arranged lengthwise along the neck. Due to the greater distance between the notes, when the melody of a 6th interval is on the first string, the harmony must be fretted on the third string.

The following example shows 6th-interval double-stop patterns for A7, D7, and E7 with the melodies all on the first string, arranged within the same region of the neck. For greatest efficiency, fret all of the notes on the third string with your second (middle) finger and use either your first or third finger on the first string, depending on the specific interval.

Fig. 5: A, D, and E Dominant Scales Harmonized in 6ths

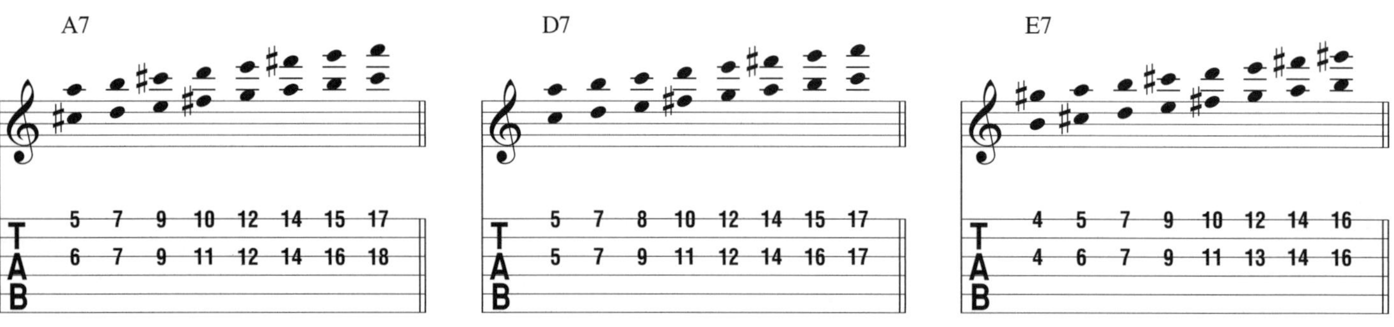

Because the notes are not on adjacent strings, the picking technique for 6th intervals is different than that for 3rds. Many players prefer to pick the strings separately using hybrid picking—i.e., flatpick on the third string and a bare finger to pick the first string. To flatpick both strings simultaneously, mute the middle string with the side of your second finger when you fret the intervals.

The following example demonstrates 6th-interval double-stop phrasing over a relaxed 12-bar shuffle.

Fig. 6: 12-Bar Solo with 6th Intervals

Performance Notes

1. Bars 1–4: The melody is based around the major 3rd, creating a sweet quality typical of 6ths. The phrasing uses a standard 6th-interval technique—i.e., picking the lower note and sliding into the next interval shape before picking the upper note.
2. Bars 5–8: This is essentially the same phrase transposed to D7.
3. Bar 9–10: Very similar to Freddie King's famous "Hide Away" lick, the position shifts are too fast to think about while you play, so you must rely on muscle memory. Practice the phrase slowly until you can make the moves with no hesitation and gradually work it up to tempo. In bar 10, the same lick is transposed to D7; to avoid running out of room on the neck, the intervals switch to the second and fourth strings halfway through, but the same fingerings apply.
4. Bars 11–12: This is a variation on the Jimmy Reed turnaround.

Demo 10-2

A7 D7 A7 E7 D7 A7 E7

let ring

Soloing with Chords

For down-home acoustic singer/guitar players who have to perform harmony and melody simultaneously, soloing with chord is a standard technique. But even when you play in a band, the distinctive texture of chords provides a welcome alternative to single-note solos—particularly when the guitar is the only harmonic instrument.

When you learn chords for the purpose of playing rhythm, you normally build the voicings up from the lowest note (usually the root), but when you solo with chords, you need to shift your attention to the highest note—i.e., the melody. To illustrate this sort of "top-down" thinking, the figure below shows three-note voicings for A7, D7, and E7 arranged on the upper three strings (three-note chords are big enough to define the harmony but still small enough to move around quickly). Each chord tone (root, major 3rd, 5th, or minor 7th) on the first string is harmonized by two other notes from the same chord on the second and third strings. Comparing the chords side-by-side you can see that, at any point on the neck, all three are within a fret or two of each other. This means that when the harmony changes, it's relatively easy to switch from one melodic voicing to another.

Fig. 7: A7, D7, E7 Voicings on the Top Three Strings

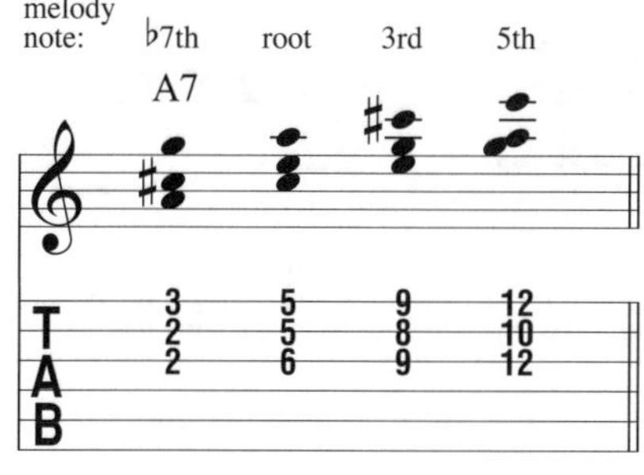

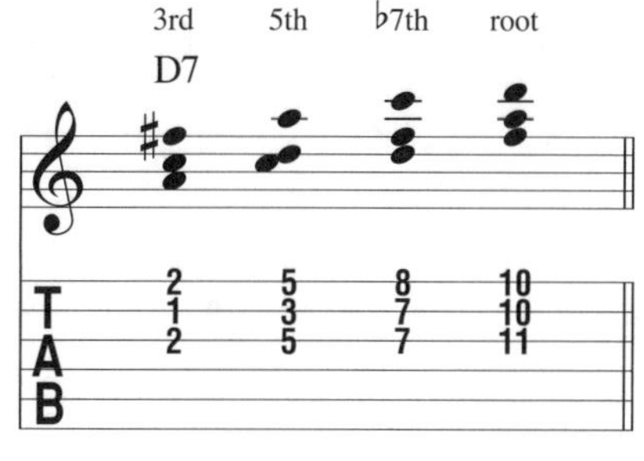

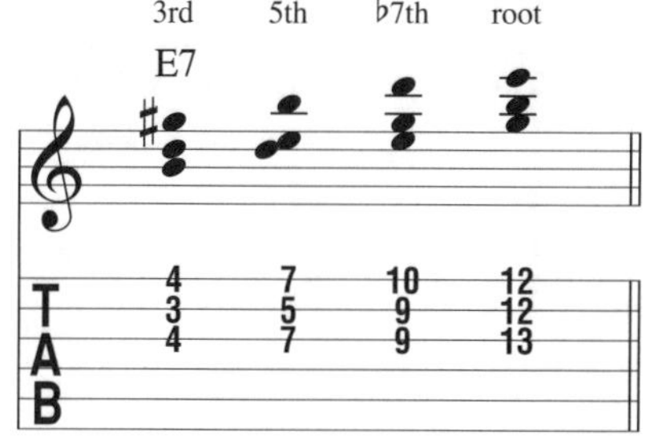

The next example demonstrates a chord solo using these voicings over a 12-bar medium shuffle.

Fig. 8: Soloing with Chords

Performance Notes

Throughout the example, half-step (chromatic) moves between the primary chord voicings are used to connect one voicing to the next. Naming each of these passing chords individually would make the solo look far more complicated than it sounds, so only the main harmony in each bar is identified.

1. Bars 1–2: As with 3rd intervals, it's common to slide into chords from a half step below as notated on the first triplet; the same effect is used throughout the example. In bar 2, lowering the A7 chord a half step (similar to Robert Johnson's "Kind Hearted Woman" or Hendrix's "Red House") suggests a quick change whether or not the band actually plays it.
2. Bars 3–4: The moving chords in bar 3 are followed in bar 4 by a fixed A chord; barre the second and third strings with your index finger and move the melody on top with your other fingers (this phrase is very common in country blues).
3. Bar 5–6: The harmony changes to D7; in bar 6, beats 2 and 3, the upper notes stay the same while the third string changes, creating subtle melodic movement within the chord.
4. Bars 7–8: In bar 7, the 6th intervals are the outside notes of the three-note chords. Fret the low A at the end of bar 7 with your thumb. In bar 8, all three notes are picked separately as an alternative rhythmic texture.
5. Bars 9–10: Barre the top four strings while moving the melody on the first string as in bar 4.
6. Bars 11–12: This is a version of the Jimmy Reed turnaround arranged with three notes instead of two (most of the other classic turnarounds covered in Chapter 8 can also be expanded to three-note chords).

The vocabulary for this style of soloing draws heavily from the Mississippi Delta acoustic blues tradition. For example, Hendrix was very likely inspired by Robert Johnson's high-string chords on "Kind Hearted Woman" when creating the intro to "Red House." In practice, most electric soloists use chords as an occasional texture, such as playing the chord figure in bars 1–4 and then switching to single-note phrasing for the remainder of the chorus.

Chicago-Style Soloing

When blues guitar was electrified in the 1940s, two main styles emerged: the uptown single-note style (represented by T-Bone Walker and his disciples) and the down home rhythm-based style (typified by Chicago blues artist Muddy Waters and his circle). Many Chicago guitarists of that era were emigrants from the rural South, particularly the Mississippi Delta region, and began their playing careers on the acoustic guitar. Chicago electric blues was typically performed by small bands, often with two electric guitars (one sometimes substituting for the bass), drums, piano, and amplified harmonica. Acoustic playing techniques influenced the approach taken by electric guitarists in these bands, and while the presence of a rhythm section freed guitarists from the need to handle harmony and melody simultaneously, Chicago-style solos still tend to blur the line between "rhythm" and "lead."

The next example is in the style of Chicago guitar icons like Jimmy Rogers (a member of Muddy's band as well as a solo artist), Robert Lockwood (who recorded with many different Chicago artists as well as on his own), Eddie Taylor (solo artist and member of Jimmy Reed's band), and Louis and Dave Myers (best known for their work behind harp great Little Walter). The Chicago influence can also be heard in the rhythm-oriented approach of powerful single-note masters Freddie King and Stevie Ray Vaughan.

Fig. 9: Chicago-Style Solo

Performance Notes

1. Bars 1–4: The opening idea consists of 3rd intervals picked as separate notes. Alternating melodic phrases and rhythm parts is typical of the Chicago style.
2. Bars 5–6: A classic Chicago IV chord riff, the phrase is based around D7 with the melody moving on the top string against the 3rd of the chord on the second string.
3. Bars 7–8: Bend the C on the second string (the minor 3rd) a quarter tone without bending the high E (a lick that can be traced back to Blind Lemon Jefferson, the original blues guitar hero). In bar 8, descending 3rd intervals set up the change to V7 in the style of Chicago guitar great Jimmy Rogers.
4. Bars 9–10: Fret the E7 chord voicing, pick the notes individually, and let them ring together. In bar 10, the phrase outlines a D9 chord, also reminiscent of Jimmy Rogers.
5. Bars 11–12: The turnaround is in the style of Robert Lockwood; the final transition back to A7, like that in Fig. 8, reflects the Delta-Chicago connection.

Demo 10-4

A7

let ring

let ring

D7

A7

E7

let ring

D7

A7

E7

let ring

Accenting Solos with Horn-Style Chords

Another way to vary the texture of a solo is by alternating single-note phrases with *chord accents*, which creates an effect similar to the sound of a guitar solo backed by a horn section. The concept is very simple: play a short melodic phrase and answer it with rhythmic chord accents in a call-and-response format. The interplay between melody and harmony strengthens the overall sense of structure and helps to focus your phrasing. You can vary the accents in any number of ways. For ideas, listen to uptown blues with horn section arrangements to hear both how the horn accents are arranged and how soloists interact with them. The following example illustrates the idea:

Fig. 10: Solo with Chord Accents

Performance Notes

1. "Horn parts": Sixth and ninth chords are typical of horn-section-style voicings; the color tones add uptown sophistication. In the picking hand, either strum the chords with up-strokes of the pick (as on the audio demo) or use hybrid technique, flatpicking the lowest note while simultaneously plucking the upper notes with your second, third, and fourth fingers. Different techniques produce different sounds; the pick is bright and punchy, while the fingers are somewhat more muted.
2. The single-note phrases in the example all stick to the blue-note pentatonic in Pattern #5, but the alternating single-note/chord accent technique is adaptable to any melodic style.

Soloing in the Lower Register

The high strings of the guitar are prime soloing real estate, but by venturing occasionally into the lower register, you can put a fresh, ear-catching spin on your phrasing and also exploit the full range of the instrument. Blues guitarists who have used low-end phrasing to notable effect include Freddie King, Johnny "Guitar" Watson, Gatemouth Brown, and Albert Collins, all of whom also combine a bright sound and a strong attack to give the low strings more presence. King used thumb and finger picks, and the others used bare fingers.

A useful way to begin building your low-end vocabulary is by transposing familiar licks down an octave (see Chapter 7 "Pattern #4, Lower Octave" for examples). When you memorize phrases not just as pattern-specific fingerings but also by their relationship to the scale, you can quickly move a phrase to a different pattern or key by repeating the same sequence, which speeds up your ability to play in different patterns and eliminates "blind spots" on the neck. Most phrases fit within one octave, so apart from certain position-specific techniques, it's possible to play virtually everything you know anywhere on the neck.

The next example shows a 12-bar solo that is played almost exclusively on the two lowest strings. The key of A also offers the option of including open strings (see "Soloing in Open Position" on the next page), so these phrases include a mixture of open and fretted notes.

Fig. 11: Low-Register Solo

Performance Notes

To give the notes more presence, use a brighter tone (e.g., middle or bridge pickup) combined with an aggressive attack including bare-finger string-popping.

Soloing in Open Position

The heart of the traditional blues guitar sound is in open position. Down home blues rhythm patterns are largely based around open-position chord voicings, and the melodic phrases built from those chords also mix open strings with fretted notes, giving open-position solos a sound that evokes the roots of the blues style.

Key of A

Playing in open position requires some adjustments to fingerings and techniques, so we'll start with a look at how these affect your phrasing in the by-now very familiar key of A. To play the open-position minor pentatonic pattern shown here, fret the low C with your third finger, the fourth-string E and third-string A with your second finger, and the other fretted notes with your first and third fingers:

Fig. 12: Open-Position Minor Pentatonic Pattern in A

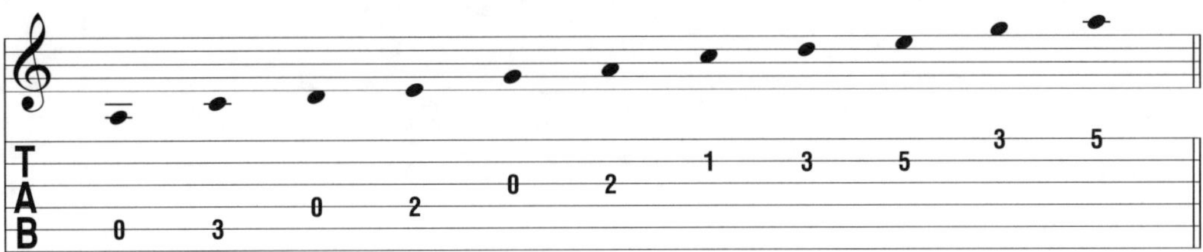

Down home blues harmony is generally based on seventh chords rather than the sixth and ninth chords of uptown blues. The seventh-chord voicings shown in the next example are the most common:

Fig. 13: Open-Position Chords in the Key of A

Performance Notes

1. A7 (I7) is typically voiced with just two fingers, leaving the other fingers free to add other melody notes while holding down the chord.
2. D7 (IV7) is often voiced with the 3rd (F♯) in the bass, which provides the chord with a deeper foundation than the fourth-string root; the F♯ is usually fretted with the thumb.
3. E7 (V7) is voiced without the fifth string (mute it with the tip of your second finger), freeing the third finger to play other notes in addition to the 7th (D).

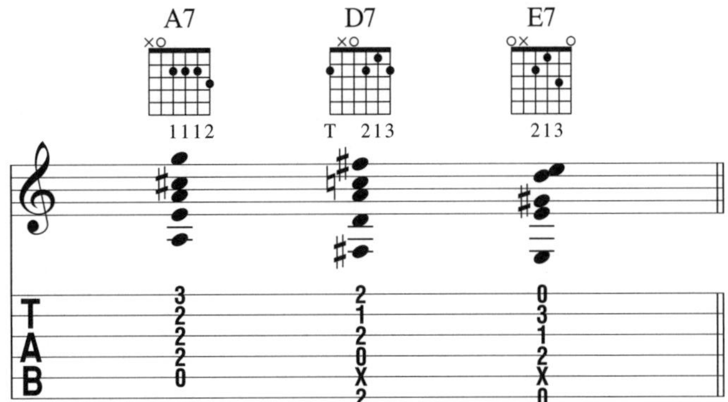

The next example is a 12-bar solo in the key of A that demonstrates some open-position down home phrases inspired by Texas blues legend Lightnin' Hopkins. As you play the phrases, notice how the melodies are related to the chord voicings; in the down home style, soloing is largely a matter of "playing around the shapes"—that is, building melodies by adding notes around the chords (often while continuing to hold at least part of the chord down) rather than playing separate scale patterns. The added advantage of this style of soloing is that, even without accompaniment, you can easily hear the chords and follow the form. Like chord-based and Chicago-style solos, open strings give you the means to be a self-contained musician.

Fig. 14: Open-Position Solo in A

Performance Notes

1. Bar 2: The trill is a rapid, repeated hammer-on/pull-off combination between the open string and your second finger.
2. Bar 4: Fret the A7 chord and hold it while playing the melody.
3. Bars 5–6: Fret the low F and F♯ with your thumb; in bar 6, fret the third-string C with your third finger and use a finger roll from A to E.
4. Bar 8: Fret the A7 chord and hold it as in bar 4.
5. Bar 9–10: The melody in bar 9 outlines the E7 chord as it moves across the strings. Fret the low F and F♯ with your thumb.

Key of E

Open position in the key of E is home to the biggest down-home blues sounds on the guitar. From acoustic blues icons Blind Lemon Jefferson and Robert Johnson, to electric pioneers Lightnin' Hopkins and Muddy Waters, to power-trio titans Hendrix and Stevie Ray Vaughan, E has always been the go-to key for what Muddy called the "deep blues."

As in the key of A, to play the "home" minor pentatonic scale pattern (Pattern #4) in open-position E, you need to modify the fingerings to account for the open strings. Use your third finger for all notes at the third fret and your second finger for all notes at the second fret; the first finger is not needed at all until you start filling in the rest of the blues tonality.

Fig. 15: Open-Position Minor Pentatonic Pattern in E

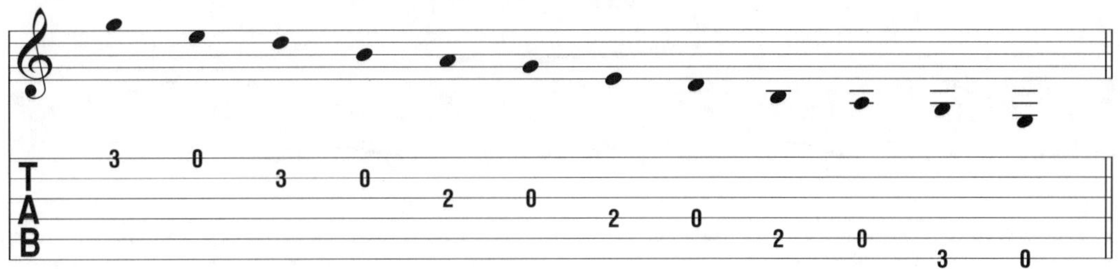

The next example is a 12-bar solo in E with a combination of chord-based and single-note phrases. Virtually every down home blues guitarist spends a lot of time in open-position E, so examples are abundant. Lightnin' Hopkins in particular favored E almost exclusively aside from a few excursions in A, and Muddy Waters, Jimmy Rogers, Hendrix, and Stevie Ray Vaughan are all known for classic open-position blues performances in the key of E.

Fig. 16: Open-Position Solo in E

Performance Notes

1. Bars 1–2: The open E and B strings are both chord tones of E7, so using them in combination with fretted notes creates fat melodic lines. The low E in bar 2 anchors the melody to the chord and exploits the full range of open position.
2. Bars 3–4: This is a re-phrasing of the initial idea answered by chords; in the down home style, melodies and chords are intertwined.
3. Bars 5–6: Here's a classic A7 phrase with the melody moving around the open A7 chord voicing. On beat 1, drag the pick upward across the strings to attack the open A string while muting with the fretting hand (a variation on the rake).
4. Bars 7–8: The blue 3rd is followed by typical open E phrases.
5. Bars 9–10: Following an arpeggiated ♭7 chord, the melody jumps briefly up the neck to fifth position over the A7 before returning to open position. This phrase is a staple of players from Jimmy Rogers to Freddy King to SRV.
6. Bars 11–12: A Jimmy Rogers-inspired variation on a barber-shop turnaround, it incorporates the open E string (listen to Rogers' "That's All Right").

Demo 10-8
Play-Along 9

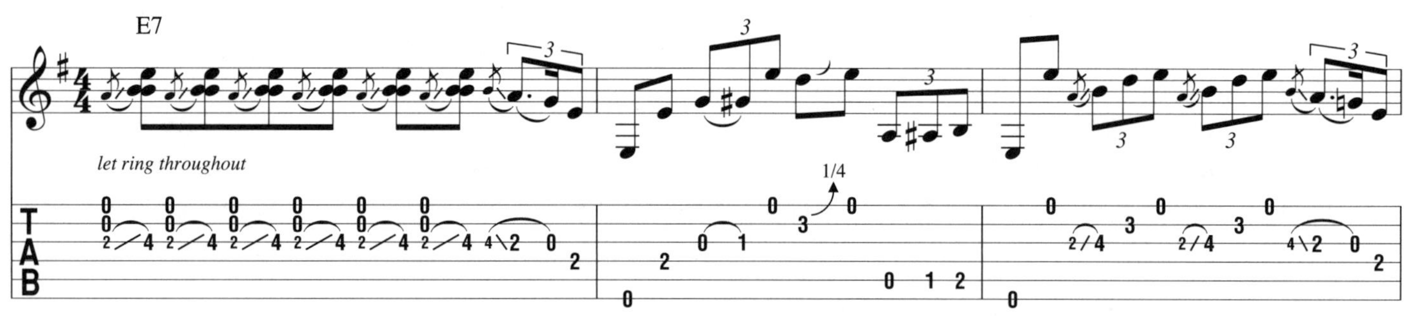
E7
let ring throughout
1/4

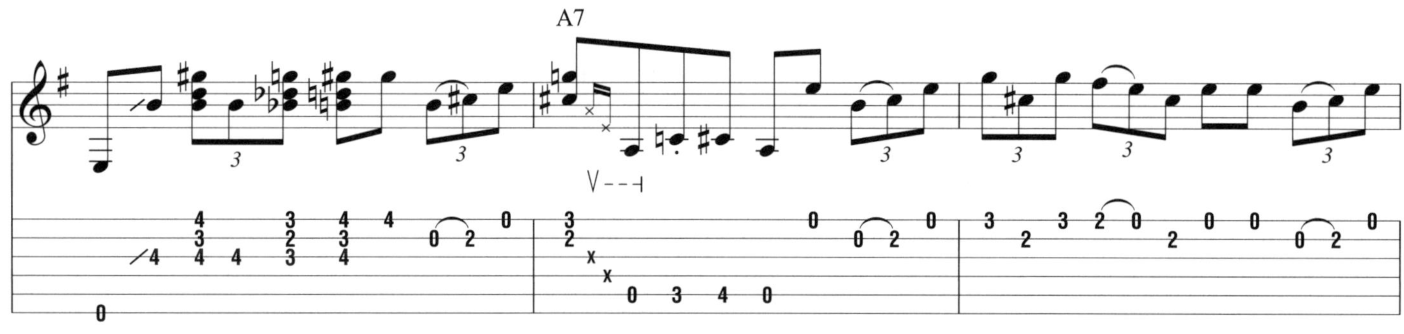
A7

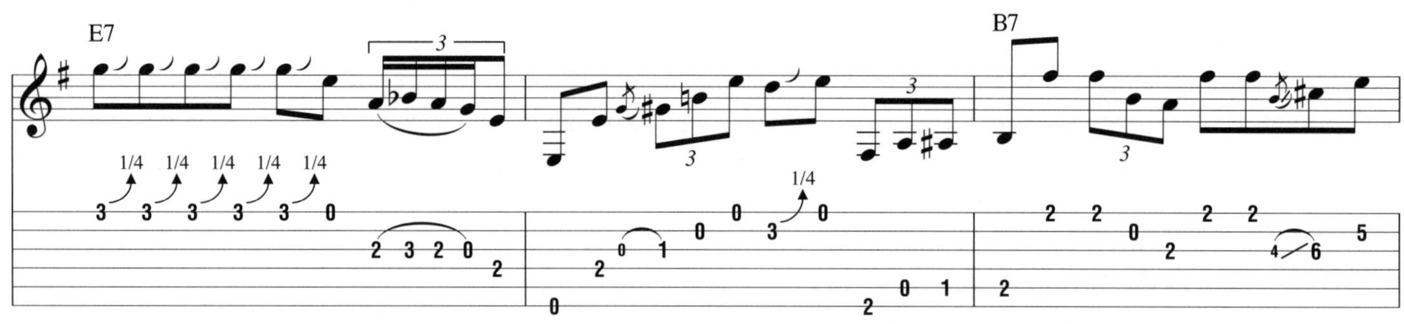
E7
B7
1/4

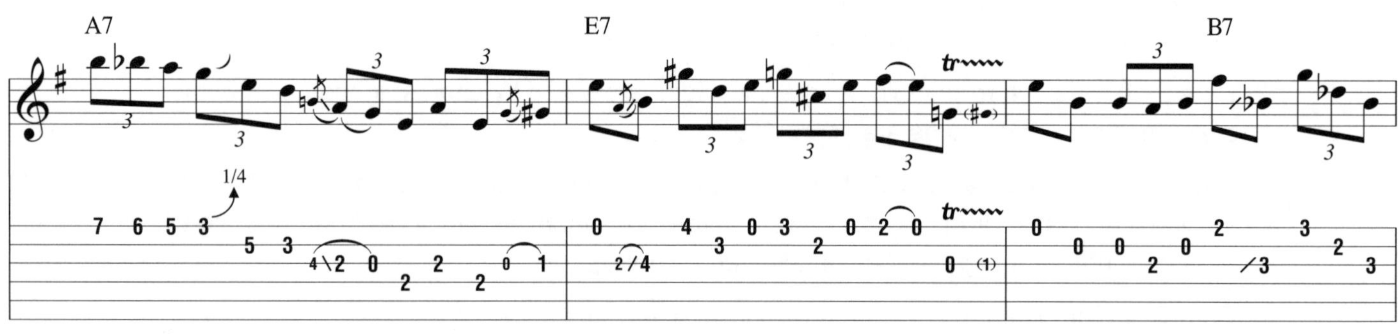
A7
E7
B7
1/4

E7

Combining Open and Moveable Patterns

Some blues guitarists stick to a certain school of playing, such as down home (open-position, chord-based) or uptown (pattern-based, single-note), but others combine both approaches in a hybrid style that encompasses the whole neck. Think Freddie King, Hendrix, and Stevie Ray Vaughan, to name just three. When you combine these approaches, your soloing retains a powerful, self-contained quality no matter how high up the neck you go. Rather than depending on a rhythm section to convey the harmony, form, and feel, it's all included in your phrasing.

The next example combines open-position and up-the-neck phrases in E—a key that's ideal for exploring the full length of the neck. To bring out the maximum tone and dynamic range, avoid using too much distortion; the huge, powerful tone of players like Stevie Ray Vaughan comes from combining a very hard attack with a relatively clean sound.

Fig. 17: Solo in E Combining Open Position and Moveable Patterns

Performance Notes

1. Bars 1–2: Fretted notes combined with the open first string are answered by the down home blues combination in seventh position (bend the G a quarter tone without bending the B).
2. Bars 3–4: The fretted notes move up the neck against the open E string to 12th position, where the answer sets up the change to IV7.
3. Bars 5–6: High, bent-note phrases emphasizing A7 chord tones contrast with the thicker texture of the first four bars. Use your third finger (supported by the first and second) to fret the whole-step bends from G to A, and then move the same fingering down one fret to bend from F♯ to G.
4. Bars 7–8: The open E string provides enough time to move your fretting hand from 12th to open position. In bar 8, use hybrid picking to cover the two-octave jump from the open low E string (flatpick) to the open high E string (bare finger); the open E string provides time to shift your fretting hand to seventh position in preparation for the V7 change.
5. Bars 9–10: The melody outlines ♭7 in bar 9 and then jumps to 12th position to emphasize A7 chord tones in bar 10.
6. Bars 11–12: After the trill on beat 1, pick the open E string and shift back to open position, ending the chorus with a classic down home turnaround.

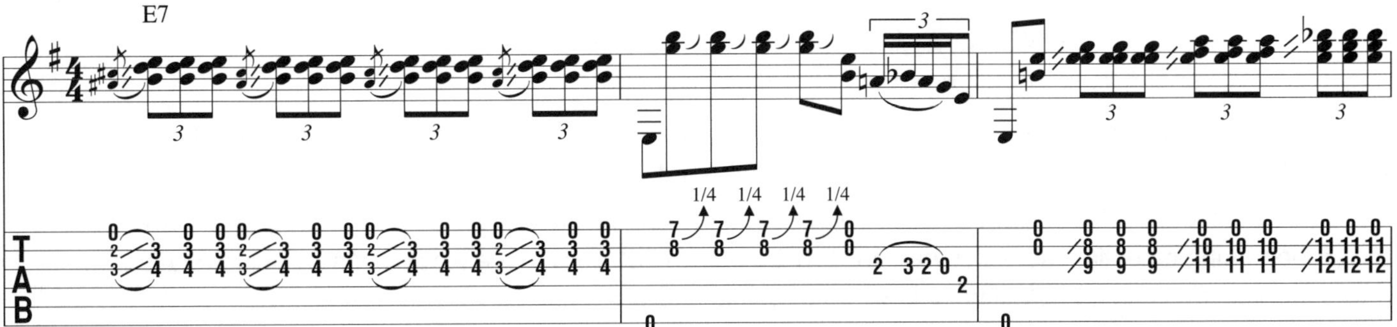

Open Position: Other Keys

A very quick and effective way to turn any key into an open key is to use a *capo*. To play in A♭, for example, place a capo at the fourth fret to access the same open-string combinations you use in E. Some players (notably Albert Collins) use a capo all the time, moving it up and down the neck for different keys. Learning to play with a capo takes practice, since it alters the familiar visual relationships between hands, frets, and patterns and creates a different feel under your fingers, but the advantages in sound and style can be well worth the effort.

In the absence of a capo, open-position phrasing is most common in the keys of A and E, but any key that has a relationship to any of the open strings is also a candidate. For example:

- **Key of G:** The open fourth, third, and second strings form a G major triad (G Pattern #3).
- **Key of B:** The IV7 chord (E7) invites open-position phrases like those in Figs. 16 and 17 (Hendrix used this approach on "Red House").
- **Key of D:** All three chords have open-string roots as well as other chord tones, so with some experimentation, you can find open- and fretted-string combinations at any point.

Whatever key you're playing in, make it a habit to analyze the I7, IV7, and V7 chords to discover any open-string potential. Moveable patterns are the same in all keys, but each key has a unique relationship to the open strings. Exploiting that difference will add new dimensions to your solos.

Chapter 10 Summary

1. **Double stops** (two notes played simultaneously) are halfway between single notes and chords. The two most common double-stop intervals are 3rds and 6ths.
2. **Three-note chords** arranged melodically provide classic style, depth, and power.
3. **Chicago blues** combines elements of down home chord-based Delta blues style with single-string soloing.
4. **Accenting solos with chords** adds both dynamic variety and harmonic awareness.
5. **Soloing in the lower octave** provides contrast to the standard high-string approach.
6. **Soloing in open position** and combining open and fretted strings provides additional texture and a traditional blues flavor. Open-position phrases are common in the keys of A and E but can also be adapted to other keys.

Practice

Intervals

Intervals are harmonized scales, so many of the same practice methods apply. The examples shown in this chapter are limited mainly to melodies on the first string in the key of A, but here are some ways to expand your repertoire:

1. **Keys**
   a. Following the cycle of fourths, find a one-octave dominant scale pattern on the first string for each of the 12 keys (some keys will require you to shift octaves mid-scale). The pattern of whole steps and half steps that make up the scale are identical regardless of key. Practice the scale patterns ascending and descending.
   b. Once you know the scale pattern for a given key on the first string, the 3rd and 6th interval shapes that accompany each melody note are identical from one key to the next. Practice the interval sequence for each key ascending and descending.
   c. Apply the intervals to 12-bar blues progressions in different keys, adapting the patterns to each chord change. The relationships between the notes and chords are the same regardless of the key, so most ideas that work in one key will work in all keys.
   d. Listen to the examples cited on the next page ("Listen") to hear how players apply these intervals in practice. Like any technique, some players use intervals more than others; it's all a matter of taste and style.
2. **Range**
   a. Repeat the double-stop exercise with melodies on the second, third, and fourth strings to cover the entire neck. The locations of the chord tones on the inner strings are not as obvious as they are on the first string, so most players avoid them, but it's mostly a matter of familiarity. The concepts and techniques are identical regardless of which string sets you use.
   b. Play the dominant scale across the neck in one position and harmonize each note as you go. Due to their nature, playing melodies with intervals requires more lengthwise motion than single notes, but moving across rather than along the neck also opens up new melodic ideas.

Soloing Variations (Chords, Chicago-Style, Horn Section, Low Register, Open Position)

All of these soloing concepts involve different applications of familiar techniques, so the most effective practice xmethod is to listen to examples like those mentioned on the next page and steal ideas. Once you learn the fundamental concepts and techniques of blues, the focus turns mostly to style, and developing your style is a continuous process of listening and playing—not practicing technical exercises. When you're inspired, you can leap a long distance in a hurry.

Listen

3rd-Interval Double Stops

Lonnie Johnson	"Away Down in the Alley Blues"
Robert Johnson	"Sweet Home Chicago"
Chuck Berry	"Thirty Days"
Freddie King	"The Stumble"
Stevie Ray Vaughan	"Love Struck Baby," "Pride and Joy"

6th-Interval Double Stops

Billy Butler (with Bill Doggett)	"Honky Tonk"
Freddie King "Hide Away,"	"The Stumble"
Steve Cropper (w/ Sam & Dave)	"Soul Man"
(w/ Otis Redding)	"Sittin' on the Dock of the Bay"

Soloing with Chords

Robert Johnson	"Kind Hearted Woman"
Robert Lockwood Jr.	"Black Spider Blues"
Jimi Hendrix	"Red House"

Chicago-Style Soloing

Jimmy Rogers	"That's All Right," "Ludella"
Eddie Taylor	"Big Town Playboy"

Horn Section Chord Accents

B.B. King	"Every Day I Have the Blues"
Albert King	"Overall Junction"

Low-Register Solos

Freddie King	"Sen-Say-Shun"
Johnny "Guitar" Watson	"Three Hours Past Midnight"
Gatemouth Brown	"Boogie Uproar"
Albert Collins	"Don't Lose Your Cool," "Collins Shuffle"

Open-Position A Solos

Lightnin' Hopkins	"Fast Life Woman"
Eddie Taylor	"Bad Boy"

Open-Position E Solos

Lightnin' Hopkins	"Short Haired Woman"
Muddy Waters	"Still a Fool"
Jimmy Rogers	"That's All Right"
Jimi Hendrix	"Come On (Part 1)"
Stevie Ray Vaughan	"Scuttle Buttin'"

Combining Open Position and Moveable Patterns

Jimi Hendrix	"Voodoo Chile (Slight Return)"
Stevie Ray Vaughan	"Pride and Joy"

Part 3
Beyond the 12-Bar Shuffle

The 12-bar three-chord medium shuffle represents the heart of the traditional blues sound, but blues isn't restricted to a certain form, type of harmony, or rhythm; it's a means of expression that can be adapted to virtually any musical setting. A typical contemporary blues set list might include elements of funk, R&B, Latin, rock, jazz, country, or any number of other popular or traditional styles mixed in with traditional blues elements. The thread that ties all of these variations together is blues phrasing, and the principles of phrasing that you have learned in the context of the 12-bar shuffle have also prepared you to handle the many stylistic and technical variations that make up the expanded blues universe. In the following chapters, we'll look at how to handle different chords, tempos, progressions, and rhythm feels from a blues perspective.

11 Harmony and Form

The three-chord 12-bar progression is by far the most popular version of blues, but there are plenty of other ways to arrange and harmonize a blues song. In this chapter, we'll look at some variations that have become part of the standard blues repertoire.

Uptown Blues Harmony

Ever since the invention of blues, composers and arrangers have been altering the 12-bar progression and chord qualities to create different pathways through the changes. Even if you mainly play three-chord blues, at some point you will almost certainly encounter arrangements that include these uptown chords, so it's a good idea to develop a strategy for dealing with them. A certain amount of theory is required to explain how these alterations work, but the main focus is to learn practical phrases that you can quickly absorb into your existing style and play with confidence.

Chromatic Passing Chords

Chromatic passing chord is not a term you're likely to hear tossed around at blues clubs, but the sound it describes—a chord that is inserted between the main blues changes to increase the feeling of anticipation and release—is very common in blues harmony.

The first point in the progression where you might encounter a chromatic passing chord is between IV7 and I7 (bar 6 of the 12-bar progression). The two options, ♯IV°7 ("sharp four diminished") or IVmi7 ("four minor"), each insert a half-step connection between chord tones of IV7 and I7. The following example demonstrates typical guitar passing-chord voicings:

Fig. 1: Chromatic Passing Chords: IV7–I7

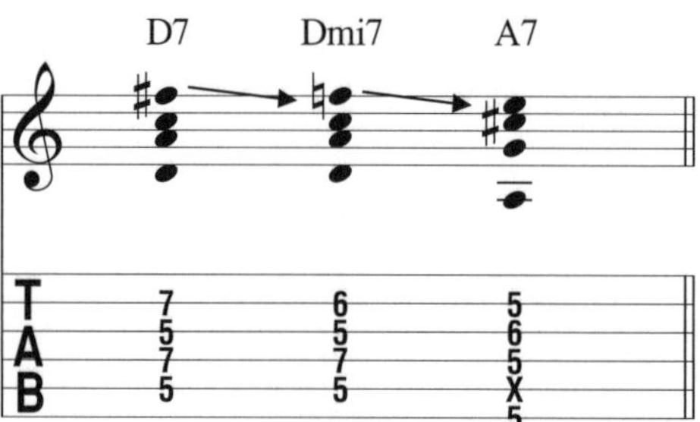

When you solo over chromatic chords, you have two basic ways to handle the melody:

1. Include the chromatic tone in your phrasing (i.e., "play the changes").
2. Play key-center phrases that avoid the chromatic tone.

The next figure demonstrates how to play the changes with phrases that incorporate each of these chromatic tones in bar 6 of the 12-bar progression (bars 5–8 are shown). The first example adds D♯ (the root of ♯IV°7), and the second adds F natural (the ♭3rd of IVmi7) to otherwise typical blues phrases:

Fig. 2: Blues Phrases with Chromatic Tones

2a: "Sharp four diminished"

2b: "Four minor"

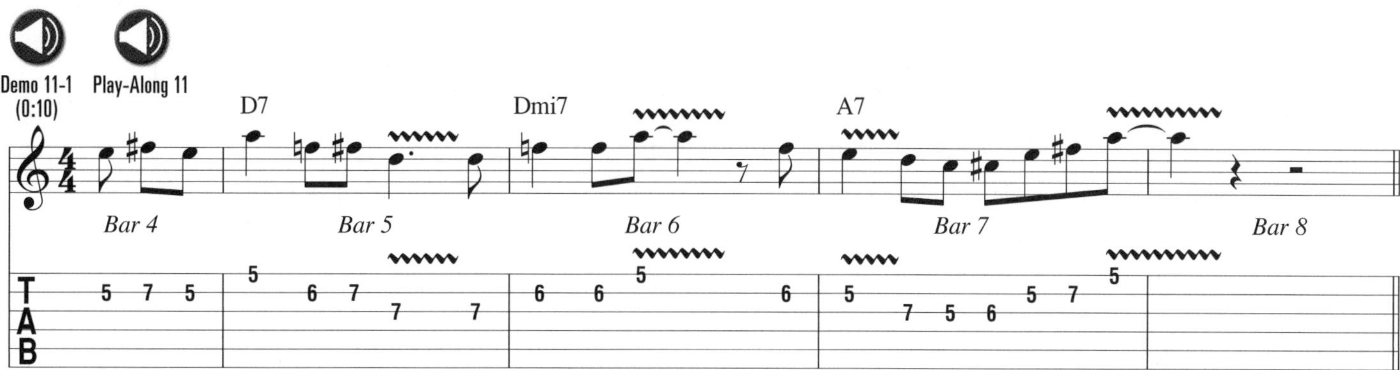

The chord-tone approach is standard in jazz-oriented blues, but mainstream blues and blues-rock guitarists who play over chromatic changes almost invariably take the second, key-center approach. The following example shows a key-center phrase that fits over either chromatic chord; the melody doesn't include any chromatic tones, but the C in bar 6 is common to both passing chords as well as the key center (on the audio demonstration you can hear the same phrase played over both sets of changes).

Fig. 3: Key-Center Phrase over Chromatic Changes

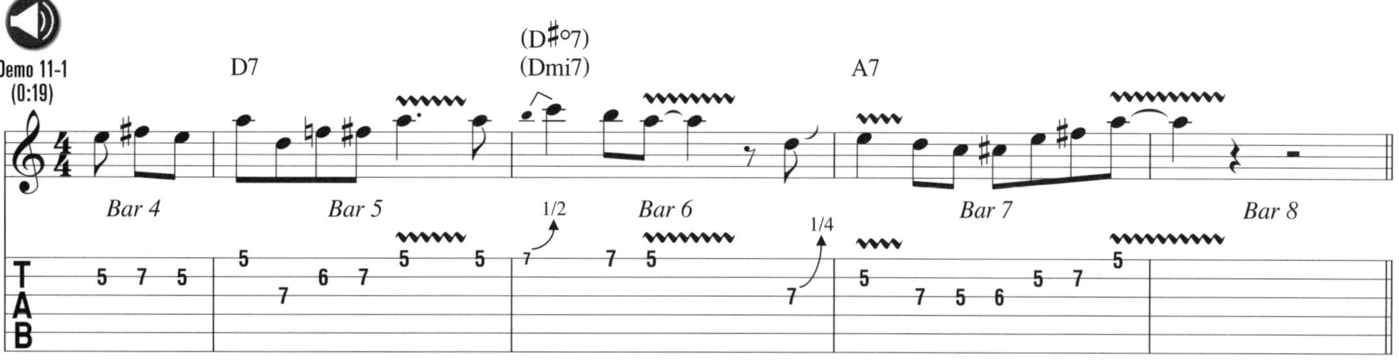

The best way to develop your ear for chromatic changes is through repetition. Loop the changes and play over them until they become familiar, identify which notes work best, and smoothly integrate the phrases into your normal style. Like color tones and chord tones, the more you listen to and play chromatic changes and melodies, the sooner they work their way into the sound of the key center and become part of your vocabulary.

Ragtime Changes

Another common way to augment the three-chord 12-bar progression is to replace the basic changes in bars 8–10 (I7–V7–IV7 or I7–V7–V7) with substitute chords that form a chord cycle known as "one-six-two-five." This progression was a common feature of ragtime, a sophisticated style of popular music that predated blues, and it has been part of the blues style since the beginning, so every blues guitar player is likely to encounter it at some point.

Fig. 4: Chord Substitution: I7–VI7–II7–V7

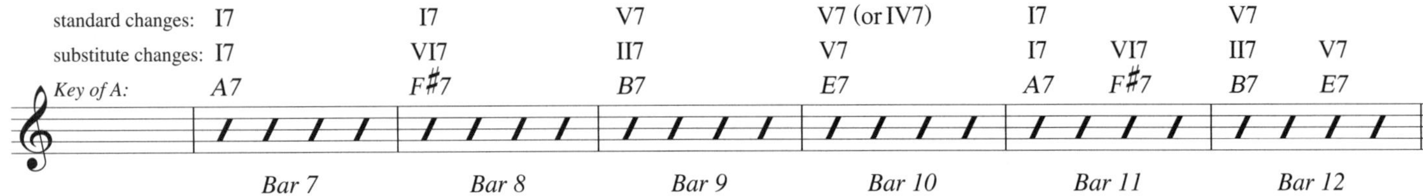

The same two basic soloing strategies—chord tones and key centers—that apply to chromatic passing chords also apply to ragtime changes. Here is a practical, blues-style way to create phrases that follow these changes:

1. Find chord voicings for I7, VI7, II7, and V7 within one area of the neck.
2. Pick a single tone from each chord and link them into a melodic line.
3. Play the tones with blues touch and add pickup phrases.

The following example illustrates a couple of versions of blues-style chord-tone phrasing based on the chord voicings shown in the diagrams above the staff. Before you play the melody, look at how the first melody note in each bar is related to the respective chord.

Fig. 5: I–VI–II–V Chord-Tone Phrasing

Performance Notes

1. Bars 1–4: The first note of each bar is a strong chord tone (3rd, root, 3rd, root, respectively). Rhythmically, the melody is arranged in two-bar call-and-response style with "breathing room" that allows time to think about the next note. When you play the line smoothly and expressively, the result is both sophisticated and intuitive.
2. Bars 5–8: Choosing different chord tones (root, 3rd, root, 3rd) creates a different melodic path through the changes. Continue developing this approach by choosing other chord tones; avoid sounding merely "technical" by giving equal attention to rhythm and touch.

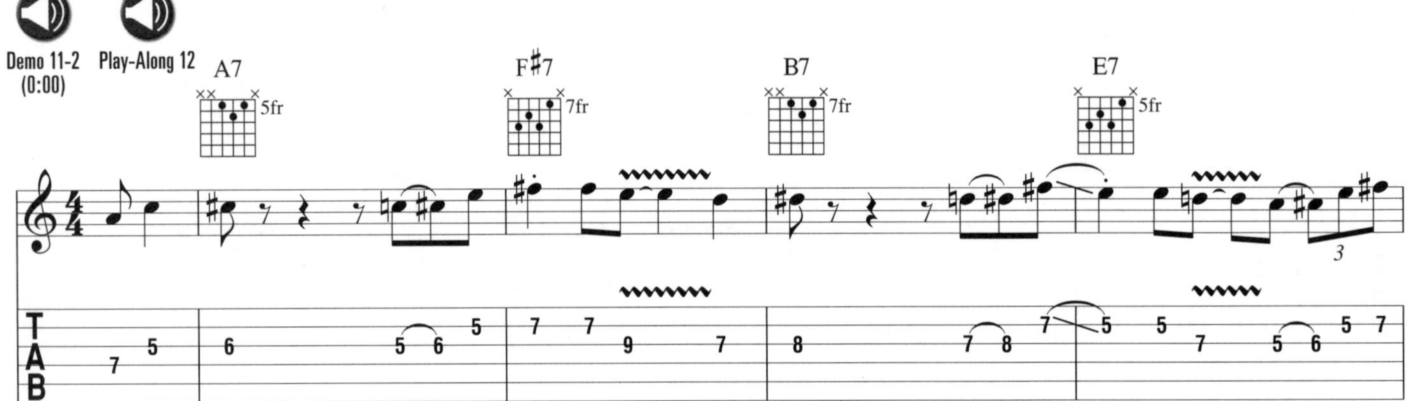

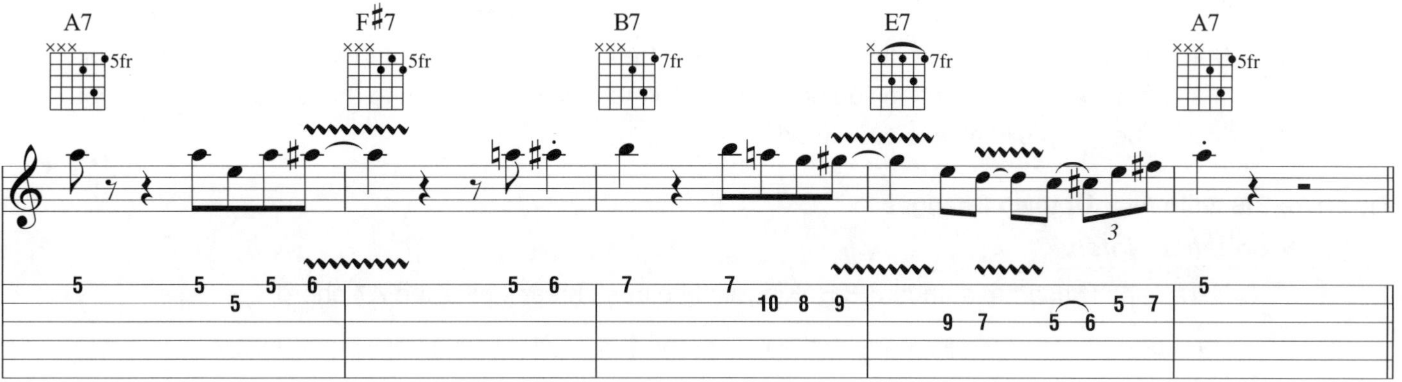

Like most mainstream electric blues guitarists, B.B. King favors a key-center approach to soloing over uptown changes, emphasizing timing and touch over melodic complexity. The first half of the following example illustrates this approach with phrasing centered on the "B.B. spot" (Chapter 7). In the second half, the melodic emphasis shifts to a bluesier approach with short, aggressive, down home phrases like those of Freddie King (the audio demos for Figs. 5 and 6 are performed back-to-back so you can compare sounds).

Fig. 6: I–VI–II–V Key-Center Phrasing

Performance Notes

1. Bars 1–4: The phrasing is all contained within Pattern #1. Notice that the melody emphasizes B over the ♭7 change. The chord tones fall easily under the fingers in this pattern, so it's relatively easy to make harmonically accurate choices by ear when you're familiar with the fingering and their related sounds.
2. Bars 5–8: The phrases are played mostly in Pattern #5 within the key-center blue-note pentatonic. The strength of the phrases and the flexibility of the blues tonality keep the melody and harmony connected even though the melody technically clashes with the changes at several points.

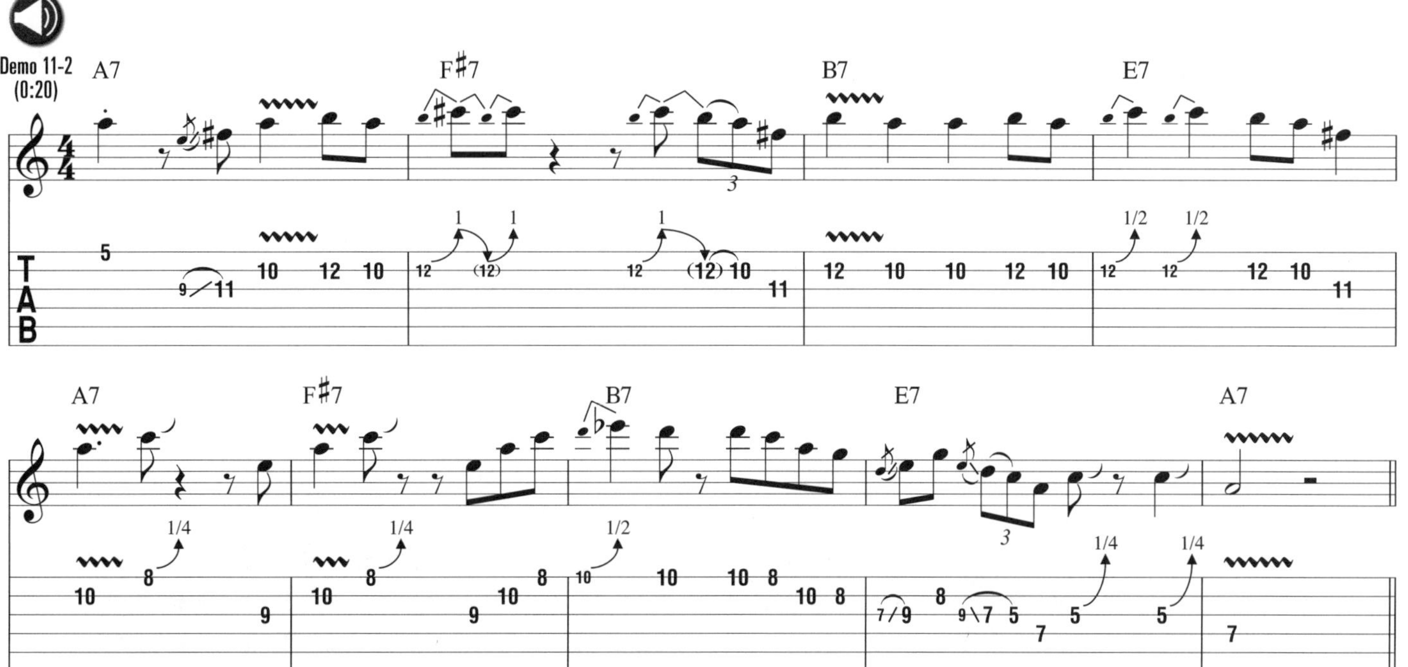

The next example illustrates a medium-tempo solo over a 12-bar progression that includes both the ♯IV°7 passing chord and the I7–VI7–II7–V7 cycle. The cycle repeats during the turnaround, which is typical, but with just two beats per chord there is very little time to think about the changes. A good rule of thumb is to play chord tones when you have enough time to think and stick to the key center when you don't, which is how this example is structured.

Fig. 7: 12-Bar Solo over Uptown Changes

Performance Notes

1. Bars 1–4: These are standard B.B. King-style blues phrases over the A7 chord.
2. Bars 5–6: A D7 arpeggio leads to the root of the ♯IV°7 (D♯); a variation on the example shown in Fig. 2a.
3. Bars 7–8: The typical A7 phrase in bar 7 leads to the 3rd of VI7 (A♯), a variation on the example in Fig. 5.
4. Bars 9–10: These are chord tone-based blues phrases over II7 (♭7) and V7 (E7).
5. Bars 11–12: The melody shifts back to B.B. King-style key-center phrases over the turnaround chords.

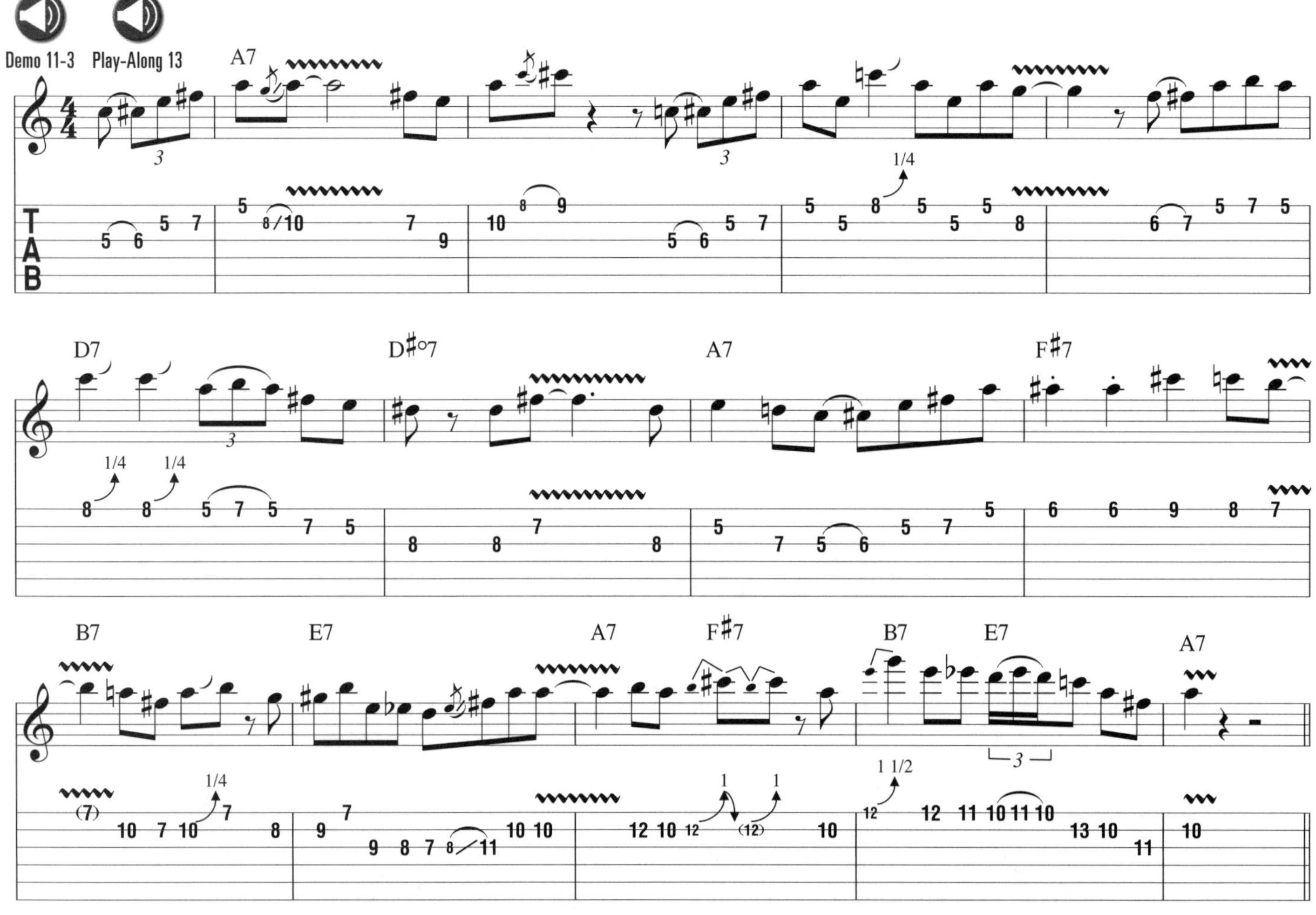

Soloing over unfamiliar chords takes considerable concentration, and when your mind is wrestling with technical issues, it often results in awkward phrasing. It's essential to push the limits of your knowledge and skill and allow yourself to make mistakes when you practice, but it's also important to remember that soloing isn't only about moving notes around; if the rhythm and touch are there to give it dimension, the melody can be very simple. Keep listening and practicing, and over time what sounded strange or complicated will become familiar, and you'll have ideas to spare.

8-Bar Blues

Next to 12-bar blues, the most common blues songwriting form is the *8-bar blues*. The 8-bar harmony can be arranged in a number of different ways, but traditional blues songs are most often based on one of two very similar 8-bar progressions.

"How Long"-Style

The timeless blues classics "How Long Blues," "Staggerlee," and "It Hurts Me Too" all share the same progression, which is similar to a shortened version of 12-bar form with the changes occurring in the same order and concluding with an identical turnaround.

Fig. 8: "How Long"-Style 8-Bar Progression

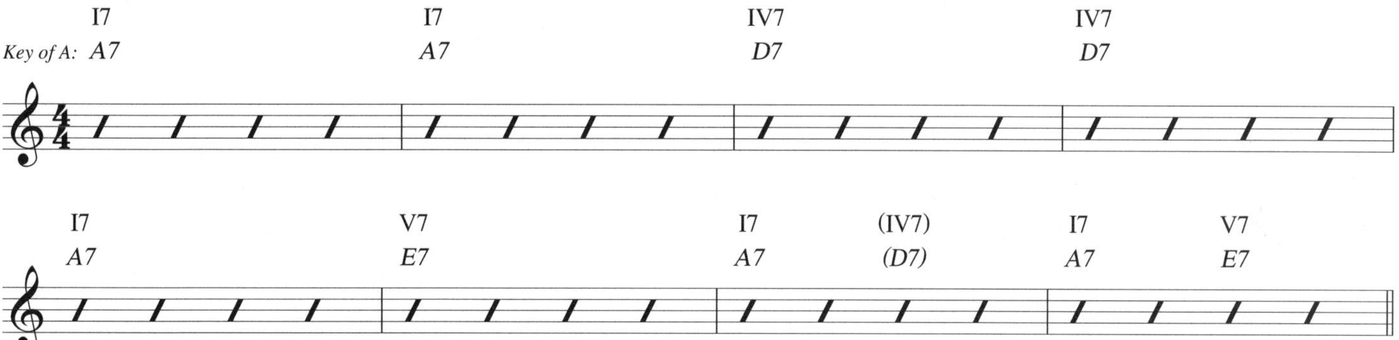

If you are only familiar with 12-bar form, the faster rate of chord changes in 8-bar form—three two-bar phrases plus a turnaround—might catch you by surprise. The best way to absorb the sound of the progression and develop a comfortable feel for the phrasing is to listen to any of the 8-bar blues classics mentioned above, study the vocal phrasing, and use it as a template for your solo. For example, the following 8-bar solo is inspired by the melody of "How Long Blues."

Fig. 9: "How Long"-Style 8-Bar Solo
Performance Notes

1. Bars 1–4: The first call-and-response phrases loosely follow the melodic contours of "How Long Blues."
2. Bars 5–6: The phrasing is based around the melodic rhythm of the song with different note choices. Over E7, the melody emphasizes B (the 5th of the chord), a very common choice for tying the melody to the V7 chord structure.
3. Bars 7–8: An improvised turnaround completes the chorus. On beat 3 of bar 7, pull off from your fourth to third and first fingers in one motion, fret the A, and then roll it over onto the D.

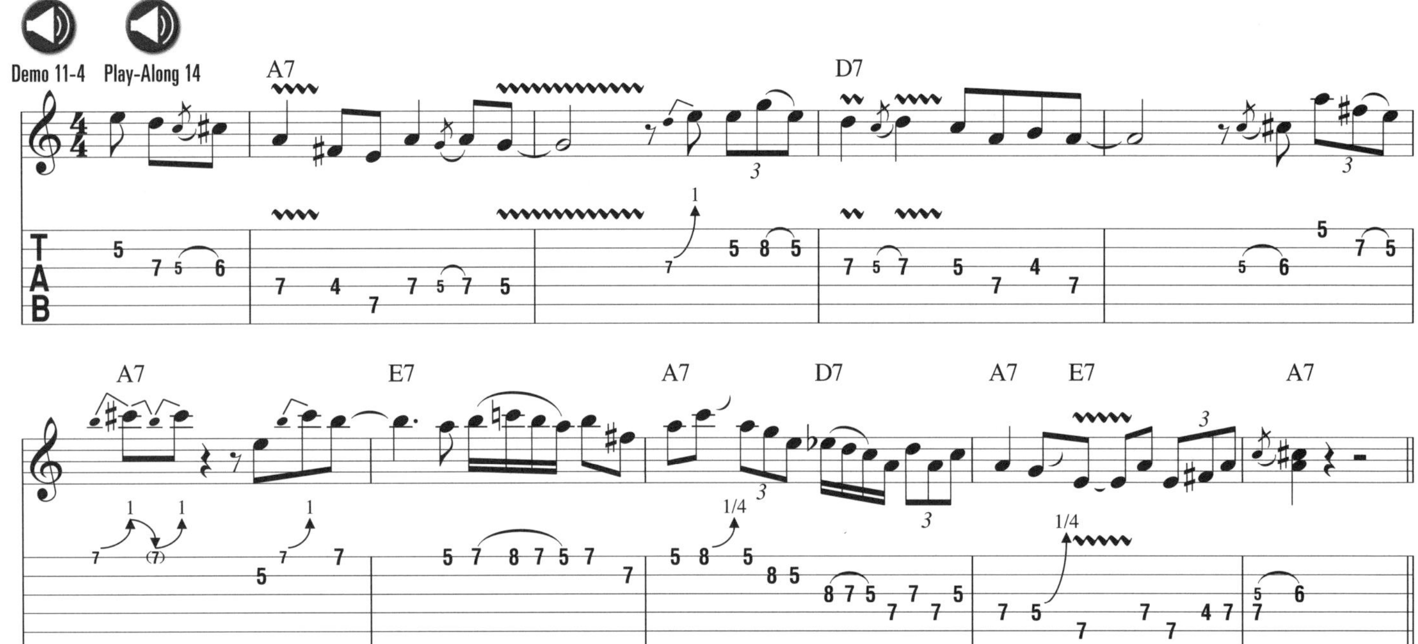

Like 12-bar blues, the 8-bar progression can be "jazzed" with passing chords and ragtime changes; a good example is the ancient Delta classic "Sitting on Top of the World" (recorded by the Mississippi Sheiks and Howlin' Wolf, among many others). In an 8-bar progression, the I–VI–II–V changes receive only two beats apiece; depending on the arrangement, the turnaround can either revert to standard I–IV–I–V harmony or repeat the ragtime cycle.

Fig. 10: 8-Bar Progression with Substitutions

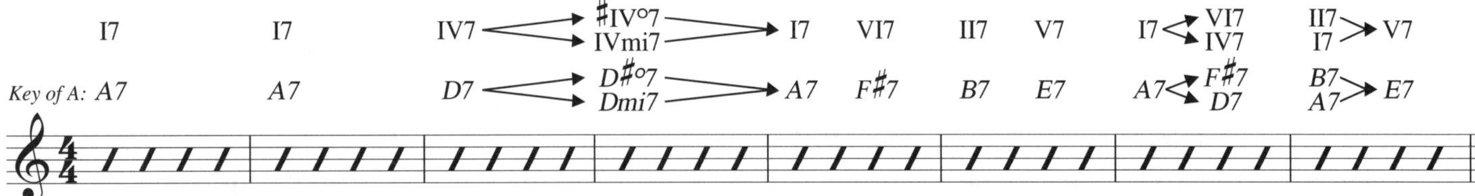

The same approaches to soloing over the substitute changes that apply to the 12-bar progression also apply here—i.e., key center and chord tones. The following example illustrates both approaches.

Fig. 11: 8-Bar Solo over Chord Substitutions

Performance Notes

1. **First Chorus:** This is played entirely in Pattern #1 (the "B.B. King spot"), which is ideal for finding bluesy melodies that fit a variety of changes. While the key-center phrases don't target specific chord tones on every change, the phrasing still depends on anticipating which tones will make a good fit—i.e., playing it by ear.
2. **Second Chorus:**
   a. Bars 1–2: Roll your third finger from E on the "and" of beat 2 onto B and immediately bend up to C♯; isolate this technique and practice it until it's smooth.
   b. Bars 3–4: A simple rhythmic phrase transitions smoothly from IV7 to ♯IV°7. To add vibrato to the D on bar 3, beat 3, fret the note with your second finger and use your fourth finger to fret the following B.
   c. Bars 5–8: As the chord changes come faster, the melody gets simpler; each chord is defined with a strong chord tone on the downbeat. When the harmony gets tricky, it's a good idea to at least initially play memorized phrases so the overall level of your soloing remains consistent.

Demo 11-5 Play-Along 15

first chorus:

A7 D7 D♯°7

A7 F♯7 B7 E7 A7 D7 A7 E7

second chorus:

A7 D7 D♯°7

A7 F♯7 B7 E7 A7 D7 A7 E7

"Key to the Highway"-Style

The second standard 8-bar blues progression differs from "How Long" by only one chord—V7 replaces I7 in bar 2—but this is enough to give the progression a much different flavor. (The same chord substitutions used on "How Long Blues" can also be applied to this progression.) Classics based on this progression include "Key to the Highway" and "Trouble in Mind."

Fig. 12: "Key to the Highway"-Style 8-Bar Progression

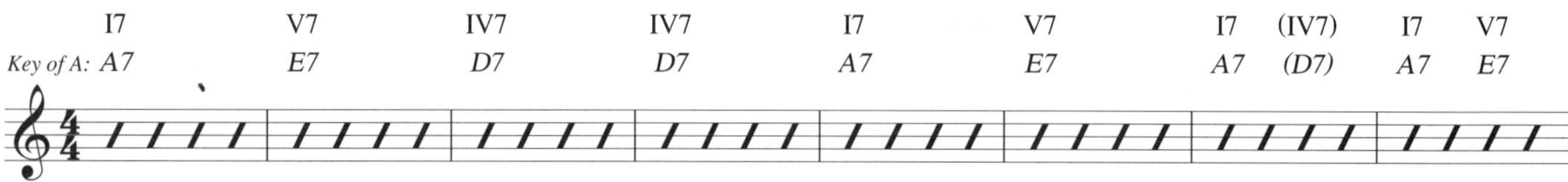

The next example shows a solo that borrows from the melody and melodic rhythm of "Key to the Highway," including Chicago-style chord-based phrasing.

Fig. 13: "Key to the Highway"-Style 8-Bar Solo

Performance Notes

1. **First Chorus:** In bar 5, bend from B to C♯ on the second string and hold the note while you pick D on the first string, then release the bend. The chorus ends with a traditional Robert Johnson-style turnaround; use hybrid picking.
2. **Second Chorus:**
   a. Bars 1–2: The melody is arranged around the chord structure of A and E7.
   b. Bars 3–4: After a classic Chicago-style phrase on the IV7 chord, slide the 3rd-interval shape up the neck.
   c. Bars 5–6: Follow the down home C/E combination with descending 6th intervals from 12th to 10th to eighth positions; fret the first string with your first finger and the third string with your second finger. Shift from eighth to fifth position on beat 4 of bar 6.
   d. Bars 7–8: This is a variation on the classic turnaround style.

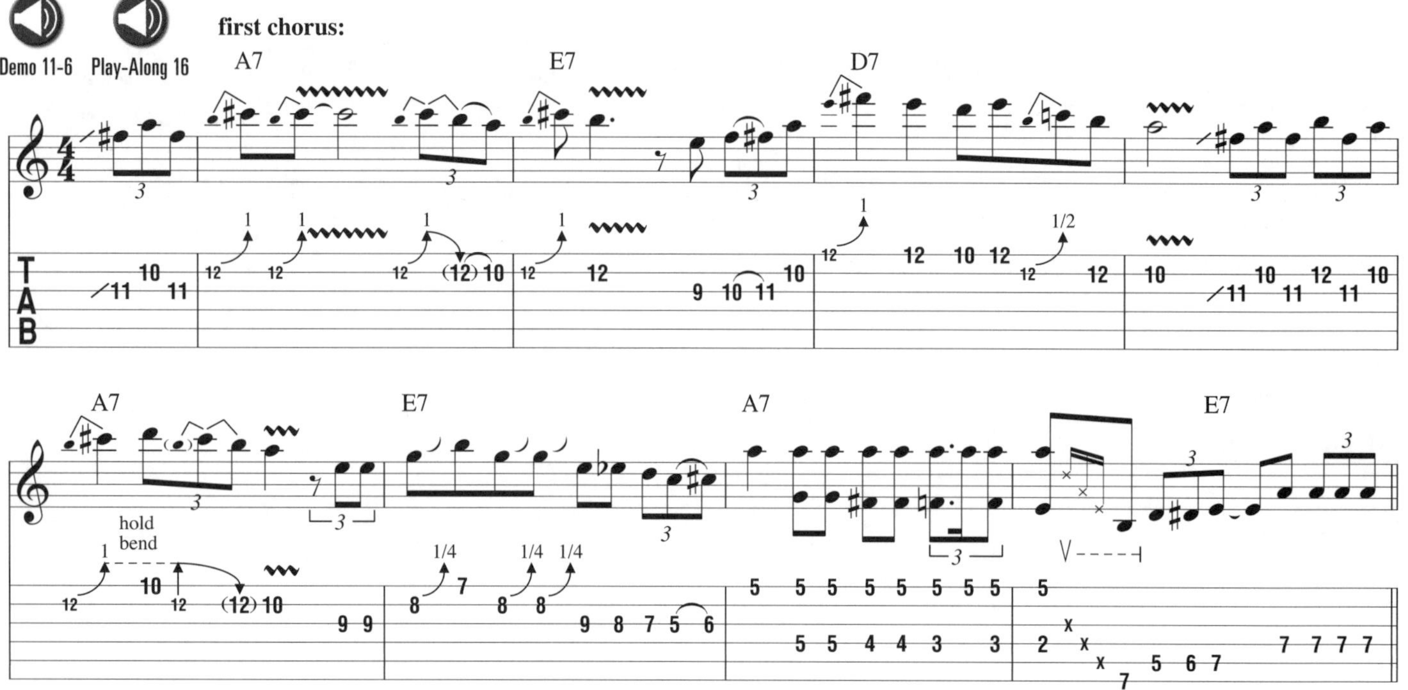

second chorus:

A7 E7 D7

A7 E7

A7 E7 A7

8-Bar Variations

Down home blues often features lyrics that are assembled out of images and rhymes that are passed from one artist to another (known as *floating verses*), but many classic blues songs have also been written by professional songwriters. Of these, many are built on the 8-bar form, including such standards as "Ain't Nobody's Business (If I Do)," "Same Old Blues," "I Need Your Love So Bad," and "Nobody Knows You When You're Down and Out." All feature sophisticated harmony that goes well beyond basic I–IV–V changes, as shown by the following example based on "Nobody Knows You When You're Down and Out."

Fig. 14: "Nobody Knows You" 8-Bar Progression

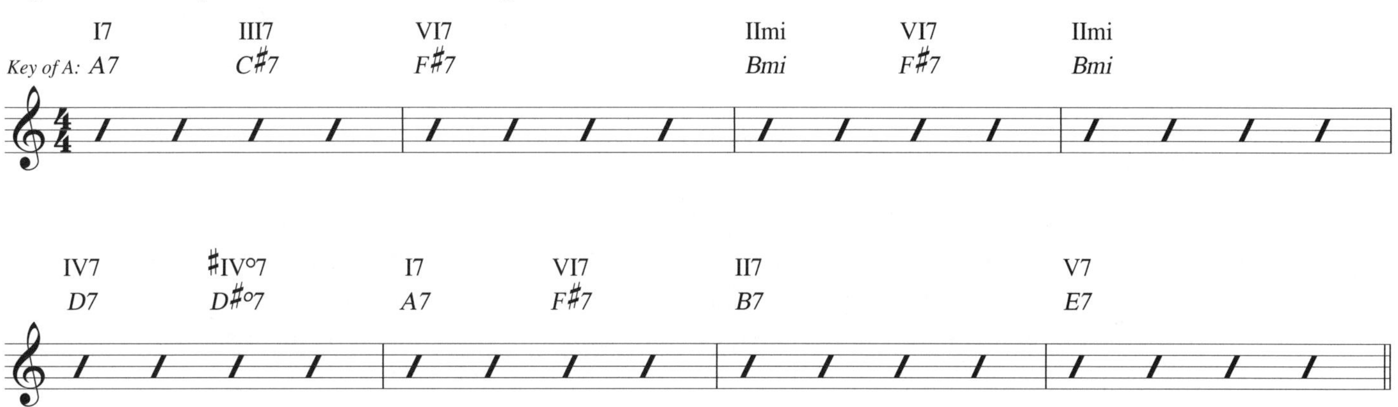

The melody and lyrics of "Nobody Knows You" have the same natural feel and flow as any blues song, but at first glance the progression presents a dizzying string of changes with few familiar resting points. Understanding the structure of a progression like this requires a level of theory beyond the scope of this book, but no matter how complex a song may appear to be at first, you can quickly play a musically coherent solo by following one of these strategies:

- **Embellish the Melody:** Professional songwriters put a great deal of effort into constructing their melodies, and the result is a ready-made foundation for soloing. Learn the melody note-for-note and embellish it with your own fills and touch.
- **Create Your Own Melody:** Arrange the chord voicings on the neck, pick a note from each chord that you can join together to form your own melody, and embellish it with touch and fills. Ironically, the more chords there are, the easier this process becomes because harmonic movement keeps the melody flowing.

It's important to note that neither of these approaches requires improvisation. Although the terms "soloing" and "improvisation" are often used interchangeably, they are not necessarily the same. Playing an improvised (i.e. spontaneously organized) solo over complex changes requires a high level of skill and experience, but you can also compose a solo in advance and perform it note-for-note; if the ideas are good, the result for the listener is the same either way. Most players do some of both, playing pre-arranged ideas over some sections and improvising over others.

The following example combines hints of the original melody with ideas derived from chord tones. The melodic "skeleton" in the first chorus is filled in with embellishments and fills the second time around.

Fig. 15: 8-Bar Solo: "Nobody Knows You"

Performance Notes

1. **First Chorus:** The melodic skeleton follows the contour of "Nobody," beginning on the major 3rd of A7 (C♯) and proceeding mostly in whole- and half steps, with each note matching the respective chord. You can create alternate melodies by beginning on a different chord tone or changing direction along the way—e.g., moving the melody up rather than down.
2. **Second Chorus:**
   a. Bars 1–2: The solo phrases here and throughout the chorus consist of setups and embellishments built around the same melodic line. The chorus begins with a standard major blues setup phrase; the melody over the first three changes is connected by step-wise lines. It's not particularly important to figure out what scale or scales the lines belong to—with only two beats on each chord, there's no time in any case to bring a scale into play. When the harmony lands on the major 3rd of F♯7, the embellishments consist of standard blue-note phrases.
   b. Bars 3–4: The melody follows the quickly-moving changes in bar 3 with more simple, stepwise lines. In bar 4, with the harmony resting on B minor, the melody answers with a B minor pentatonic fill.
   c. Bars 5–6: The IV7–♯IV°7–I7–I7 changes are just like the uptown version of "How Long Blues;" a short chromatic pickup phrase sets up the main melodic tone over each chord. Again, trying to identify scales is irrelevant when the changes are moving so quickly—just a note or two over each chord is enough to form a complete melody.
   d. Bars 7–8: The II7 and V7 each last a full bar, so each phrase is stretched out correspondingly. In bar 8, the phrase begins with E7 chord tones and then on the last two beats switches to a down home blues phrase in the key center (A).

Demo 11-7
Play-Along 17
first chorus:
A7
C♯7
F♯7
Bmi
F♯7
Bmi
D7
D♯°7
A7
F♯7
B7
E7
second chorus:
A7
C♯7
F♯7
Bmi
F♯7
Bmi
D7
D♯°7
A7
F♯7
B7
E7
A7

As you become more familiar with these changes, you'll naturally begin to hear more opportunities for bluesy key-center phrasing. It takes considerable practice before they begin to feel as natural as I–IV–V, but when you learn to handle changes like these, you gain access to a world of classic, sophisticated blues/R&B repertoire as well as an entry point into jazz. Even if your tastes lean toward three-chord blues, stretching your ears and comprehension to include a wider range of harmony and melody will benefit your playing on every level.

16-Bar Blues

Another songwriting pattern found in the basic blues repertoire is *16-bar form*, epitomized by the early 20th century New Orleans standard "Careless Love." The most well-known 16-bar tune in the electric blues repertoire is undoubtedly "My Babe." Recorded by blues harp legend Little Walter, "My Babe" is based on the earlier gospel hit "This Train" by singer/guitarist Sister Rosetta Tharpe. In the early 1960s, B.B. King also had success with "Help the Poor," which combines 16-bar form with minor harmony (see below) and a Latin feel (see Chapter 13).

The next example shows the progression for "My Babe"; the variations shown in parentheses are used in "Careless Love," among others. Like 12- and 8-bar blues, 16-bar form can be modified in various ways without altering the overall structure.

Fig. 16: 16-Bar Blues

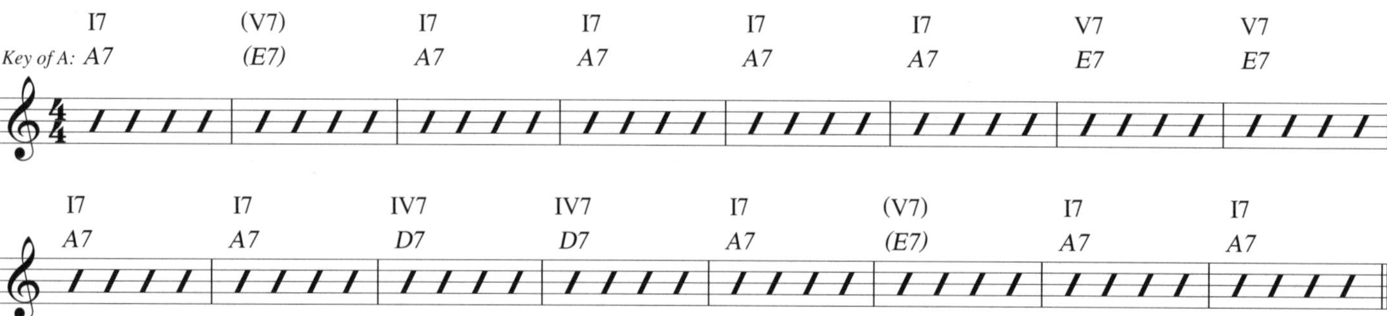

As with 8-bar progressions, the most intuitive way to learn 16-bar form is not to count bars, but to memorize the vocal melody from "My Babe" or any other song based on the form and keep it in mind as you play. (On Little Walter's version, the vocals are 16-bar, but the harp solo is actually played over a 12-bar progression.) The rest of the basic principles of blues soloing—two-bar phrases, call-and-response, rhythm, and touch—that apply to the 12- and 8-bar progressions also apply to 16-bar tunes.

The following example is loosely based on "My Babe." The tempo is faster than previous examples, and the phrasing compensates by using less notes and more breathing room (see the next chapter for more on soloing at faster tempos).

Fig. 17: 16-Bar Blues Solo

Performance Notes

1. Bars 1–6: The solo roughly echoes the melody to "My Babe" with improvised answering fills (note that the progression remains on I7 for six bars rather than the usual four).
2. Bars 7–8: The second "answer" falls on the V7 chord, so the melody "aims" for the root.
3. Bars 9–16: In the second half of the solo, the melody is improvised. The melody is based on the key center with emphasis on chord tones within the scale.

Minor Blues

So far, we have focused exclusively on soloing over dominant seventh-based progressions, but blues songs are also written in *minor keys.* In fact, the biggest-selling blues record of all time, B.B. King's "The Thrill Is Gone" (adapted from Roy Hawkins' 1951 original), is a minor blues. The most basic version of 12-bar minor blues harmony involves simply converting all three chords from dominant to minor. (A classic based on this progression is "All Your Love [I Miss Loving]" by Otis Rush, later covered by Eric Clapton with the Bluesbreakers; see Chapter 13 "Latin Blues.") As with standard 12-bar progressions, minor blues can include variations such as a quick change in bar 2 or V7 in place of V minor (indicated in parentheses on the following example).

Fig. 18: Basic 12-Bar Minor Blues Changes

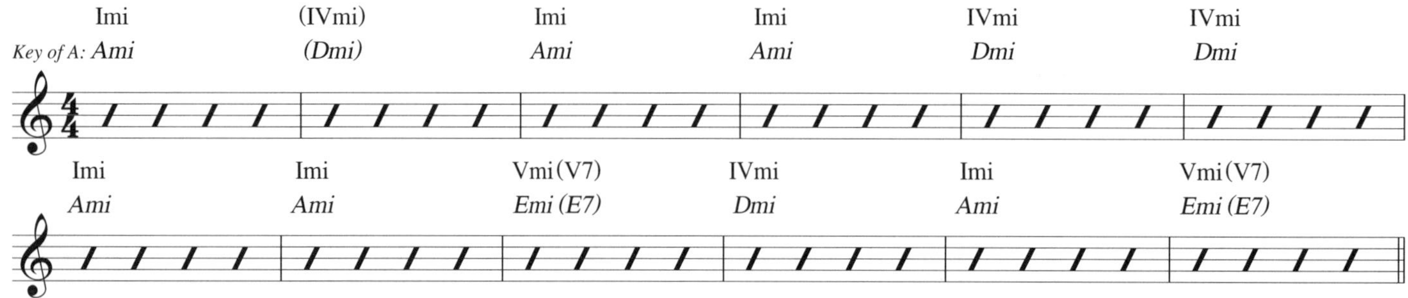

All of the methods we have developed for phrasing over dominant blues progressions also apply to minor progressions with one main exception: when you solo in minor keys, you need to take special care to avoid emphasizing the major 3rd of the I minor and IV minor chords (the V7 chord may be either minor or dominant); rather than sounding bluesy, a major 3rd over a minor chord sounds just plain wrong. Otherwise, key-center minor pentatonic melodies fit all three chords very comfortably, which makes minor blues very accessible for soloists of all different backgrounds and playing levels.

Medium Shuffle Minor Blues

Nearly a decade before "The Thrill Is Gone," another minor blues—the instrumental "Green Onions" by Booker T. & the M.G.s—was one of the best-selling records of its own era. The band, featuring Steve Cropper on guitar, was both a recording act in its own right and the house rhythm section for Stax Records in Memphis, home to some of the biggest soul music artists of the 1960s (see Chapter 13 "Soul-Blues") as well as Albert King. After more than 50 years, "Green Onions" remains a universal blues jam-session platform and is an ideal introduction to minor blues.

"Green Onions" is built around a catchy Hammond organ riff played over a minor key, three-chord, 12-bar medium shuffle (a somewhat rare combination since minor blues progressions are more often paired with grooves such as Latin, funk, or rock). The recording features an iconic two-chorus solo by Cropper that is a model of both attitude and simplicity, and the following example borrows from both Cropper and Otis Rush before exploring other minor-key ideas.

Fig. 19: Medium Shuffle Minor Blues Solo

Performance Notes

First Chorus:

1. Bars 1–8: The first theme is inspired by Otis Rush's classic chord-based solo on "All Your Love (I Miss Loving)," alternating with a theme similar to Steve Cropper's solo on "Green Onions." Use an aggressive attack on both figures and add finger vibrato to the chords.
2. Bars 9–12: The moving minor triads over the Vmi–IVmi change are again inspired by Otis Rush.

Second Chorus:

1. Bars 1–4: The second chorus builds energy with a simple, repetitive blues lick; over a driving groove, the melody can be very simple.
2. Bars 5–8: The phrasing leaves a lot of breathing room to release some of the energy built up in the first four bars. Decisions about when and how to use space to raise or lower the energy are essential parts of a personal style.
3. Bars 9–10: This phrase is similar to the organ melody on "Green Onions;" emphasizing the 5th of the V chord (dominant or minor) is a classic, simple way to play the changes.
4. Bars 11–12: The solo winds down with a standard blues phrase that segues back into the groove.

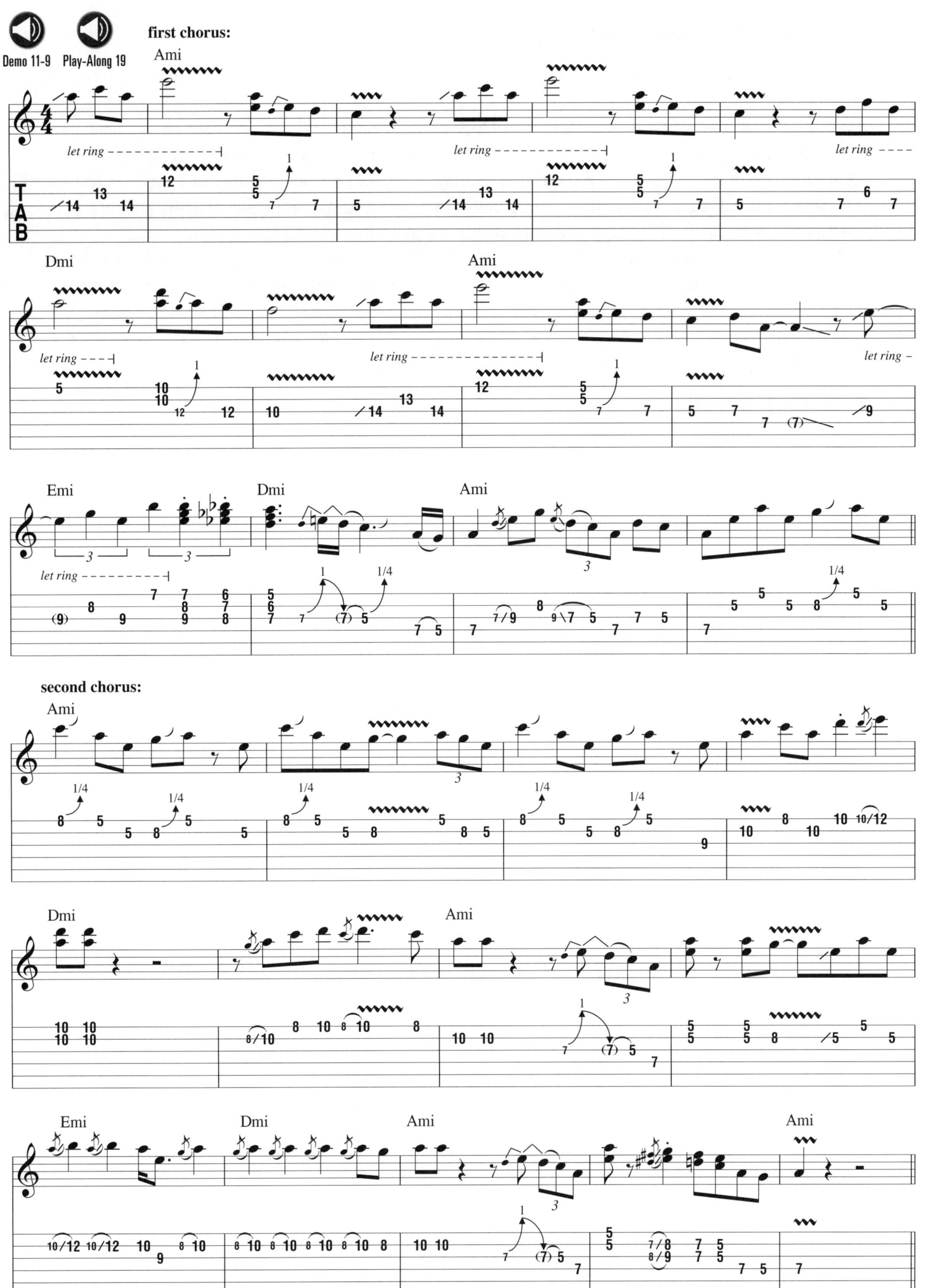
Demo 11-9
Play-Along 19
first chorus:
Ami
let ring
Dmi
Ami
Emi
Dmi
Ami
second chorus:
Ami
Dmi
Ami
Emi
Dmi
Ami
Ami

One-Chord Blues

Some of the most powerful blues ever recorded has been played over the most minimal progression of all: a single chord. Muddy Waters, Howlin' Wolf, and Hendrix, to name just a few, all created stripped-down, one-chord masterpieces—a sound that Muddy called "deep blues." One-chord blues eliminates the complications of thinking about changes and chord tones, but it poses a different challenge: how to create a sense of form and manage the flow of energy with your phrasing alone. The solution is to use the same two- and four-bar phrasing structure that works over a 12-bar progression; in the absence of a fixed form, a solo can keep going for as long as your imagination can feed it.

The following example demonstrates a 16-bar solo over a one-chord medium shuffle. The solo consists of two eight-bar halves, each made up of two four-bar call-and-response phrases. The first half of the solo is inspired by Howlin' Wolf's one-chord classic "Spoonful" (a recording that also includes a stellar solo by guitarist Hubert Sumlin), and the second half takes a more improvised approach. The melody is straightforward, but the solo introduces two new phrasing techniques:

Pedal Points

A *pedal point* is single note sustained against a moving melody; the effect is to anchor the melody to a central note, creating a melodic texture somewhere between single notes and double stops. In contemporary blues/rock, the best-known example of a pedal point is probably the main solo theme of Stevie Ray Vaughan's "Cold Shot," which is reminiscent of "Leave My Girl Alone" by Buddy Guy and "Why" by Lonnie Mack (both of whom were major influences on Vaughan).

Tremolo Picking

Tremolo picking, or rapidly and evenly picking a single note or double stop, simulates the effect of a single, sustained tone. The technique is widely used in classical guitar to compensate for the instrument's lack of sustain, but on the electric it provides an alternate melodic texture as well as a means of maintaining dynamic control while sustaining a single note over time. In blues, examples of tremolo picking are found in Billy Butler's solo on Bill Doggett's "Honky Tonk," Pete Lewis' wild solo on Willie Headon's "Fun on Saturday Night," Magic Sam's rocking intro to "Love Me with a Feeling," and Stevie Ray Vaughan's "Stang's Swang."

Listen to the accompanying audio to hear how the techniques are applied; the Performance Notes describe the techniques in more detail.

Fig. 20: 16-Bar, One-Chord Solo

Performance Notes

1. Bars 1–4: The opening idea echoes the melody of "Spoonful." In bars 3–4, the same melody is repeated against the high pedal point. Hold down the top three strings with a first-finger barre while you fret the melody with your other fingers; flatpick the moving phrase while you simultaneously pluck the A on the first string with your bare third finger.
2. Bars 5–6: The answering phrase ends with a trill between the open G string and second fret.
3. Bars 7–8: After the melody concludes in bar 7, bar 8 begins the transition into the next eight-bar segment with another version of a pedal point. In this case, alternate between A on the fourth string and the moving line; hold down A with your third finger and roll from the tip to the side to fret the D on the third string at the same fret.
4. Bars 9–10: Here we see a combination of pedal point and tremolo (indicated by the diagonal slashes on the note stems). Rapidly alternate-pick the A and jump back and forth to

the first string as the melody ascends. The tremolo has no fixed number of pick-strokes per beat—just pick as fast as you can while maintaining an even attack. The movement from string to string is technically challenging, so practice the phrase slowly and gradually work up to tempo.

5. Bars 11–12: The melody echoes the original theme in a higher octave, ending with another tremolo on high A.
6. Bars 13–16: The final phrase begins with a classic down home lick in Pattern #2 and then descends with shifts and slides to conclude in Pattern #4.

Demo 11-10 Play-Along 20

A7

The Rules and the Blues

We have now covered most of the standard versions of blues form, but it's important to remember that all of these technical rules and variations are only part of the blues spectrum. Some of the most exciting moments in blues take place when the music goes outside the lines and players throw away the playbook. For down-home blues artists such as Muddy Waters, Howlin' Wolf, Lightnin' Hopkins, John Lee Hooker, Robert Burnside, and Frankie Lee Sims, structures like 12-bar blues are treated more as suggestions than requirements. Chord changes, if they happen at all, might occur on the "*if of and*," and players rely on their ears rather than following a pre-determined arrangement. This book, like most instructional methods, focuses on teaching the techniques and approaches used by most players most of the time, but for every rule that attempts to define how blues is supposed to work, you'll find someone who brilliantly does it "wrong." To be the best blues player you can be, learn the rules but keep your ears open and your inspiration unchained.

Chapter 11 Summary

1. **Expanded 12-Bar Changes**
   a. **Passing Chords:** ♯IV°7 ("sharp four diminished") or ivmi7 ("four minor") create chromatic (half-step) transitions from IV to I.
   b. **Substitutions:** The I7–VI7–II7–V7 (one-six-two-five) progression creates additional harmonic energy in bars 6–10 as well as on the turnaround.
   c. The two basic approaches to soloing over expanded blues changes are:
      i. **Key Center:** Phrase within the key-center blue-note pentatonic (usually favoring the major side of the tonality) and use your ear to find the best note choices.
      ii. **Chord Tone:** Play phrases based on the structure of each chord.
2. **8-Bar Blues**
   a. "How Long" variation: similar to compact 12-bar changes.
   b. "Highway" variation: V7 change in bar 2.
   c. Expanded 8-bar changes include passing chords and substitutions similar to uptown 12-bar changes.
3. **16-Bar Blues:** "My Babe" is the best-known blues standard based on 16-bar form.
4. **Minor Blues:** In its simplest form, convert each chord in a standard 12-bar progression from dominant to minor, as found in "Green Onions."
5. **One-Chord Blues:** When there are no changes or arranged form to solo over, build solos in 8-bar cycles made up of two- and four-bar phrases.
   a. **Pedal Point:** A single note sustains against a moving melody.
   b. **Tremolo Picking:** Rapidly and evenly pick a single note or double stop to simulate the effect of a single, sustained tone.

Practice

Uptown Blues Harmony

The most effective way to practice phrasing over unfamiliar changes is to isolate the portion of the progression that includes the new chords, loop it, and play over it repeatedly until you can feel the changes. Then integrate the phrases back into your normal style (audio tracks designed for this purpose accompany this book). Uptown harmony is standard in jazz-blues, so most jazz improvisation methods offer many ideas for how to solo over these changes. But jazz-style phrasing tends to be more melodically complex than mainstream blues. Listen to the recordings cited on the next page to hear examples of how mainstream blues players navigate sophisticated changes.

8-Bar, 16-Bar, Minor and One-Chord Blues

Different progressions require somewhat different ways of organizing a solo over time, but the individual two-bar phrases remain essentially the same. The biggest challenge presented by these variations is familiarity, so the best way to absorb the differences and hear the changes in a musical way (rather than just a technical one) is to listen to the examples cited on the next page and learn from their example.

Pedal Points and Tremolo Picking

Each of these techniques requires careful coordination between the fretting and picking hands as well as a higher degree of pick control than is required by most blues phrases. As with specific techniques discussed earlier in this book, the most important thing is to slow each technique to the tempo at which you can perform it perfectly and build it over time. Isolate each phrase apart from the solo and practice it individually. Then join it with the phrases that come before and after; before a phrase is useable, you have to know how to get in and out properly.

Listen

Uptown Blues Harmony

Chord-Tone Phrasing

Examples of chord-tone phrasing over chromatic substitutions, while common in jazz, are much rarer among mainstream electric blues guitar influences. For perspective, check out recordings by blues-influenced jazz guitarists including Charlie Christian, Herb Ellis, Barney Kessel, Kenny Burrell, and Grant Green as well as guitarists who crossed between the two worlds, including Billy Butler, Mickey Baker, and Bill Jennings (in particular, check out his track "Big Boy").

Key-Center Phrasing

B.B. King, Freddie King (different versions of the same songs)	"Please Send Me Someone to Love," "Ain't Nobody's Business (If I Do)"
Freddie King	"The Stumble" (non-standard 16-bar progression)
Allman Brothers (Duane Allman, Dickey Betts, guitars)	"Stormy Monday" (*Live at Fillmore East*), "Not My Cross to Bear" (*The Allman Brothers Band*)

8-Bar Blues

Leroy Carr	"How Long Blues"
Elmore James	"It Hurts Me Too"
Mississippi Sheiks, Howlin' Wolf	"Sitting on Top of the World"
Nina Simone, Big Bill Broonzy	"Trouble in Mind"
Little Walter, Eric Clapton (w/ Derek & the Dominos)	"Key to the Highway"

8-Bar Progressions with Harmonic Variations

Bessie Smith, Louis Jordan, Eric Clapton (w/ Derek & the Dominos)	"Nobody Knows You When You're Down and Out"
Peter Green (w/ Fleetwood Mac), Little Willie John (original vocal version)	"I Need Your Love So Bad"
Freddie King, Peter Green (w/ Fleetwood Mac)	"Same Old Blues"
Jimmy Witherspoon, B.B. King	"Ain't Nobody's Business (If I Do)"
Charles Brown (Johnny Moore, guitar)	"Fool's Paradise"

16-Bar Blues

Lonnie Johnson, Big Bill Broonzy	"Careless Love"
Sister Rosetta Tharpe	"This Train"
Little Walter	"My Babe"
Dave Dudley, Taj Mahal	"Six Days on the Road"
Stray Cats	"Rock This Town"

Minor Blues

Booker T. & the M.G.s (Steve Cropper, guitar)	"Green Onions"
Otis Rush, Eric Clapton (w/ John Mayall's Bluesbreakers)	"All Your Love (I Miss Loving)"
Otis Rush	"Double Trouble"
Fleetwood Mac (Peter Green, guitar)	"Black Magic Woman"
Magic Sam	"It's All Your Fault," "My Love Will Never Die"
B.B. King, Roy Hawkins	"The Thrill Is Gone"
Albert King	"I Will Play the Blues for You"

One-Chord Blues

Muddy Waters	"Rolling Stone," "Still a Fool"
Howlin' Wolf (Hubert Sumlin, guitar)	"Back Door Man," "Wang Dang Doodle," "Spoonful," "Hidden Charms"
Little Willie John	"Fever"
Jimi Hendrix	"Hear My Train a' Comin'," "Voodoo Chile"

Pedal Points

Stevie Ray Vaughan	"Cold Shot"
Buddy Guy	"Leave My Girl Alone"
Lonnie Mack	"Why"

Tremolo

Stevie Ray Vaughan	"Stang's Swang"
Billy Butler (w/ Bill Doggett)	"Honky Tonk"
Pete Lewis (w/ Willie Headon)	"Fun on Saturday Night"
Magic Sam	"Love Me with a Feeling"

12 Tempo – From Ballad to Boogie

Medium shuffles are the meat and potatoes of the traditional blues style, but you can play the blues at any point on the metronome. In this chapter, we'll look at concepts and techniques that apply to soloing at both slower and faster tempos.

Slow Blues

Slow blues is the emotional heart of the blues tradition. Slowing the tempo and lowering the volume puts the listener's focus squarely on the smallest details of each note, making slow blues both the most emotionally expressive form of blues and the most challenging to perform at a high level. To get the most out of a slow blues solo, it's important to understand how slowing the tempo affects the harmony, feel, and phrasing.

Harmony

At slower tempos, 12-bar chord options like the quick change and additional chords on the turnaround are almost always added to the progression in order to maintain the harmonic energy and provide more melodic options for soloing (other common variations are discussed later in this chapter).

Fig. 1: Typical Slow Blues Harmony

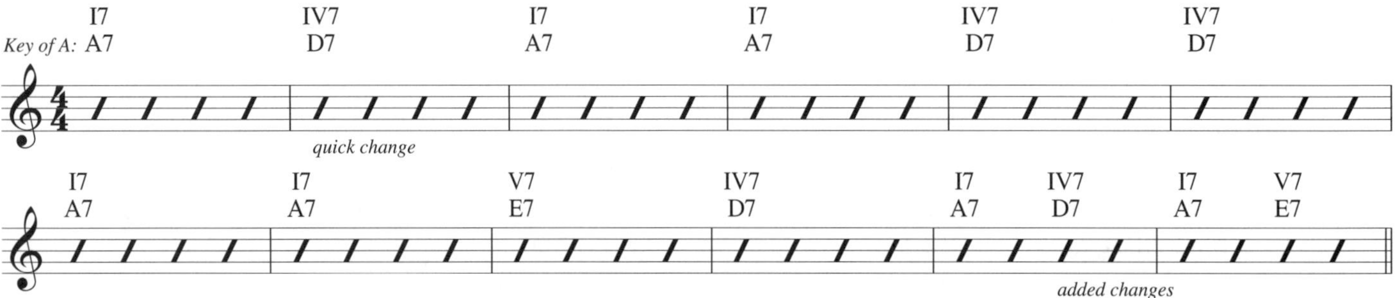

12/8 Meter

As with medium tempos, "slow" is a relative term. Classic slow blues recordings range from 60 bpm on the lower end up to more than 90 bpm. (If the beat is *too* slow, it tends to feel sluggish, so traditional slow blues rarely goes below 60 bpm.)

As the tempo slows and the beats lengthen, the middle eighth note of the triplet shuffle emerges to become part of the basic rhythm pattern (meter). The layering of steady triplets over an underlying four-to-the-bar pulse is indicated by a time signature of *12/8* ("twelve eight"), which in practical terms feels like "4/4 with triplets" (a *6/8* time signature, while technically different, is often used interchangeably with 12/8).

It's important to note that, in 12/8 meter, the *dotted quarter note* (equivalent to three eighth notes) gets one beat. This eliminates the need to notate triplet signs, but the difference can also make the rhythms confusing to read at first. Since 12/8 and "4/4 with triplets" are identical to the ear, the best way to familiarize yourself with 12/8 notation is to listen to the examples while you read them.

Fig. 2: 4/4 vs. 12/8 Meter

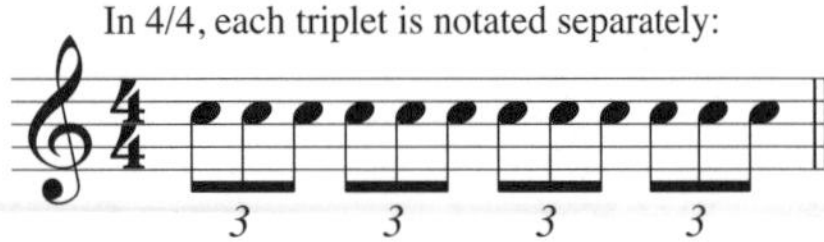

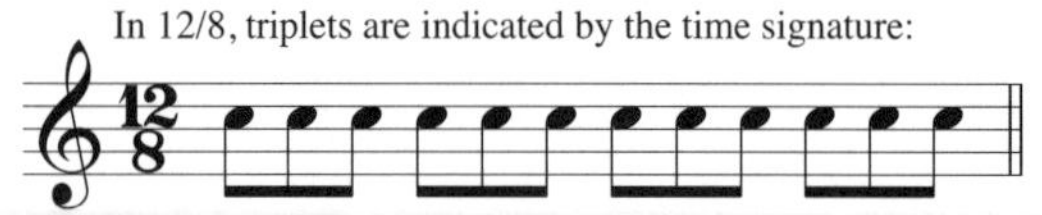

Conversational Phrasing

Tempo does not have a direct effect on the notes you choose or how you structure a solo, but a slower tempo does give you more time to manipulate the expressive details. One common slow-blues technique is to loosen up the melodic rhythm to create a more "conversational" style—i.e., phrase with the irregular rhythmic and dynamic flow of casual speech as opposed to the more regular, beat-driven rhythms that are typical at faster tempos (for examples of conversational phrasing, see Fig. 3 on the next page).

A favorite conversational technique is to add a quick note-cluster—a sudden slide down the neck, rapid pull-offs, or a sweep-picked burst—onto the end of a phrase. This is akin to throwing "know what I mean?" onto the end of a sentence––in fact, it has no intrinsic meaning, but it establishes a loose, casual tone. Conversational phrasing is a matter of taste and style. B.B. King and Albert King, for example, use it only occasionally, while Johnny "Guitar" Watson, Buddy Guy, Albert Collins, Jimi Hendrix, and others make it a centerpiece of their approach.

The following two-chorus solo over a 12/8 groove demonstrates some standard slow blues techniques such as conversational phrasing, dynamics, and pickup phrases.

Fig. 3: Slow Blues Solo

Performance Notes

First Chorus:

1. Pickup/Bars 1–2: This is a classic slow blues pickup followed by an emphasis on the major 3rd—sweet and romantic. On the transition to the quick change (IV7), using chords within the solo creates call-and-response interaction and also helps to tie the melody to the harmony and form.
2. Bars 3–4: Here, 6th intervals broken into single notes also tie the melody directly to the harmony.
3. Bars 5–8: The phrasing becomes more conversational—i.e., less rhythmically strict. In bar 5, the cluster of pull-offs and consecutive down-strokes are typical of Freddie King; 6th intervals between bars 5–6 suggest the D9 chord. In bars 7–8, the fast phrase ending on C♯ (the major 3rd) is typical of B.B. King.
4. Bars 9–10: The phrases emphasize chord tones on E9 and D9.
5. Bars 11–12: Steady rhythm, hard attack, and melodic repetition combine to increase the energy level in preparation for launching the second chorus; the phrasing is similar to Albert King.

Second Chorus:

1. Bars 1–4: The second chorus begins with a series of high, string-bending phrases in the style of Albert King. Like King, the bends include "in-between" pitches that create different shades of emotion.
2. Bars 5–6: The energy continues to build over IV7; the chord accents in bar 5 are another B.B. King trademark, as is the extremely hard pick attack used on the repeated bends in bar 6.
3. Bars 7–8: The solo approaches the climax with more B.B. King-style phrases, including the bend from E up to high G and the second-string slide from G down to E followed by a fast run down the neck that winds up again on the low C♯. The notes go by quickly, and the rhythm is irregular, but it is carefully timed so that the end of the phrase lands squarely on a downbeat to keep it from sounding random.
4. Bars 10–11: The solo peaks with a chord-based phrase on E followed by the rhythmically simple but very melodic line over D.

5. Bars 11–12: The energy gradually eases, and the melody drops to a lower range as the solo concludes over the turnaround. The E augmented triad arpeggio in bar 12 is a classic R&B touch; the dissonance of the augmented chord is relieved when the harmony returns to the I7 chord.

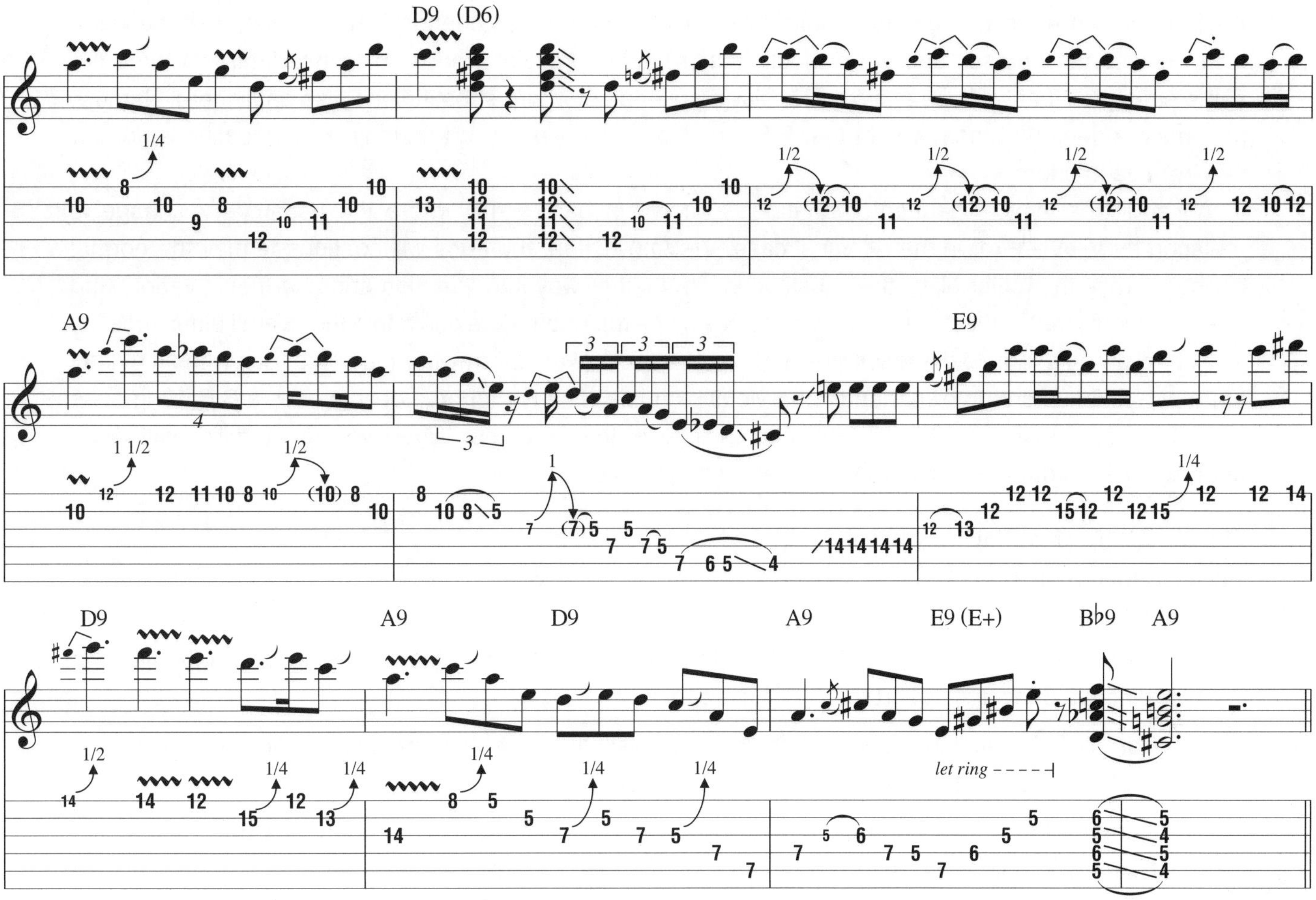

"Stormy Monday" Changes

Not long after its release in 1947, T-Bone Walker's signature slow blues "They Call It Stormy Monday (But Tuesday's Just as Bad)" became one of the most-performed classics in the blues repertoire. T-Bone's distinctive, sophisticated rhythm guitar style included passing chords that lent a jazzy flavor to the basic changes, and subsequent interpretations—notably Bobby "Blue" Bland's 1962 recording (featuring a sterling performance by guitarist Wayne Bennett) and the Allman Brothers' 1969 rendition from *Live at the Fillmore East*—built on the foundation of Walker's arrangement by modifying the second half of the chord progression as shown here:

Fig. 4: "Stormy Monday" Changes

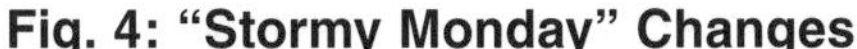

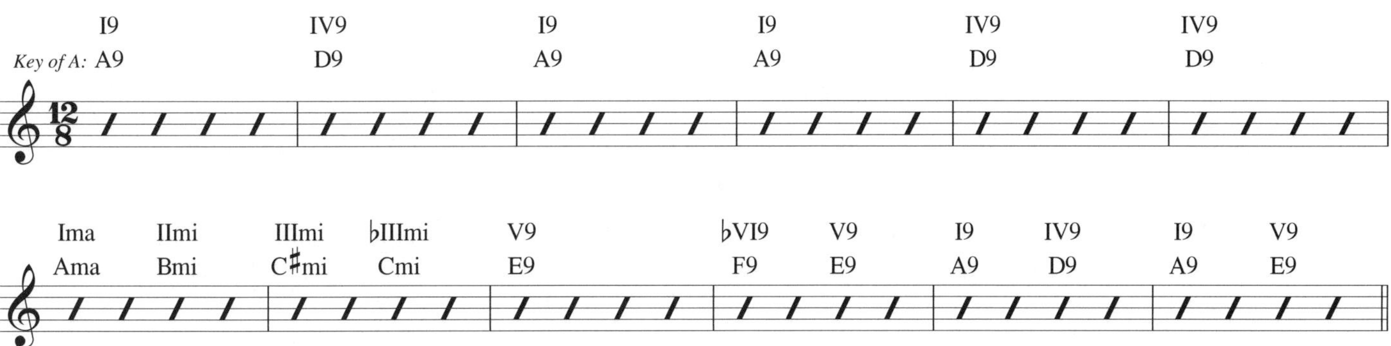

The variations occur in bars 7–8, where the usual I7 chord is replaced by a short progression based on the harmonized A major scale. For soloists used to standard blues changes, the sudden clash between minor key-center phrases and the distinctly major-key progression can be disconcerting. However, the same strategies that we have explored for playing over other chord substitutions also apply here. Namely, play major-oriented phrases within the "B.B. spot" or compose a short melody by connecting a note or two from each chord.

An additional typical harmonic variation is shown in bars 9–10, where the usual V–IV change is replaced by V–♭VI–V (or in the Allmans' case, V–IVmi). Often, the bass will continue to play the normal changes while the guitar plays the substitutions, but either way, the variation adds harmonic variety and does not significantly affect your melodic choices since the chords are still within the overall blues tonality.

The following example demonstrates a two-chorus solo over "Stormy Monday" changes with an overall approach that is more uptown than the previous example. The first chorus of solo uses a B.B. King-style key-center approach, and the second chorus follows the changes. When you are familiar with both approaches, of course you can mix them any way you like.

Fig. 5: "Stormy Monday"-Style Solo

Performance Notes

First Chorus:

1. Bars 1–6: The solo is roughly based on the melody to "Stormy Monday" plus answering fills, all located mostly around the B.B. King spot.
2. Bars 7–8: Repeating a short phrase over sophisticated changes creates an effective blend of straight-ahead blues melody and smooth, uptown harmony.
3. Bars 9–10: The melody in bar 9 emphasizes B, the 5th of E9. Bar 10 features a B.B. King trademark: attacking the high tonic note with a rake and quickly sliding away.
4. Bars 11–12: This is an interpretation of a traditional turnaround line.

Second Chorus:

1. Bars 1–4: The melody begins by outlining the changes and then moves into a longer melodic line that incorporates rhythmic emphasis on chord tones. The half-step moves in the rhythm guitar part are in the T-Bone Walker style (echoed by both Wayne Bennett and the Allmans), creating a jazzy effect without actually altering the 12-bar harmony.
2. Bars 5–6: The repeated diminished chord over IV7 is another T-Bone Walker trademark. It's technically "wrong," but the dissonance creates an effective contrast with the sweeter melodic lines that precede it and begins to build energy toward the climax.
3. Bars 7–8: The intensity builds with the melody closely following the structure of the substitute chords.
4. Bar 9–10: The arpeggio-based phrase over E9 is followed in bar 10 by another B.B. King trademark: a short, repetitious phrase with a rake into the first note and a very hard pick attack for maximum intensity (listen to King's live recordings of "Worry, Worry" or "Gambler's Blues" for exceptional demonstrations of this sort of dynamic control).
5. Bars 11–12: The turnaround begins with a flashy legato pentatonic lick followed by a much more relaxed conclusion to wind down the end of the solo. Practice fast licks like this very slowly at first to work out the fretting-hand details; you need a strong, consistent legato technique in order to match dynamic levels between the picked notes and the hammer-ons and pull-offs.

Demo 12-2
Play-Along 22
first chorus:
A9
D9
A9
D9
A
Bmi
C♯mi
Cmi
E9
F9
E9
A9
D9
A9
E9
second chorus:
A9
D9
A9
D9
A
Bmi

Telling the Story

Techniques and phrasing concepts are not ends in themselves; their purpose is to help us tell a musical story, and nowhere does that become more apparent than on a slow blues. Listen to great recorded slow blues performances like "Sweet Little Angel" by B.B. King, "Personal Manager" by Albert King, or "Red House" by Jimi Hendrix and focus on how the stories that they tell with their vocals and lyrics relate to the choices they make in their solos. Each player uses familiar techniques and phrases, but each solo is a unique event, a personal expression of a deeply felt message. To make that connection yourself, you have to practice and internalize your skills to the point that you can focus your attention on the feeling you want to create rather than the physical challenges of playing the guitar. Like all method books, this book concentrates on processes and techniques, but if like these players you persist to the point where you can hear the music rather than the notes, that is the ultimate payoff.

Jump Blues

Electric guitars first became commercially available in the mid-1930s, and its first true star—jazz guitarist Charlie Christian—arrived before the end of the decade. But it wasn't until T-Bone Walker unveiled his revolutionary electric guitar style in 1942 that the instrument was widely accepted as a lead instrument in blues.

Walker was a master of the style known as *jump blues*, a stylistic descendent of the piano boogie-woogie craze of the late 1930s that featured polished horn arrangements over a hip, up-tempo urban swing beat. Walker's commercial success established the electric guitar as a rival to the still-dominant saxophone, and his sophisticated chord voicings, swinging single-note lines, and distinctive phrasing techniques defined the sound of electric blues guitar for an entire generation.

The feature that most obviously distinguishes jump blues from the medium shuffle is tempo. As the name implies, jump is a high-energy style with tempos that range from a relatively sedate 160 bpm to 250 bpm and up. Characteristic rhythm section patterns include a four-on-the-floor bass drum, walking bass (a bass line that outlines the harmony with a steady, quarter-note pulse) answered with a piano chord on every upbeat, and syncopated, two-bar, call-and-response horn-section riffs. During the 1940s and early 1950s, jump rhythm sections were acoustic—upright bass, piano, drums, and horns—with guitar as the only electrified instrument (the electric bass did not become commonplace until the mid-1950s).

Most of the medium-tempo soloing concepts and techniques covered so far in this book also apply to jump blues, but as the tempo speeds up, the emphasis in the phrasing shifts increasingly from melody to rhythm. Unlike slow tempos, where the melody has to carry most of the weight, at fast tempos the excitement generated by the rhythm section makes even very simple melodies effective; in fact, some classic jump saxophone solos consist of just one note played with a catchy groove. A good rule of thumb is "the faster the tempo, the simpler the melody."

Even today, T-Bone Walker's personal stylistic trademarks still define the jump guitar vocabulary, including snappy bent-string phrases and dissonant chord punctuations like those shown in the following example. (Note that, since jump blues arrangements usually included horn sections, the jump repertoire usually favors saxophone-friendly flat keys—F, B♭, E♭, etc.—rather than the key of A as demonstrated here.)

Fig. 6: Jump Blues Solo

Performance Notes

First Chorus:

1. Bars 1–8: Phrasing based around one-note syncopated patterns was especially popular among tenor sax players known as "honkers," a group that included Big Jay McNeely and Joe Houston (whose melody on the instrumental "All Night Long" consisted almost exclusively of one note repeated with different rhythms).
2. Bars 9–12: In bars 9–11, the opening phrase evolves into a chromatic phrase that is also typical of the jump style; many jump saxophonists were trained as jazz musicians and worked more sophisticated melodies into their jump blues solos. Bar 12 acts as a pickup into the second chorus.

Second Chorus:

1. Bars 1–4: This syncopated bent-string phrase was a T-Bone Walker trademark; after you pick the bent third string, immediately bring your pick into position to pluck the second string and simultaneously mute the third string with the side of your thumb. The result is snappy and staccato.
2. Bars 5–8: Bend the diminished chord a quarter tone and repeat it with a syncopated rhythm to create harmonic dissonance that pumps up the tension and excitement—another T-Bone trademark (Walker also used the same effect on slow blues, as shown in Fig. 5).
3. Bars 9–10: Incorporating chords into the solo provides a dynamic contrast that also ties the solo directly to the harmony.
4. Bars 11–12: The ending phrase is similar to that used by Gatemouth Brown on his jump guitar masterpiece, "Okie Dokie Stomp."

first chorus:

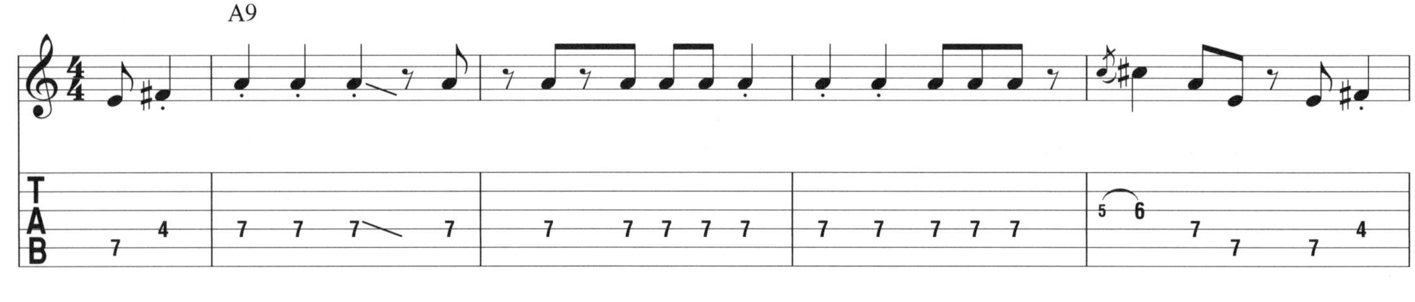

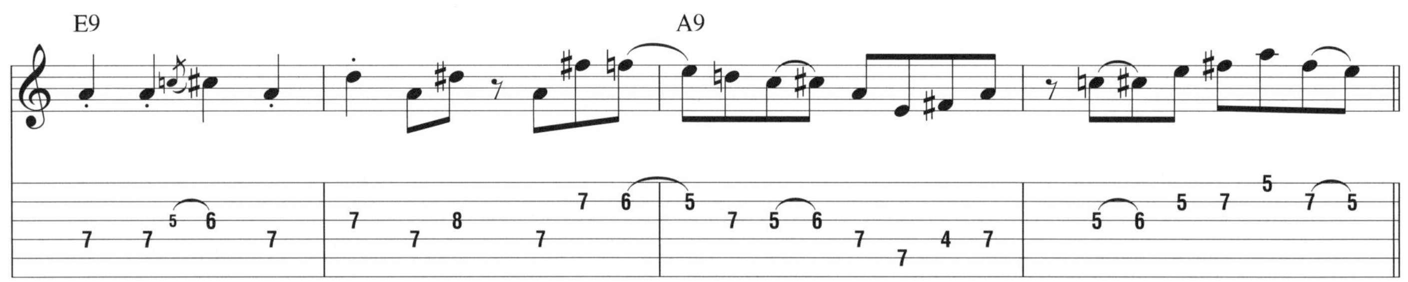

second chorus:

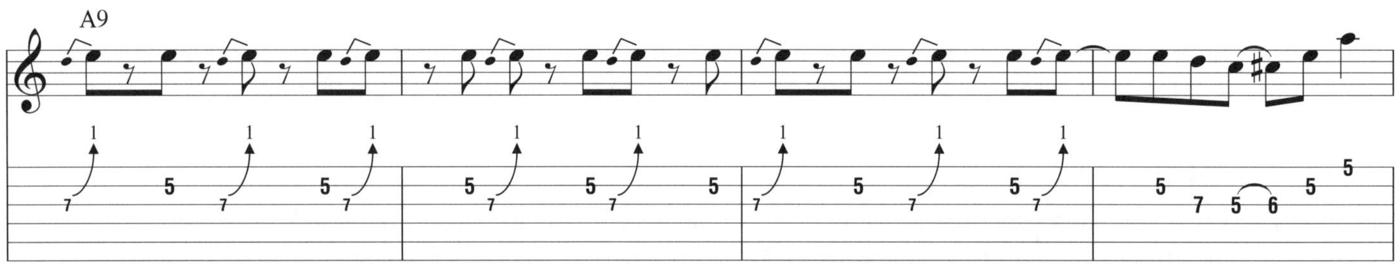

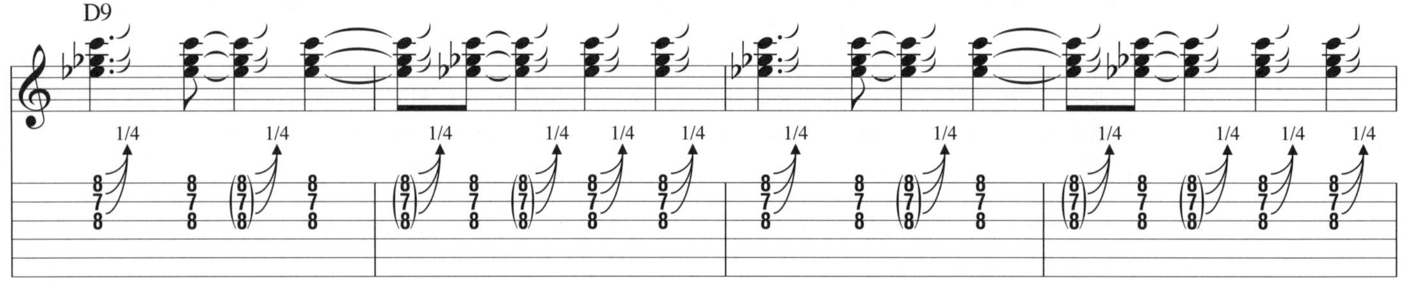

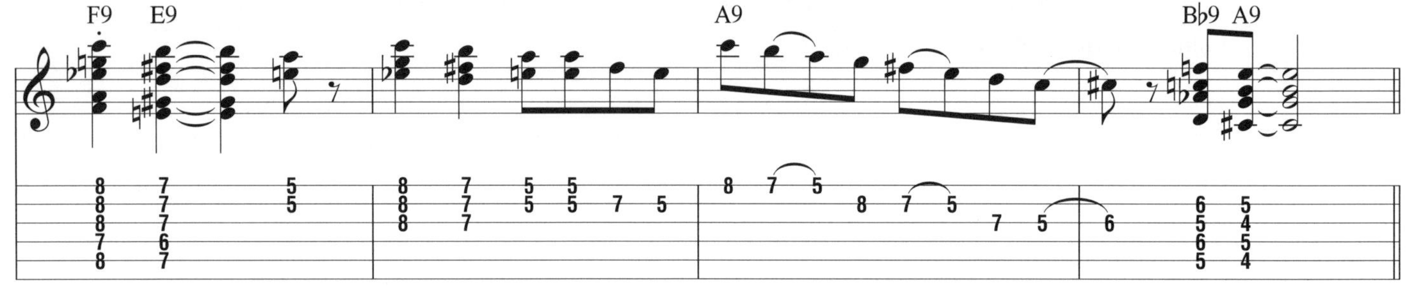

This example only scratches the surface of the jump blues guitar style. As with any style, the key to developing a convincing approach to jump blues is to listen to influential players and absorb their rhythmic feel, phrasing, and tone. While T-Bone had a fairly restrained attack and a very clean tone, his disciples, such as Johnny "Guitar" Watson, Guitar Slim, and particularly Clarence "Gatemouth" Brown, combined his melodic phrasing with a much more aggressive and distorted sound that set the stage for rock 'n' roll.

In particular, Brown's 1951 instrumental guitar showcase "Okie Dokie Stomp" ranks as a must-learn jump blues classic not only based on the performance, but also for the way Brown brilliantly arranges simple blue-note pentatonic phrases into a cohesive extended solo. The following example is inspired by one chorus of "Okie Dokie." (The original recording is in the key of E♭; to transpose, move the same fingerings up six frets.) In contrast with the saxophone-like one-note themes and T-Bone-style chords in the previous example, Brown's style utilizes single-note key-center melodies that are rhythmically simplified to fit a fast tempo. Brown picked with his bare finger and thumb, and the audio demonstration is played the same way, but hybrid or straight flatpicking are fine. The most important thing is to maintain accurate timing and feel.

Fig. 7: Gatemouth Brown-Style Jump Blues

Performance Notes

1. Bars 1–2: The strong, simple opening phrase repeats with slight rhythmic variations that "breathe" like a vocal melody. Brown typically used a capo, which allowed him to play the tonic (A) as an open string. Without a capo, the shift from A on the second string into the bend on the first string requires a very fast "hop" with the third finger. An alternative is to fret A on the first string and make an equally fast shift with your third finger up to the 10th fret to start the bend. For either technique, practice slowly in tempo and gradually speed up.
2. Bars 3–4: The answer continues with the same phrase before beginning the transition to IV7. At the beginning of bar 4, shift from eighth to fifth position (G to E) with your first finger.
3. Bars 5–6: The second call is a sequence moving stepwise through the minor pentatonic scale.
4. Bars 7–8: The response continues the sequence before building toward the V7 chord.
5. Bars 9–10: Another simple pentatonic phrase emphasizes the root of V7 (E).
6. Bars 11–12: The turnaround phrase outlines A7 before ending on E; although the rhythm section plays a "no turnaround" arrangement, it is still typical in blues solos for the melody to suggest the V7 chord.

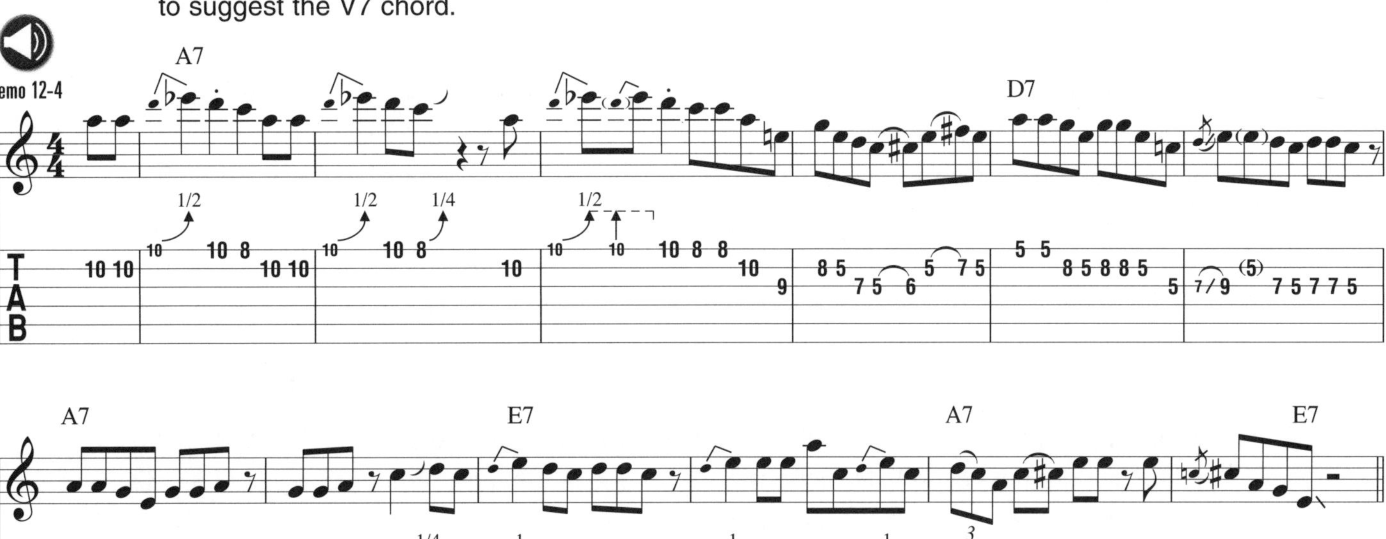

Other notable guitarists of the era include Tiny Grimes (who played an electric four-string tenor guitar), virtuoso soloist Slim Gaillard, and Bill Jennings (with Louis Jordan), all of whom favored a jazzier, melodically complex approach. You can also apply the concepts and techniques of soloing that you learn from jump blues to other up-tempo swing-based styles ranging from jazz-blues to rockabilly, rock 'n' roll, and Western swing.

One-Chord Boogie

In 1948, John Lee Hooker's catchy single "Boogie Chillen" reached the top of the R&B charts. Hooker's instrumentation and approach were the opposite of polished big-band jump blues arrangements—just a voice, guitar, and tapping foot driving a hypnotic, up-tempo shuffle groove that was known from then on simply as the *boogie*. Hooker's success inspired a number of rhythmically similar recordings over the years that range in style from blues and R&B to rock and pop.

A boogie shares some features with jump blues (e.g., walking bass, shuffle rhythm, tempos ranging from 160 bpm to 200 and up), but whereas the jump groove emphasizes the downbeat, the boogie places more emphasis on the upbeat, creating a feeling like that of continuously falling forward. Boogie rhythms have been adapted to various song arrangements including 12-bar blues, but in a classic Hooker-style boogie, the changes, if any, are few and far between.

As described in the previous chapter, one-chord solos maintain structure and direction by linking a series of two- and four-bar phrases. As the tempo speeds up and the rhythm becomes the center of energy, you can reduce the amount of melodic movement proportionately (check out the guitar solo on Slim Harpo's boogie "Shake Your Hips" for a classic example). When the tempo gets very fast, an effective strategy for maintaining a steady rhythm is to tap your foot on every other beat—i.e., 1 and 3 (called *cut time*). It doesn't change the actual tempo, but it helps you to relax and gain some breathing room.

The following example illustrates a 32-bar one-chord boogie solo divided into four eight-bar sections, each based on a different concept as described below.

Fig. 8: One-Chord Boogie Solo

Performance Notes

1. Bars 1–8 ("A" section): The intense, one-note attack is a trademark of Albert Collins, whose first single "The Freeze" is a one-chord masterpiece consisting of just four different phrases repeated throughout. ("The Freeze" is not based on a boogie rhythm, but the concept applies equally well.) For extra intensity, rake with the pick across the muted lower strings and slide quickly into the A; pick with bare fingers like Collins to pop the strings with dynamic intensity.

2. Bars 9–16 ("B" section): The rhythm of the phrasing becomes more active, which picks up the energy level. This melodic idea is loosely based on Chicago guitarist Jody Williams' wild solo on Bo Diddley's "Who Do You Love"—another one-chord masterpiece based on a different but related rhythm.

3. Bars 17–24 ("C" section): The classic down home double stops are a feature of the guitar solo on Junior Parker's 1953 boogie classic "Feelin' Good." The second half of the section consists of simple, rhythmic pentatonic phrasing.

4. Bars 25–32 ("D" section): The repeated bends and double stops build intensity; pick the double stops with your second and third fingers to enhance the attack. The sliding triplets in the final four bars echo Billy Gibbons' solo on one of the most famous boogies of all: ZZ Top's "La Grange." Pick the second string with your bare second finger (the same phrase also references John Lee Hooker's short guitar break on "Boogie Chillen," which started it all).

Demo 12-5 Play-Along 24

D

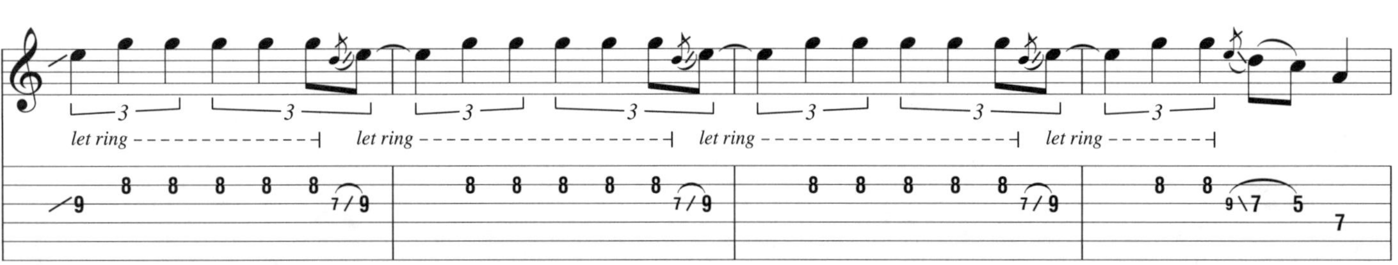

Chapter 12 Summary

1. **Slow Blues**
   a. **Harmony:** 12-bar progressions at slower tempos usually feature a quick change and additional chords on the turnaround.
   b. **Meter:** The typical slow blues meter is 12/8, which is equivalent to 4/4 with steady triplets.
   c. **Conversational Phrasing:** Slower tempos allow for more rhythmic freedom in the phrasing, creating a "conversational" quality.
   d. **Solo Development:** A good slow blues solo extends the message and feeling of the lyrics; as on any blues, basing the solo on the vocal melody is an excellent way to tailor the solo to the song.
   e. **"Stormy Monday" Changes:** This variation on slow blues harmony features common chord substitutions; as with other blues substitutions, the two most common soloing approaches are to play within the key center (the "B.B. King spot") or incorporate chord tones into the melody.
2. **Jump Blues**
   a. Jump blues is up-tempo blues with a swing feel. The basis of the jump blues guitar style was established by T-Bone Walker.
   b. At faster tempos, simplify the melody and emphasize the rhythm.
3. **Boogie**
   a. Boogie is an up-tempo version of the shuffle with an emphasis on the upbeat that originated with John Lee Hooker's "Boogie Chillen."
   b. Organize one-chord boogie solos into four- and eight-bar phrases with an emphasis on rhythm.

Practice

The melodic choices and techniques of expression for blues soloing are essentially the same at any tempo, so the most important thing to learn about playing at different tempos is the way in which the feel of the rhythm and details of the arrangement affect your phrasing. As such, practicing is mainly a matter of listening and playing. This is true not only of solos but the rhythm parts that accompany them; one of the best ways to improve your soloing over different grooves is to improve your rhythm playing.

Listen

Slow Blues

T-Bone Walker	"They Call It Stormy Monday (But Tuesday's Just as Bad)"
B.B. King	"Sweet Little Angel" (*Live at the Regal*), "Gambler's Blues"
Albert King	"The Sky Is Crying," "Personal Manager"
Jimi Hendrix	"Red House"
Guitar Slim	"The Things That I Used to Do"
Bobby Bland (Wayne Bennett, guitar)	"Stormy Monday"

Conversational Phrasing and Dynamics

B.B. King	"Worry, Worry" (*Live at the Regal*)
Freddie King	"Have You Ever Loved a Woman"
Johnny "Guitar" Watson	"Three Hours Past Midnight"
Buddy Guy	"Stone Crazy"
Albert Collins	"Dyin' Flu"
Jimi Hendrix	"Red House"

Jump

T-Bone Walker	"Strolling with Bone," "T-Bone Boogie"
Gatemouth Brown	"Okie Dokie Stomp," "Boogie Uproar"
Red Prysock (sax)	"Hand Clappin'"
Joe Houston (sax)	"All Night Long"

Boogie

John Lee Hooker	"Boogie Chillen"
Junior Parker	"Feelin' Good"
Slim Harpo	"Shake Your Hips"
Magic Sam	"Lookin' Good"
Canned Heat	"On the Road Again"
ZZ Top	"La Grange"
Albert Collins	"The Freeze" (different groove/same attitude)
Bo Diddley	"Who Do You Love" (see above)

13 Blues Fusions

The core musical values of blues phrasing—blue notes, touch, call-and-response—can be applied to any stylistic setting, as proven by the proliferation of hyphenated styles like rhythm-and-blues, blues-rock, jazz-blues, Latin blues, and funk-blues. In fact, mainstream blues guitarists such as B.B. King, Albert King, and Buddy Guy all achieved their greatest commercial success with stylistic fusions. From the other side of the musical equation, major pop stars who have incorporated blues into their repertoire include David Bowie featuring Stevie Ray Vaughan on his glossy album *Let's Dance* and U2 adding B.B. King to the straight-up rock of "When Love Comes to Town." When done well, blues fusion is a marriage that benefits both sides of the hyphen, and in this chapter we'll look at some of the most common forms.

Rhythm and Blues (R&B)

Rhythm and blues is a term that was introduced to the music industry in the late 1940s to describe popular music performed by African-American artists and aimed at African-American audiences (a category known previously as "race music"). Over the decades, R&B has encompassed jump blues, doo-wop, soul, New Orleans, Motown, funk, and a multitude of other sub-categories, all rhythmically different but all built around a core of blues melodic phrasing. As swing and shuffle blues faded from the commercial airwaves in the late 1950s, other R&B rhythm patterns took their place in the repertoire of mainstream blues artists.

Soul-Blues

By the early 1960s, new dance rhythms were quickly replacing the swing-based grooves that had dominated both black and white popular music since the 1920s. In the world of R&B, artists such as Otis Redding, Joe Tex, Sam & Dave, and Wilson Pickett began combining blues and gospel-influenced vocal styles with syncopated dance grooves to form the fusion known as *Southern soul.* The style achieved huge commercial success, and as the traditional shuffle blues audience disappeared, artists such as Freddie King, Buddy Guy, Magic Sam, Albert King, and Little Milton began populating their set-lists with similar rhythms.

In its most basic form, soul-blues is a fusion of 12-bar form and dominant-seventh harmony with syncopated eighth-note rhythms, typified by the rhythm pattern shown in the following example. The beat is based on straight eighth notes (i.e., divide the beat into two equal parts) with a strong accent on beats 2 and 4 (the *backbeat,* or main snare drum accent), and the syncopation is reminiscent of soul-era classics by artists like Otis Redding, Wilson Pickett, and Booker T. & the M.G.s.

Fig. 1: Soul-Blues Groove

Performance Notes

The key of A offers the option of using open-position chords, but to achieve the most consistent rhythm sound, it's best not to mix open and movable voicings and/or chords voiced on different string sets. For this reason, the chords shown in the example are all voiced around fifth position. In each bar, accent beat 3 as indicated by the accent symbol above the staff. (**NOTE:** The following notated example is demonstrated on the rhythm track that accompanies the solo in Fig. 3 as well as on the soul-blues play-along track.)

Demo 13-1 Play-Along 25

Chicken-Picking

The tight, snappy feel of soul-blues rhythm is also reflected in the solo phrasing. In addition to a sharp, dynamic attack, common stylistic techniques include 6th intervals (Chapter 10) and *chicken-picking*, a technique related to hybrid picking (Chapter 4) that produces an effect reminiscent of a clucking chicken—a symbol of down-home Southern culture.

To learn the basic technique, fret D on the third string, seventh fret with your third finger and follow these steps:

- While holding the pick normally between the thumb and index finger, rest the tip of the middle finger of your picking hand on the third string, muting it.
- While the string is muted, pick it with a down-stroke of the flatpick to produce a muted "thunk" and then immediately pluck the string with an up-stroke of your middle finger to produce the actual pitch; the combination of the two strokes creates the "cluck."
- Return your fretting-hand middle finger to its resting position and repeat; the chicken-picking effect emerges with repetition.
- Enhance the effect by bending the string while applying chicken-picking technique.
- A similar effect is created by fretting a note without pressing the string down fully and picking it with either the flatpick or a bare finger, creating a sound that is about 90% percussion and 10% pitch. Enhance the effect by picking with a combination of skin and fingernail.

The following example illustrates basic chicken-picking technique (the same techniques are demonstrated in context in Fig. 3). Down-strokes with the pick are indicated by "⊓." Pluck the other notes with up-strokes of the bare finger (indicated by "V"). In the first two bars, notes indicated by "x" are muted with the picking-hand finger; in the third bar, "x" means press the string down only part-way.

Fig. 2: Chicken-Picking Technique

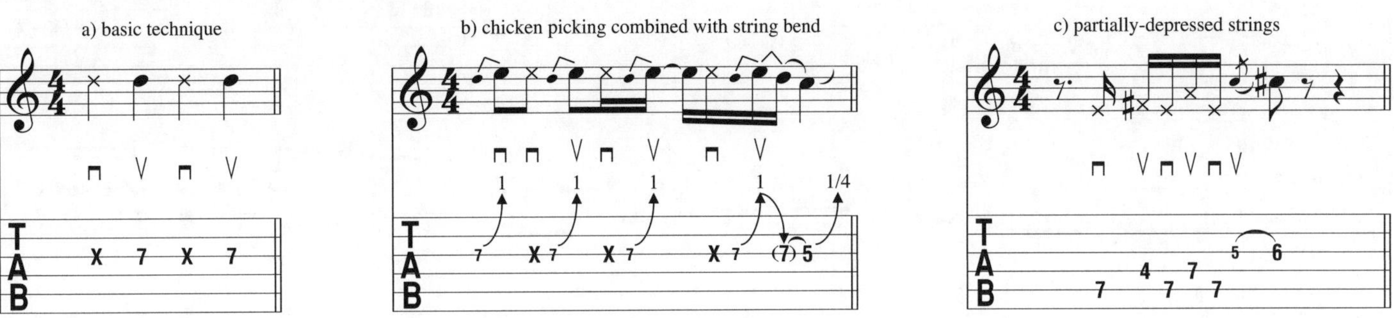

Chicken-picking is more than just a gimmick. When mastered, it adds considerable expressive range to your repertoire. Texas blues giant Albert Collins, for example, used bare thumb-and-fingers picking techniques to create not only a unique percussive, dynamic attack but also effects ranging from human voices to automobiles and household appliances (for a sample, check out his recording "Conversation with Collins").

The following example demonstrates a soul-blues solo that features both the pick/finger and partially-depressed string techniques for chicken-picking along with 6th intervals and other examples of stylistic phrasing.

Fig. 3: Soul-Blues Solo

Performance Notes

1. Throughout, partially-fretted notes are indicated by an "X."
2. Bars 5–6: Bend the third string up a whole step and chicken-pick; release slightly and re-bend before each attack for a more evocative effect.
3. Bars 9–10: Play the 6th intervals using the pick on the third string and bare finger on the first string.

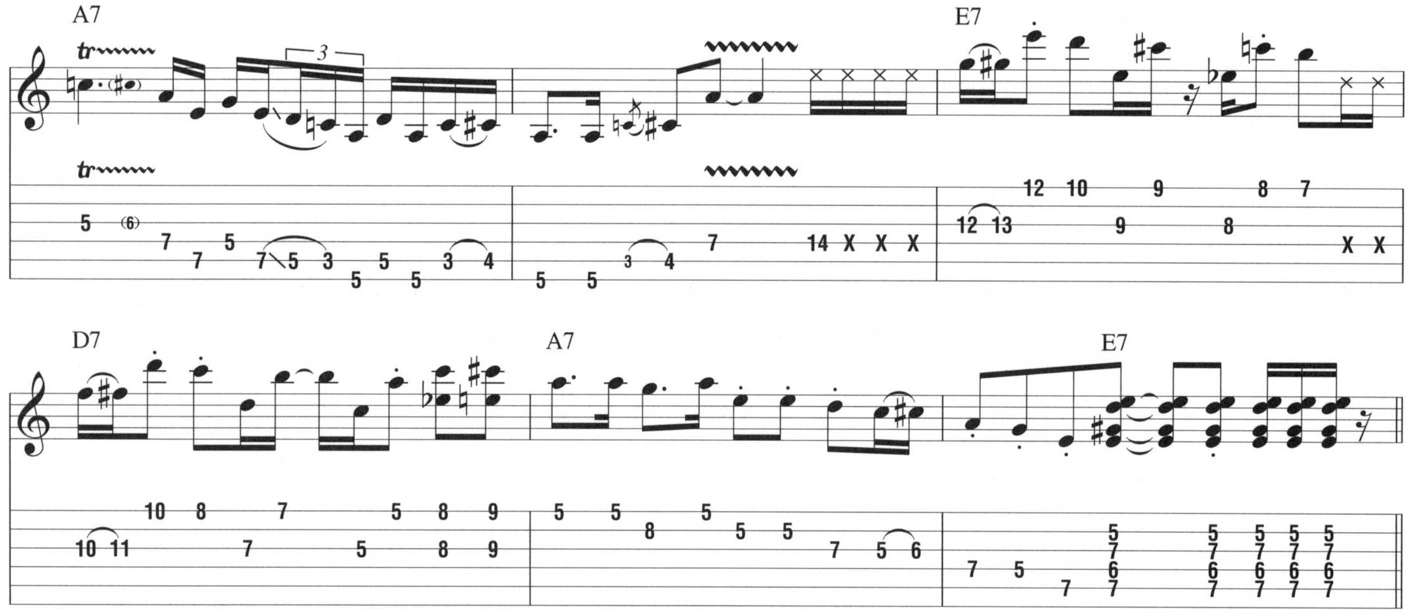

Smooth Blues

Smooth blues describes the sound of an R&B-blues sub-genre that took off following the massive success of B.B. King's "The Thrill Is Gone." King's reinvention of Roy Hawkins' early-1950s blues ballad as a contemporary dance track broke into every radio format—from blues to R&B to pop—sold in huge numbers, and earned King long-awaited mainstream recognition. Blues-based artists from Albert King, Little Milton, and Bobby "Blue" Bland to Z.Z. Hill, Robert Cray, and a host of others followed in King's stylistic footsteps, and smooth blues (analogous to "smooth jazz") remains a popular "crossover" blues format to this day.

Hawkins' original "Thrill" represented an earlier version of smooth blues, the mellow 1940s West coast style that was dominated by piano player/vocalists including Amos Milburn, Charles Brown, Nat "King" Cole, and early Ray Charles. B.B. King updated the 12/8 groove of the original recording with a mellow-funk dance groove that was more polished and restrained than soul-blues (hence "smooth" blues). He also expanded the minor-key three-chord progression by replacing the normal V7 chord in bar 9 with ♭VIma7—a substitution that extends the harmonic palette without going outside the minor key-center—and his use of minor seventh and major seventh chord qualities lent the changes a sophisticated urban flavor.

Fig. 4: Minor Blues – "Thrill" Changes

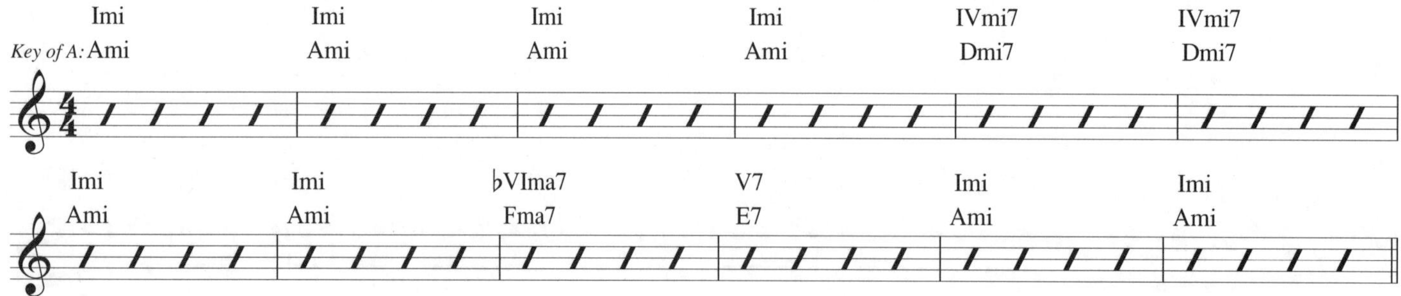

Chicks & Fills

The standard rhythm guitar style for this feel is known as *chicks & fills*, a combination of sharp chord accents on the backbeats ("chicks") and fills consisting of sparse chord embellishments as shown in the following example.

Fig. 5: "Chicks & Fills" Rhythm

Performance Notes

1. **Chicks:** Listen carefully to the snare drum and place each chick directly on the "crack" of the snare as if harmonizing the drum. To improve your timing, move your picking hand silently up and down in tempo between chicks, keep your picking hand relaxed, and "snap" with your wrist; for extra bite, play the chicks with up-strokes.
2. **Fills:** The purpose of a fill is to answer the main voice (in this case, the solo). Playing a guitar fill during a vocal or solo phrase can be distracting—like talking while someone else is talking—so if you're in doubt about whether a fill might interfere with the main voice, play chicks instead. When you accompany a vocalist or soloist live or on a recording, you can wait for the "holes" or pauses and place the fills there, but if you're playing to just a rhythm track, the most common location for a fill is during the second half of every other bar. (**NOTE:** The example notated here is performed on the rhythm track that accompanies Fig. 6 and on the smooth blues play-along track.)

Ami

Dmi Ami

Fma7 E7 Ami

B.B. King's solos on "Thrill" are masterpieces of melodic phrasing. As opposed to his normally sweet, major-oriented approach, B.B. stays almost exclusively within the key-center minor pentatonic. The non-traditional changes also provide the opportunity to expand the melody to include additional chord tones. The following two-chorus solo demonstrates both approaches, with the first chorus staying close to King's stripped-down style and the second chorus including additional tones on the changes.

Fig. 6: Minor Blues Solo over "Thrill" Changes

Performance Notes

1. The first chorus is played almost entirely in minor pentatonic Pattern #5, roughly modeled on B.B.'s "Thrill" phrasing. A simple melody played with a clean tone puts the emphasis on timing and touch—attack, dynamics, bending, and vibrato.
2. The second chorus raises the energy with more driving rhythms and also includes more color tones to create smooth, step-wise lines and pickup phrases that resolve into chord tones, including the following:
   a. Bar 5: F, the minor 3rd degree of D minor.
   b. Bar 9: F again, this time the root of Fma7, followed by A, the major 3rd of the chord.
   c. Bar 10: The melody drops a half step to G♯ (the major 3rd of E7); this is a particularly strong melodic tone because it emphasizes the quality of the chord and also stands out from the minor pentatonic.

Demo 13-2

Play-Along 26

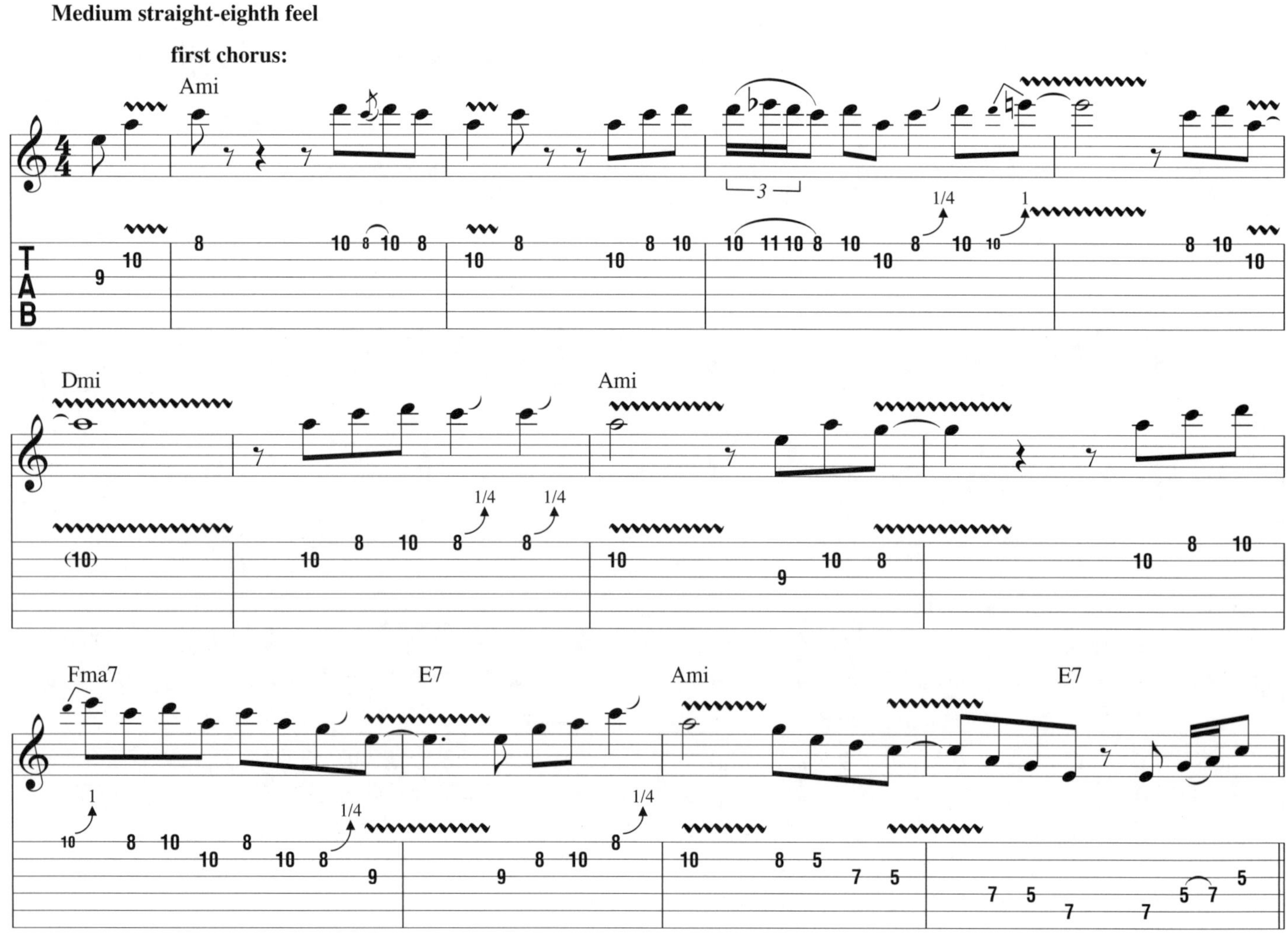

Medium straight-eighth feel

first chorus:

Ami | Dmi | Ami | Fma7 | E7 | Ami | E7

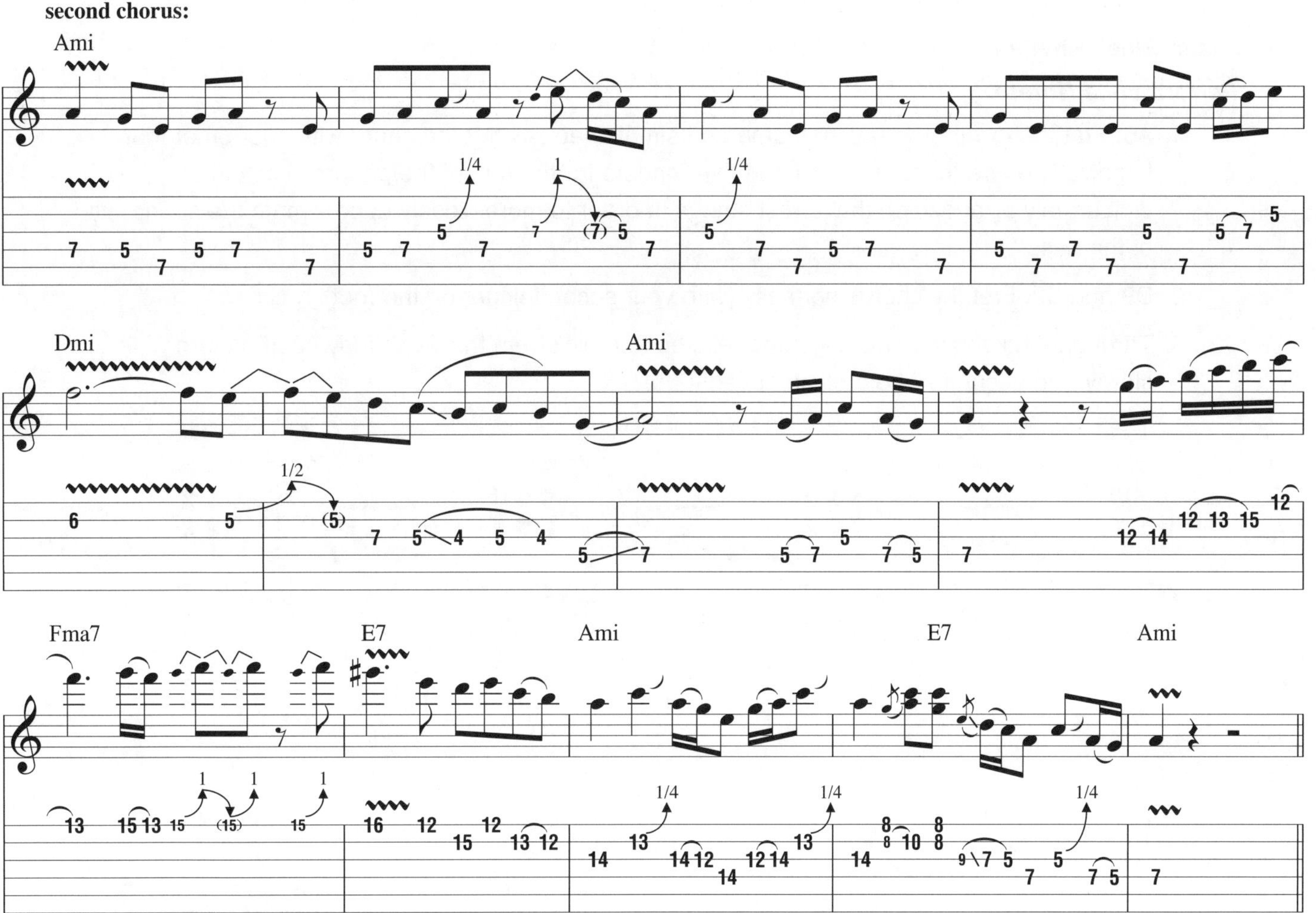

Other Rhythm and Blues Variations

Many more styles can be included under the broad R&B umbrella, ranging from James Brown-style funk to regional variations from New Orleans, New York, the West coast, and elsewhere. Each has distinct qualities, but all are more or less related to the styles described here. "Rhythm and blues" is just what the name describes—different rhythmic textures tied together by the common language of blues phrasing—so learning different styles of R&B is mostly a matter of learning different rhythm patterns. Whatever the rhythm may be, when it's time to solo, play the blues.

Latin Blues

Latin (specifically, Afro-Cuban) music has been intertwined with blues and jazz since the earliest days, when influential New Orleans jazz pianist Jelly Roll Morton declared that a syncopated "Spanish tinge" was an essential element of the jazz style. From the 1940s on, Latin-blues fusions were featured in the discographies of electric blues stars, including T-Bone Walker, B.B. King, Earl Hooker, Otis Rush, and Albert King, all long before Santana made it the centerpiece of his sound in the late 1960s. (Santana's first huge hit, the Peter Green composition "Black Magic Woman," is traceable to Otis Rush's Latin-infused "All Your Love (I Miss Loving)," which was itself derived from Chicago guitarist Jody Williams' "Lucky Lou.")

While Afro-Cuban music encompasses a multitude of sophisticated rhythmic variations, Latin-blues is almost invariably based on a simplified version of the straight-eighth *rumba* groove adapted for small-band instrumentation. The following example shows a rhythm guitar figure that combines elements of the typical Latin-blues bass and drum figures into a single pattern (in a band arrangement, the bass and chord patterns may be split between two guitars).

Fig. 7: Latin-Blues Rhythm

Performance Notes

1. A6: Fret the low root with your thumb and simultaneously fret the chord with your other four fingers. Then switch to your first and third fingers for the rest of the pattern. The pattern is deliberately arranged on the lowest strings in order to more closely approximate the sound of the bass.
2. D9 and E9: Fret the chords normally (with your second finger on the root).
3. Throughout, keep your picking hand relaxed and pick from the wrist. Play each pattern slowly and accurately before you speed it up.

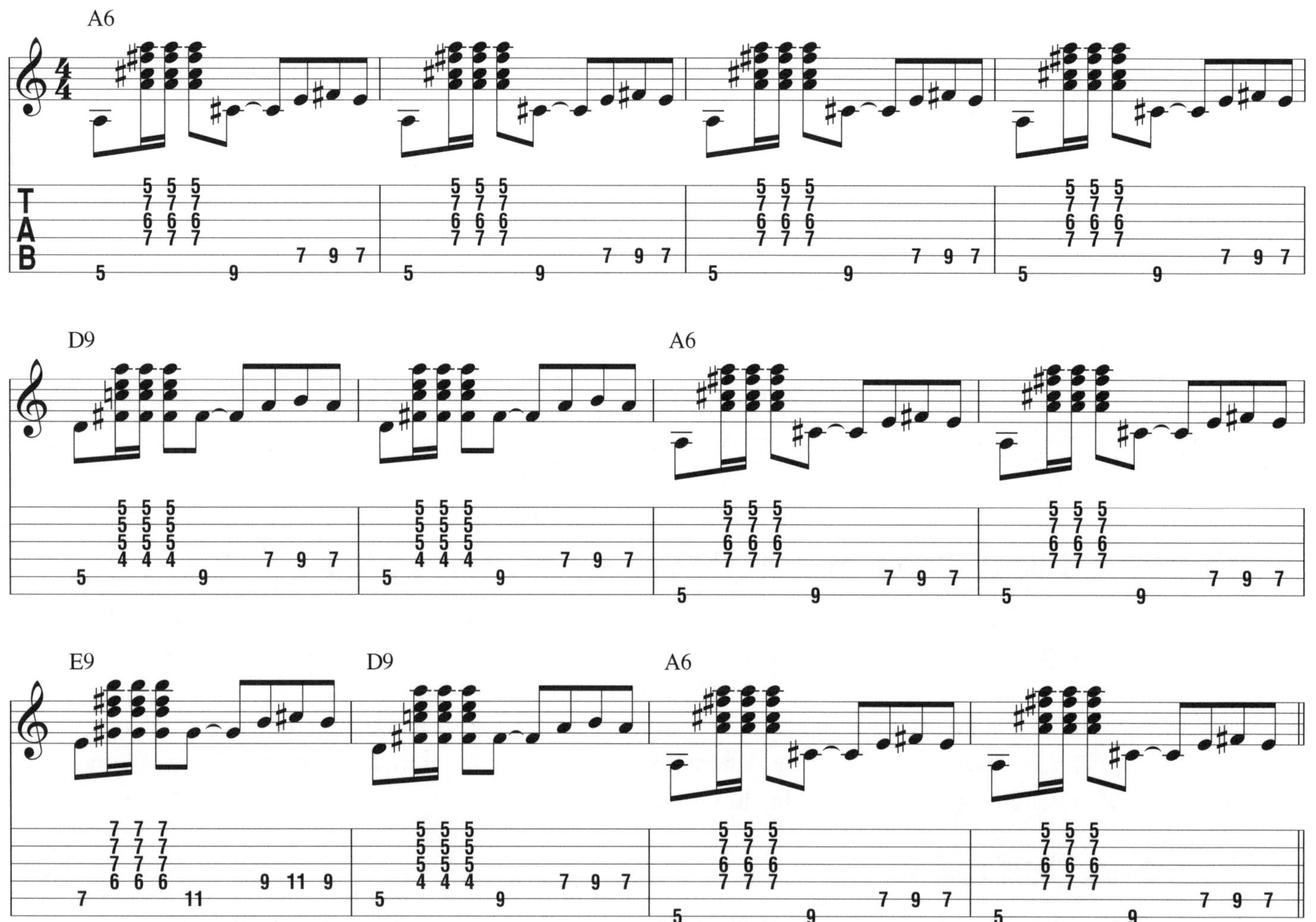

NOTE: The guitar accompaniment for the Latin-blues solo example in Fig. 8 incorporates an Americanized horn section-style rhythm; to hear a solo Latin-blues guitar arrangement similar to Fig. 7, check out New Orleans guitarist Snooks Eaglin's rendition of "Looking for a Woman."

The best-known example of Latin blues by a mainstream blues artist is probably Albert King's "Crosscut Saw." King converted Delta singer/guitarist Tommy McClennan's down home "Cross Cut Saw Blues" into a multi-layered fusion of rumba rhythm, a funky Memphis R&B horn section arrangement, and King's straight-ahead blues guitar and vocals. The following example is inspired by King's approach; aside from the straight eighth-note feel, all other aspects of the phrasing are the same as they would be on a medium shuffle.

Fig. 8: Latin-Blues Solo

Performance Notes

To emulate King's sound, pick with your bare fingers and thumb (the audio demo is performed without a pick) and attack the strings hard for maximum dynamic range. King plays simple melodies, but he infuses each phrase with a great amount of detail in the timing, dynamics, and touch.

First Chorus:

1. Bars 1–4: Typical of King's style, the opening phrases leave lots of space. The bend and gradual release that begins in bar 4 and extends through bar 5 are a King trademark. When you bend the first string, deliberately capture the second string under your fingers and pluck both strings together; this deliberate dissonance is another feature of King's style.
2. Bar 6: Shift from eighth to fifth position before the bend on beat 2.
3. Bars 9–10: Here we have more double-string bends from C to D.

Second Chorus:

1. Bars 1–4: The opening phrase locks into the rhythm, raising the energy level to start the chorus.
2. Bar 6, beat 1: In 10th position (Pattern #1), fret C (13th fret, second string) with your third finger and bend up two whole steps; the rest of the bar is based around different-sized bends using the same fingering.
3. Bars 11–12: We go out with more big bends typical of King's style using the same position and fingering.

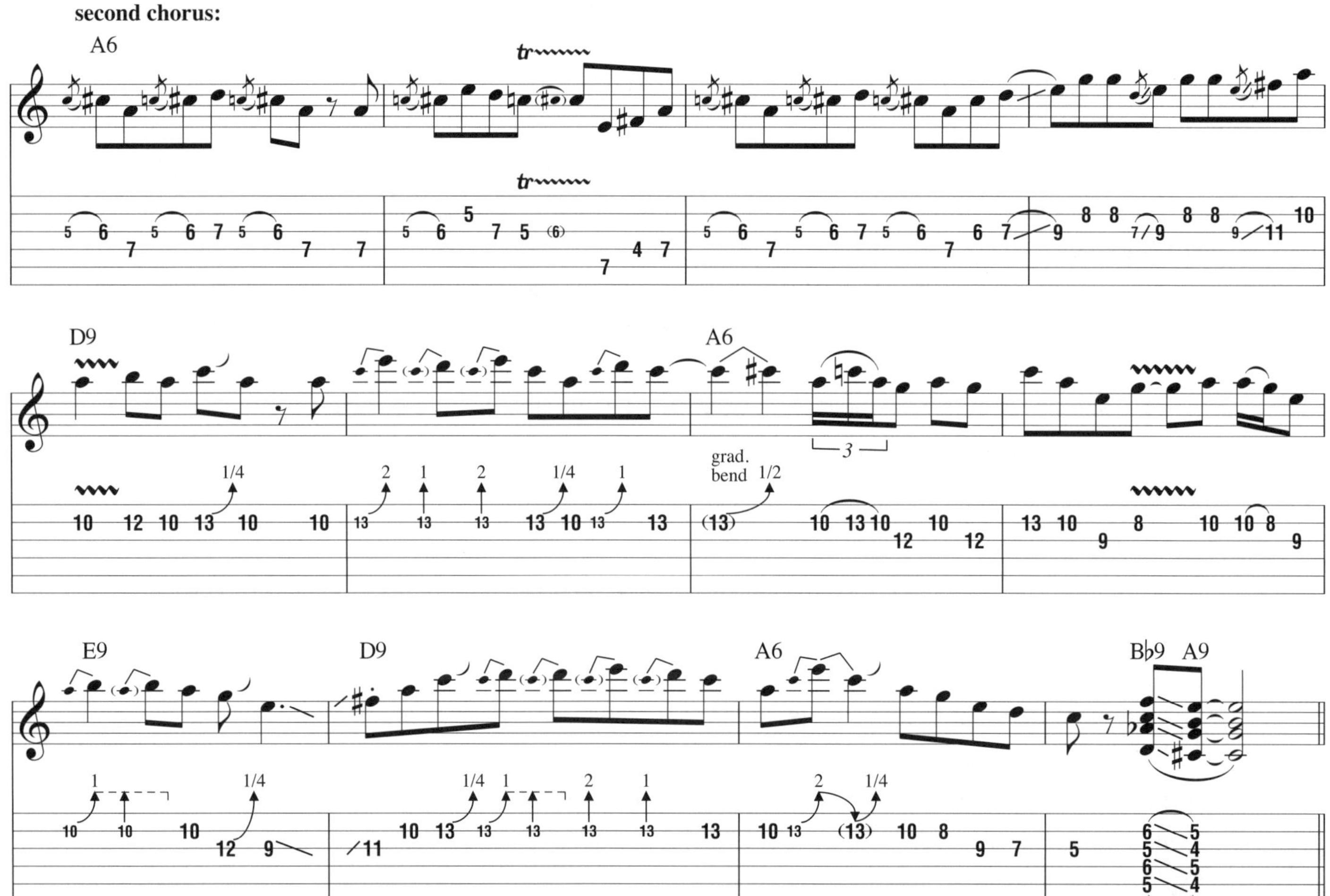

Several well-known Latin-blues recordings—"Woke Up this Morning" by B.B. King and "All Your Love (I Miss Loving)" by Otis Rush, for example—feature rhythm arrangements that switch from Latin to shuffle and back again. Aside from providing an interesting arranging feature, the smooth interchange between styles also illustrates how easy it is for blues to cross musical boundaries; it is the true world music.

Rock 'n' Roll

Rocking and rolling were common themes in blues for decades before Cleveland radio DJ Alan Freed combined them to coin a name for a new popular music phenomenon. In the 1956 film *Rock, Rock, Rock,* Freed described rock 'n' roll as "…a river of music that has absorbed many streams: rhythm and blues, jazz, ragtime, cowboy songs, country songs, folk songs." This depiction applies equally well to blues itself.

The standard form and rhythm of rock 'n' roll—12-bar progressions with a heavy backbeat-driven swing beat—emerged from sources including jump blues and New Orleans R&B. Rock 'n' roll guitar influences ranged from down home blues to country fingerpicking to jazz with a strong dose of T-Bone Walker—particularly in the case of Chuck Berry.

"Johnny B. Goode," recorded by Berry in 1958, provides a snapshot of the stylistic evolution of jump guitar to rock 'n' roll. Berry closely patterned his famous opening lick on guitarist Carl Hogan's intro to Louis Jordan's 1946 jump classic "Ain't That Just Like a Woman," converting Hogan's gently swinging single notes to high-energy double stops. Likewise, Berry based his solo phrasing around signature T-Bone phrases but replaced Walker's dynamic subtlety and laid-back swing with constant high-energy drive. And Berry's straight-eighth rhythm laid over the swing of the Chess Records house rhythm section created a magical "in the cracks" feel. Within a few years, the transition to a straight-eighth universe would be complete, but "Johnny B. Goode" stands squarely between two eras of popular music: the age of swing and the age of rock.

The following example illustrates Chuck Berry-style 12-bar solos over a combined swing-straight groove similar to "Johnny B. Goode," "Roll Over Beethoven," and other Berry classics. (This example is in the key of A, but another legacy of the swing era was Berry's preference for saxophone-friendly flat keys—"Johnny B. Goode," for one, was recorded in B♭.)

Fig. 9: Rock 'n' Roll Solo

Performance Notes

First Chorus:

1. Bars 1–4: We kick off with typical Berry-style double stops in Pattern #4; the repeated "call" in the first two bars is "answered" in the next two.
2. Bars 5–6: A stripped-down version of T-Bone Walker's trademark diminished chord, bend both notes of the double stop a quarter tone.
3. Bars 7–8: Continuous down-strokes add energy to the phrase; bar 8 is a series of one-finger double stops in the Chuck Berry style.
4. Bars 9–10: This syncopated double-stop phrase has been borrowed by Lonnie Mack, Keith Richards, and Stevie Ray Vaughan among others.
5. Bars 11–12: The chorus wraps up with a phrase similar to that at the beginning of the chorus. Like jump blues, rock 'n' roll 12-bar arrangements are often based on a simplified progression and forego the turnaround.

Second Chorus:

1. Bars 1–4: Here are two variations on T-Bone's signature syncopated string-bend.
2. Bars 5–8: The 3rd-interval double stops create a melody that connects chord tones of D and A; Berry has cited acoustic blues-jazz virtuoso Lonnie Johnson, who frequently used similar 3rd-interval melodies, as an influence.
3. Bars 9–12: Double-stop phrases similar to those at the beginning of the solo are transposed to E7.

Demo 13-4

Play-Along 28

Other Blues Fusions

The examples in this chapter demonstrate just a few of the most popular blues fusions that have evolved over the years. There are almost as many others as there are styles of American music, but the principles and methods of adapting blues phrasing to these styles remain the same whatever the setting. (fusions where the non-blues side of the equation is more dominant, such as jazz-blues and blues-rock, involve concepts and techniques that are beyond the scope of this book.)

Blues was a brilliant invention—a combination of musical styles, instruments, and cultural traditions that transcended the harsh circumstances of its origin to become a universal means of expression. You can learn the knowledge and techniques presented in this book fairly quickly, but shaping them to express the unique experiences and perspectives of your own life is a process that will never end as long as you play the guitar.

Chapter 13 Summary

1. **Rhythm and Blues**
   a. **Soul-Blues:** This is a combination of blues phrasing and syncopated straight eighth-note dance grooves.
   b. **Chicken-Picking:** A hybrid picking technique, it evokes down home Southern musical culture.
   c. **Smooth Blues:** A combination of blues phrasing and contemporary R&B dance grooves, it was epitomized by the B.B. King classic "The Thrill Is Gone."
2. **Latin-Blues:** This is a combination of blues phrasing and a variation on the Afro-Cuban rumba; a prime example is Albert King's "Crosscut Saw."
3. **Rock 'n' Roll:** A combination of jump blues and straight-eighth rhythms, this is typified by the style of Chuck Berry.

Practice

By definition, blues fusions consist of the familiar concepts and techniques of blues phrasing adapted to fit different rhythms; as such, practicing is mainly a matter of learning, transcribing, and jamming over the various rhythm feels. For example, study the rhythm arrangement of "San-Ho-Zay," "The Thrill Is Gone," "Crosscut Saw," or "Johnny B. Goode," including not only the guitar but also bass, drums, and other instruments. Play rhythm along with the recordings until you can keep time accurately with the appropriate feel and then transcribe one or more solo choruses by ear. This is equivalent to studying directly with the masters of the style, and any amount of time you invest in studying these and other classics will be rewarded proportionately by the improvements in your own playing.

Listen

Soul-Blues

Freddie King	"San-Ho-Zay"
Little Milton	"Feel So Bad"
Albert King	"Wrapped Up in Love Again"
Buddy Guy	"Mary Had a Little Lamb"
Magic Sam	"Just a Little Bit"
Booker T. and the M.G.s (Steve Cropper, guitar)	"Hip-Hug-Her"
Otis Redding and Carla Thomas (Steve Cropper, guitar)	"Tramp"

Chicken-Picking

Albert Collins	"Conversation with Collins"
Slim Harpo	"Scratch My Back"
Clarence Samuels	"Chicken Hearted Woman"

Smooth Blues

Charles Brown (Johnny Moore, guitar)	"Drifting Blues," "Black Night," "Fool's Paradise" (1940s West Coast predecessor of smooth blues)
Roy Hawkins	"The Thrill Is Gone" (1952 version)
B.B. King	"The Thrill Is Gone"
Albert King	"I Will Play the Blues for You"
Z.Z. Hil	"Down-Home Blues"

Robert Cray	"Smoking Gun"
Tracy Chapman	"Give Me One Reason"
Shemekia Copeland	"When a Woman's Had Enough"
Bettye Lavette	"When the Blues Catch Up to You"

Latin Blues

Albert King	"Crosscut Saw"
T-Bone Walker	"Plain Old Blues"
B.B. King	"Woke Up This Morning," "Help the Poor"
Muddy Waters	"She's Into Something"
Snooks Eaglin	"Looking for a Woman"
Earl Hooker	"Guitar Mambo"
Jody Williams	"Lucky Lou"
Otis Rush	"All Your Love (I Miss Loving)"
Fleetwood Mac (Peter Green, guitar)	"Black Magic Woman"

Rock 'n' Roll

Chuck Berry	"Johnny B. Goode," "Roll Over Beethoven"
Lonnie Mack	"Memphis"
Stevie Ray Vaughan	"Love Struck Baby"

Appendix I: Sound

Every major blues guitar influence is known not only for signature techniques and phrasing, but for a personal *sound*. As this book has attempted to demonstrate, the most important single element of your sound is your touch—how you physically fret and attack the strings—but equipment obviously also plays a big role. Aside from your touch, your sound is affected by every element that goes into shaping a note from the time you pluck the string until the sound waves strike your eardrums, including picks, strings, guitars, amplifiers, and effects.

Choosing gear involves a series of emotional as well as technical decisions, and with so many options available it can be difficult to even figure out where to start. One logical approach is to replicate the gear that your favorite players use, but if that involves top-of-the-line or rare, vintage equipment, the cost is likely to be disproportionate to the results—especially if you're not an experienced player. When you start out, relatively inexpensive new gear is usually a better investment than pricy relics. "Old" doesn't always mean great-sounding, and in the 1950s and 1960s there were more manufacturing inconsistencies than there are today. Before you make a significant investment, check out online discussions or reviews and consult with experienced friends and/or teachers. But most of all, trust your ears and your hands; what counts is the way a piece of gear feels and sounds—not the cosmetics or brand name.

Guitars

The most basic requirements for any guitar are that it stays consistently in tune and is properly set up (string height, intonation, neck adjustment, frets, electronics, etc.) so that you can play it comfortably. If you don't know how to set up a guitar yourself, spend some money to have it done professionally. It's not terribly expensive, and a guitar that won't stay in tune or is difficult to play will just frustrate you and sap your inspiration.

Aside from basic playability, almost every other judgment about guitars is a matter of taste. In the context of blues, here are some relevant factors:

Strings

It's a physical fact that thicker strings produce a bigger sound, but the thickness of a string alone is not the only factor. Stevie Ray Vaughan, for example, used notoriously heavy strings (high E = .013), but he also tuned his guitar down a half step, which deepened the sound of the instrument while also relieving a significant amount of that extra tension. By comparison, B.B. King tunes to standard pitch and uses a standard set (.010), and Albert King, who tuned below standard pitch, used very light-gauge strings. In each case, the choice of string gauge is suited to the player's touch. Vaughan used an extremely hard attack for both rhythm and lead, while B.B. (who essentially plays only single-note melodies) has a much lighter touch and Albert (also primarily a soloist) liked to bend great distances; in each case, the ideal string gauge is the one that allows the player to express their personal sound most effectively.

Fortunately, string gauges are available in nearly unlimited variety. For example, if you play music such as Chicago shuffle blues, which requires an aggressive rhythm style, heavier bottom strings provide an advantage since they don't go sharp when you dig in hard with the pick. If at the same time you also like to bend the high strings and don't want to struggle, a "skinny top/heavy bottom" set may fill both requirements perfectly. The choice of strings is also affected by factors including string height, scale length, and bridge type. For example, a Les Paul will respond to your touch differently than a vibrato-equipped Strat with identical strings, so you may need to use different strings on different guitars.

If you're not sure what's best for you, start with middle gauge—a standard set based on .010 for the high E will provide tone without too much resistance—and as you gain more skill and experience, experiment with different string gauges to see how they feel. (If you change string gauges significantly, you may also need to adjust your setup in order to accommodate differences in string diameter and tension.)

Picks

Electric blues has been performed using every possible style of picking—from no pick at all to thumbpicks, finger picks, and flatpicks of every shape and size. Your picking style is one of the major factors affecting your sound, and while most players settle on one basic approach, learning to use both picks and fingers provides maximum versatility.

When choosing a flatpick, a medium-heavy gauge (around 1mm) provides maximum dynamic range for blues. Thin picks flex easily, which impedes a strong attack, and are also prone to cracking (light picks are good for strumming acoustic guitars since they bring out more of the high-end frequencies). The small, very thick picks with rounded edges that are favored by some jazz and metal guitar players make it easier to pick fast scale passages, but they also reduce your control over dynamics, which is an essential component of blues phrasing. Even after you settle on a certain style of pick, however, it doesn't hurt to keep a variety of different pick gauges and sizes on hand for special circumstances.

Pickups

The three most common pickup types for blues are "Fender-style" single-coils (Stevie Ray Vaughan, Buddy Guy, Albert Collins, late Clapton), "Gibson-style" humbuckers (B.B. King, Albert King, early Clapton), and "P-90s," which are a high-output single coil used on early Gibsons (T-Bone Walker, early Freddie King, Guitar Slim). In terms of sound, Fender-style pickups are clean and bright, humbuckers are louder but also darker-sounding, and P-90s are in the middle. Like most musical decisions, choosing pickups is not a matter of right or wrong but of personal taste, and like guitars themselves, different pickups suit different playing styles and purposes.

If you like the way your guitar feels but not the sound, replacing the pickups may provide a fairly easy remedy. Pickup manufacturers produce endless variations on each pickup type, and installing them generally requires only basic soldering skills. Pickups respond differently to various body configurations, wood, and hardware, so the number of possible combinations is essentially limitless. However, you can't turn a Strat into a Les Paul just by changing the pickups. If you want a sound that's significantly different from what your guitar was designed to produce, it's usually best just to get a different guitar.

Capo

The capo—a.k.a. "clamp" or "cheater"—has long been used by blues guitarists in order to play and sing in different keys without wrestling with barre chords, but even if you know how to get around the neck comfortably, the capo can be very useful. For example, clamping at the first fret to play in F or B♭ allows you to retain the open-string sound and phrasing of down home blues in E and A, respectively. Some outstanding soloists (notably Albert Collins) use a capo all the time so that they are always playing in open position (Collins also used an open tuning). Chords and licks played against a capo sound different from the equivalent barre chords and moveable patterns, so even if you don't need it for technical reasons, sometimes a capo is the best choice. It takes some getting used to since it affects the feel of the guitar and can be visually confusing at first, but learning to use a capo is well worth the effort, and it may even wind up as one of your favorite accessories.

Amps

The classic blues tone is a tube amp just beginning to break up (distort). With too much distortion, you lose dynamic control; with too little, the sound can be thin and unresponsive. Amp design has come a long way since the early days, but that "in between" sound is an elusive target, and as a result most players wind up with a closet full of different amps.

When you evaluate an amp, a good rule of thumb is to listen first for the rhythm sound. The ideal blues rhythm sound can be described as "transparent distortion"—clean enough to transmit the details of your touch with just a hint of edge to fatten and sustain the tone. When you solo, it's easy to add distortion with external foot pedals, so for blues purposes, an amp that produces a good rhythm tone is much more versatile than one that's designed mainly for soloing.

Among blues guitarists, the general consensus is that you should be able to plug straight into an amp and get a good all-around tone with little or no knob-twisting; in fact, it seems that there's an inverse relationship between the number of controls and the likelihood of finding a good tone. However, the proof is in the results. If extra controls help you dial in your sound (and you know what you're looking for), then that's the right amp for you.

A number of other factors affect an amp's tone and usability: power rating, the number and size of speakers, closed- or open-back cabinets, master volume, EQ, tube or solid-state circuits, and on and on. Whatever an amp's specifications may be on paper or how it sounds when you play by yourself, the only way to properly evaluate an amp for live performance is to actually try it out on stage and find out if it provides the tones you need to play the music you like at a useable volume. Like guitars, the brand name, price, rarity, or age of an amp is not always an indicator of quality or a guarantee that you'll like the sound. You have to learn to analyze the tone critically and trust your ears.

Effects

Traditionally, the only effects available to blues guitarists were reverb and natural amp distortion; everything else was a product of the hands. Hendrix once and for all erased any doubt that blues can co-exist with any amount of distortion, feedback, and tone-shaping effects, but what made Hendrix great was not the electronics; it was his touch. He sounded just as good when he played entirely clean.

The most common effect that most players use today is distortion, with options ranging from "boost" or "edge" (making the signal louder, which causes the amp to break up slightly) to "drive" (simulated tube distortion) to "fuzz" (full-on artificial distortion). Whatever result you seek, it's important to be aware that distortion also compresses—in other words, reduces your dynamic range, making soft notes louder and loud notes softer. This creates sustain, but it can also make the guitar sound smaller and more distant while at the same time limiting one of the most expressive dimensions of your phrasing. A great blues sound depends on wide dynamic range, so let your attack speak louder than your pedal.

To get a sound approaching that of the electric blues originators, it's essential to first develop your un-aided touch to the fullest extent. When your playing sounds good without extra help, effects can make it sound even better, but electronics cannot replace touch.

Appendix II: Style and Influences

Between digital music and the Internet, guitarists today can access more music more easily than at any time in history, but that begs the question: when everything is available, who do you listen to? The names and recordings described here attempt to provide some guidance as it relates to electric blues soloing, but it's only a beginning. As you listen, form your own opinions about which players move you and let your natural curiosity inspire you to find out who influenced them, who was in their peer group, and who carried on their legacy.

Each of the players described here has a distinct musical personality that can only be fully absorbed by listening directly to the original source. Relying on tablature or watching videos of players demonstrating someone else's style can provide valuable perspectives, but the true magic lies in each player's unique touch. With the tools you have gained from this book and a pair of ears, you are in a position to study directly with the greatest players in blues history.

> **NOTE:** This is a limited selection of players and recordings and is not intended to be comprehensive or to suggest that these are the only ones worthy of attention. A web search of any artist listed here will suggest other related artists whose music will provide you with a wider and deeper perspective on the development of the blues style.

Pre-Electric Blues Guitar Influences

The first time most of the listening public heard an electric single-note guitar solo was in the late 1930s, when star bandleader and virtuoso clarinetist Benny Goodman began featuring a phenomenal young electric guitarist from Oklahoma named Charlie Christian on records and radio broadcasts. Goodman included some blues-based material in his repertoire, but Christian's sophisticated, saxophone-influenced style was far removed from the sounds of the Delta or Chicago clubs. It wasn't until 1942 (the same year that Christian died of tuberculosis) that guitarist-vocalist T-Bone Walker first featured an electric guitar playing single-note solos on recordings aimed squarely at the African-American blues audience. With the very first notes of his first single, "Mean Old World," T-Bone presented a model for electric blues guitar technique and phrasing that still echoes today. While he had no direct predecessors on the electric blues guitar, T-Bone and most other early electric innovators consistently cited the influence of two acoustic blues guitar giants:

Blind Lemon Jefferson (1897–1929) is generally regarded as the father of Texas blues. In 1925, he became the first male blues singer/songwriter/guitarist to achieve commercial success as a recording artist. Prior to Jefferson, blues was dominated by sophisticated, professionally-written "classic" blues featuring female vocalists backed by jazz orchestras, but Jefferson, who wrote his own material as well as adapting it from traditional sources, created the commercial market for down home blues. Although few could match his virtuosic and idiosyncratic skills as a guitarist and singer, Jefferson's success opened the door for similar artists and his records were widely distributed throughout the South. Particular favorites include "Match Box Blues" and "That Black Snake Moan."

Lonnie Johnson (1894–1970) was one of the most versatile, prolific, virtuosic, and influential guitarists in American history, with hundreds of recordings both under his own name and as an accompanist for artists ranging from Louis Armstrong and Duke Ellington to down-home shouter Texas Alexander. A native of New Orleans, Johnson's professional recording career as a guitarist and singer began in 1925 and continued (despite numerous setbacks) until the end of his life. His most influential guitar recordings were made during the mid-to-late 1920s; check out "Away Down in the Alley Blues," featuring solo phrasing that foreshadows both B.B. King and Chuck Berry, and his dazzling single-line improvisations on duets with fellow virtuoso Eddie Lang ("Hot Fingers," "A Handful of Riffs").

Other notable pre-World War II acoustic blues influences include:

Blind Blake (c.1890–1933): The Florida-born musician is regarded as the most technically adept guitarist of his generation based on his mastery of the piano-like ragtime style—a combination of alternating bass patterns and syncopated melodies. Also an accomplished vocalist, Blake's popularity rivaled that of Blind Lemon during the late 1930s but almost nothing is known about his life apart from the recordings themselves. Check out "West Coast Blues" and "Wabash Rag" for two examples of his seemingly effortless virtuosity.

Big Bill Broonzy (1893–1958) was a master of both finger-style and flatpicked guitar and one of the best-known singer-songwriter-guitarist-recording artists of the 1930s and 1940s. Along with renowned slide guitarist Tampa Red, Broonzy was an early kingpin of the Chicago blues scene and nurtured the careers of many up-and-coming blues performers who would make Chicago synonymous with electric blues. Later in his career he performed frequently in Europe where he became a significant influence on young musicians including Eric Clapton. Check out the finger-picked "Hey Hey Baby" and, for a flatpicking tour-de-force, "How You Want It Done."

The **Mississippi Delta** was a hothouse for blues singer-guitarists in the 1920s and 1930s and although no Delta guitarists of the era achieved the commercial success of Blind Lemon and Lonnie Johnson, the region's influence on electric guitar styles was felt through its slide virtuosos and sophisticated accompaniment styles.

Today, some of the best-known Delta singer/guitarists are **Charlie Patton** ("Pony Blues," "High Water Everywhere"), **Tommy Johnson** ("Big Road Blues," "Canned Heat Blues"), **Skip James** ("Devil Got My Woman," "Hard Time Killing Floor Blues"), **Son House** ("My Black Mama," "Preachin' the Blues"), and of course, **Robert Johnson**. Although he is now by far the best-known name in Delta blues, during his lifetime Johnson was little known outside the region. From his death in 1938 until his recordings were re-released in the 1960s, his influence was felt mainly through contemporaries such as Elmore James, Muddy Waters, and Robert Lockwood, all of whom continued to perform his music and use his techniques (see below).

Electric Blues Guitar Influences

The first name in the history of electric blues guitar is Aaron "T-Bone" Walker (1910–75). Walker was by far the greatest single influence on electric blues guitar soloists during the 1940s and early 1950s, and even today his approach remains at the core of the electric blues style.

Walker was born in 1910 in Dallas, Texas and by the late 1920s was already established as a singer, dancer, banjoist, and all-around entertainer. He began experimenting with the electric guitar soon after its introduction in the late 1930s, made his first recordings on the instrument in 1942, and went on to become one of the most popular African-American entertainers of his generation. In contrast with more the down home blues sound of Chicago, T-Bone's style featured sophisticated swing-band horn arrangements and single-line, saxophone-influenced phrasing that formed the model for lead guitar as we know it today. His popularity as a recording artist faded by the mid-1950s but he continued to perform nearly until his death. He made dozens of records of consistently high quality; a few recommendations include his very first electric guitar recordings, "Mean Old World" and "I Got a Break, Baby," his best-known tune, "Call It Stormy Monday (But Tuesday's Just as Bad);" and his signature up-tempo guitar showcase, "Strolling with Bone."

Appendix II: Style and Influences

T-Bone's success inspired many to follow in his stylistic footsteps. Some of T-Bone's most prominent disciples include:

Clarence "Gatemouth" Brown (1924–2005) broke into the music scene in the late 1940s with a style that was derivative of T-Bone, but he soon established a unique identity based on a bare-handed, aggressive attack. He covered many musical styles and played a number of different instruments over his lengthy career, but his blues guitar legacy is featured most prominently on his early recordings for the Peacock label, including "Okie Dokie Stomp" (the bible of jump blues guitar soloists) and the wild "Boogie Uproar."

Guitar Slim (1926–59), a.k.a. Eddie Jones, scored a huge hit in 1954 with "The Things That I Used to Do," which featured his rough-hewn version of the T-Bone/Gatemouth guitar style. An early adopter of the solid-body guitar, Slim's legendary over-the-top live performances inspired a very young Buddy Guy.

Chuck Berry (1926–) modeled his iconic guitar style directly on that of T-Bone, adapting Walker's jump-blues phrasing to the "big beat" of rock 'n' roll. Virtually all of Berry's classic solos bear T-Bone's stamp, and in turn they provided models for electric rock guitar stylists including Keith Richards.

T-Bone disciples are too numerous to mention, but just a few notable names include **Pee-Wee Crayton** ("Blues After Hours"), **Lowell Fulson** ("Reconsider Baby"), **Wayne Bennett** ("Stormy Monday," with vocalist Bobby "Blue" Bland) and in later years, **Hollywood Fats**, **Ronnie Earl**, **Duke Robillard**, **Junior Watson**, **Dave Gonzales**, **Kid Ramos**, and virtually everyone else who has carried on the tradition of jump-influenced blues. Like many other Texas-based artists, T-Bone did most of his recording in Los Angeles, and his influence remains particularly strong among West coast guitarists.

Texas

Beyond the legacy of Blind Lemon and T-Bone, Texas has spawned more than its share of guitar legends. A few of the most prominent include:

Lightnin' Hopkins (1912–82) was a Houston native who carried on the Blind Lemon tradition of volcanic, idiosyncratic guitar playing. With a vast catalog of traditional songs and an uncanny ability to improvise material on the spot, Hopkins was one of the most-recorded blues artists in history. His guitar style ranged from deep and sensitive to fast and flashy; although his extensive catalog contains many gems (and provides a virtual catalog of open-position phrases in the keys of E and A), for starters check out "Short Haired Woman" (his first single) and "Hopkins Sky Hop," which was the inspiration for Stevie Ray Vaughan's "Rude Mood."

Albert Collins (1932–93), known as the "Ice Man" and "Master of the Telecaster," possessed one of the most personal and instantly-identifiable guitar styles in electric blues history. The Houston native plucked the strings bare-handed, played in open tuning, and used a capo, all of which contributed to his original rhythmic and melodic combinations, wide dynamic range, and laser-beam intensity. Check out "The Freeze" and "Collins Shuffle," two early instrumental classics, plus his signature tune, "Frosty."

Johnny "Guitar" Watson (1935–96) combined intense, bare-handed guitar playing with phenomenal vocal skills (he inspired Etta James) and a wild stage act. His mid-1950s recordings are all classics, but in particular check out the intense slow blues "Three Hours Past Midnight" and the near-psychotic instrumental, "Space Guitar."

Jimmy Vaughan (1951–) came to prominence in the early 1980s with he Fabulous Thunderbirds, an Austin-based band that resurrected the sound of hard-hitting shuffle blues à la Jimmy Reed. Vaughan's heavy-string, hard attack, no-frills, straight-up Strat sound epitomized the younger (1970s–80s) generation of Texas blues. Check out the T-Birds' "Full-Time Lover" and "Marked Deck."

Stevie Ray Vaughan (1954–90) needs no introduction. His debt to Albert King and Jimi Hendrix is well known, but he also wore out recordings by Jimmy Reed, Lonnie Mack, and a host of other players on his way to becoming arguably the most versatile and technically accomplished blues guitarist in history.

The Three Kings

Three guitarists named "King" (all unrelated) also happen to be three of the most influential electric guitarists in blues history.

B.B. King (1925–), after over six decades as a recording star and headline attraction, has unquestionably earned the sole right to be called "King of the Blues." Although strongly influenced by T-Bone at the start of his career, King soon developed a distinctive personal style and technique that featured evocative string-bending, vibrato, and a vocabulary of signature phrases. He made dozens of great records during the 1950s and scored his biggest commercial hit in 1970 with "The Thrill Is Gone," but many consider his greatest recording to be the album *Live at the Regal* from 1964 with performances like "Every Day I Have the Blues" and "Sweet Little Angel" that are simply unmatched.

Albert King (1923–92) made his first recordings in 1953 and finally rose to international prominence in the mid-1960s with a series of records on the Stax label that seamlessly blended his deep blues style with contemporary R&B rhythms. His powerful solos, featuring massive string bends executed with delicate precision, have inspired generations of blues-rock soloists—none more than Stevie Ray Vaughan. Check out the Latin-tinged classic "Crosscut Saw" and his hair-raising slow blues masterpiece, "Personal Manager."

Freddie King (1934–76) combined his Texas roots and Chicago upbringing to create the most hard-edged, aggressive style of the Three Kings. In addition to his powerful, gospel-influenced vocal style, King's first hit, "Hide Away," established him as a premier instrumentalist. Eric Clapton, for one, modeled his playing on that of King, and in turn King was one of the few bluesmen to cross over successfully into blues-rock. Early instrumentals such as "The Stumble," "San-Ho-Zay," and "Side Tracked" are loaded with instantly-useable blues phrases; also check out "Going Down" for a powerful example of his late-career blues-rock sound.

Chicago

The 1950s were the golden years of Chicago blues, when hole-in-the-wall clubs regularly featured performances by a host of now-legendary musicians who inspired the birth of rock. Chicago blues was a rough-edged style featuring small electrified bands in contrast with the smooth, uptown big-band swing of T-Bone and his disciples. The list of great players associated with the city is enormous; here are just a few:

Muddy Waters (1915–83) left the Delta for Chicago in the mid-1940s and re-invented himself as an urban, electric bluesman. His powerful electric performances of what he labeled "Deep Blues"—the no-frills, emotionally hard-hitting style of the Delta—made him the godfather of the Chicago scene. Muddy was not a technically sophisticated player, but his performances are hypnotic; check out "Still a Fool" and "Rolling Stone."

Jimmy Rogers (1924–97) was Muddy's guitarist during the "golden years" and a popular singer and recording artist in his own right. Together with Muddy, he was one of the prime architects of small-band electric guitar arrangement as well as a major influence on Freddie King, among others. Check out his recordings of "That's All Right" and "Walking by Myself."

Jimmy Reed (1925–76) created one of the greatest song catalogs in blues history—classics that form the core of the all-time blues set-list. Together with his guitar partner Eddie Taylor and sometimes a third and even fourth guitarist, Reed sang and played harmonica while simultaneously performing effortless-sounding but elusive rhythms that epitomize the boogie shuffle style. Check out "High and Lonesome," "Bright Lights, Big City," or just about anything else he ever recorded (Eddie Taylor's solo recordings "Big Town Playboy" and "Bad Boy" are classics in a similar style and also feature his first-rate soloing skills).

Elmore James (1918–63) carried Robert Johnson's "Dust My Broom" into the modern era, recasting it as a nasty electric boogie shuffle topped with the most-recognized slide guitar lick ever. James was also a frighteningly intense vocalist who inspired a legion of disciples from Peter Green to John Lennon. Check out "Dust My Broom" (which he re-recorded several times) and "The Sky Is Crying."

Earl Hooker (1930–70), best known for his brilliant slide playing, was considered by many to be the best all-around guitarist in Chicago (no small claim). Check out his solo instrumental "The Hucklebuck," his work behind Junior Wells on "Little by Little," and for slide, "Blue Guitar" (the identical track with an over-dubbed vocal by Muddy Waters and lyrics by Willie Dixon is better known as "You Shook Me").

Buddy Guy (1936–) cultivated one of the most unpredictable guitar styles and wild stage acts in blues. Born in Louisiana, he moved to Chicago in 1957 and with Muddy's help established his name as a session guitarist and solo artist. His partnership with harp player Junior Wells resulted in a number of classic recordings in the 1960s and 1970s, and he was often praised by rock guitarists including Hendrix, Clapton, and Stevie Ray Vaughan. However, he didn't emerge as a marquee name in his own right until his 1991 album, *Damn Right I've Got the Blues.* Check out "Let Me Love You" and "Stone Crazy" from his Chess Records years.

Otis Rush (1934–) made some of the most influential recordings in blues guitar history for Chicago's Cobra label between 1956 and 1958. His vibrato-heavy guitar playing and intense vocals had a major influence on blues-rock artists, including Clapton, Peter Green, and Stevie Ray Vaughan. Check out "All Your Love (I Miss Loving), "Double Trouble," "It Takes Time," "I Can't Quit You Baby," or any of his other recordings on Cobra.

Magic Sam (1937–69), a.k.a. Sam Maghett, was a contemporary of Buddy Guy, Freddie King, and Otis Rush, working the clubs on Chicago's West Side during the late 1950s and 1960s. Sam's biting, reverb-drenched Strat tone was matched by his high, clear vocals, and he had a gift for writing and arranging blues with a contemporary twist. His John Lee Hooker-inspired boogie instrumental "Lookin' Good" was a show-stopper, and he was on the verge of breakout success when he suddenly died of heart failure at only 32 years of age. Check out "Lookin' Good" and "Mama Talk to Your Daughter" (*West Side Soul*).

Hubert Sumlin (1931–2011) was the backbone of Howlin' Wolf's band throughout Wolf's Chicago years. His intense, bare-handed attack and inventive, extended solos inspired a generation of blues-rock virtuosos. Check out Wolf's "Spoonful" and "Hidden Charms."

A few other guitarists of note that were also associated with Chicago include **Robert Nighthawk** (brilliant slide guitarist and mentor to Earl Hooker), **Luther Allison** and **Jimmy Dawkins** (high-energy soul-influenced guitarists and singers), **Dave & Louis Myers** (brothers who played guitars on many Little Walter classics), **Pat Hare** (white-knuckle soloist), **Robert Lockwood Jr.** (in-demand accompanist to Sonny Boy Williamson II, Little Walter, and many others), **Jody Williams** (under-recognized, highly accomplished, and influential guitarist with Bo Diddley, Howlin' Wolf, and others), and **Willie Johnson** (Wolf's Memphis guitarist and sometime partner to Hubert Sumlin).

Many great Chicago guitarists made their reputations while working with singers, harp players, and piano players who also defined the Chicago sound. Some of the greatest Chicago-style guitar work can also be found on records by:

John Lee "Sonny Boy" Williamson (a.k.a. "Sonny Boy Williamson I") was a hugely influential harp player, singer, and recording artist who, along with Big Bill Broonzy, Tampa Red, and others, created the first wave of Chicago blues in the 1930s and 1940s ("Good Morning Little Schoolgirl," "Checking Up on My Baby").

Rice Miller (a.k.a. "Sonny Boy Williamson II") was a Memphis-based harp legend who moved to Chicago in the 1950s, where he recorded a string of all-time electric blues classics ("One Way Out," "Help Me," "Bring It on Home").

Little Walter Jacobs developed the amplified, saxophone-influenced harmonica style that defined electric Chicago blues and with it made some of the greatest recordings in blues history, both with Muddy Waters and as a solo artist ("Juke," "Blues with a Feeling").

Junior Wells, a disciple of Sonny Boy, joined Muddy's band after Walter departed to pursue his solo career; Junior's recordings and shows with Buddy Guy are blues legend ("Messin' with the Kid," "Hoodoo Man").

Howlin' Wolf, a.k.a. Chester Burnett, was Muddy's rival for "King of Chicago Blues" and one of the most intense vocalists and personalities in the history of blues. His recordings—many featuring the guitar work of Hubert Sumlin and/or Willie Johnson—are virtually all classics ("Spoonful," "Back Door Man").

Otis Spann, best-known as Muddy's piano player during the Chicago "golden era," made many classic recordings under his own name, including a number with guitarist Robert Lockwood. His powerful, flowing, inventive style represented the epitome of Chicago blues piano ("It Must Have Been the Devil," "Going Down Slow").

Other Blues Guitar Greats

It's much easier to start a list of guitarists who have influenced the sound of blues than to finish it, but here are a few more, in no particular order:

Lonnie Mack, from southern Indiana, was recording intense, guitar-driven blues-rock in 1963, before the style had a name. Like Freddie King, he became known for instrumentals ("Wham," "Memphis"), but as a vocalist he has few equals ("Why"). Mack's high-energy, technically accomplished phrasing was a major influence on Stevie Ray Vaughan.

Snooks Eaglin was a guitarist/singer from New Orleans with a unique, flamenco-style attack and an enormous solo repertoire developed during years as a street musician. Check out *New Orleans Street Singer*—a virtual "greatest hits" album of blues standards from 1959, all impeccably sung and played on solo acoustic guitar. His electric style was also remarkable; listen to "Traveling Mood" and "Is It True" from his Imperial recordings.

Billy Butler, from Philadelphia, performed one of the most-quoted electric blues solos of all time on Bill Doggett's 1956 instrumental hit "Honky Tonk Part 1." He later made a number of solo recordings in the style once known as "soul blues" and now re-dubbed "acid jazz."

Mickey "Guitar" Baker, based in New York City, turned from jazz to blues and rock 'n' roll in the early 1950s and played on many classic blues/R&B sessions. Best known for the single "Love Is Strange" (Mickey & Sylvia), his solos and fills on Big Maybelle's "One Monkey (Don't Stop No Show)" and "Don't Leave Poor Me," to name just two, define the sound of classic rock 'n' roll.

Appendix III: Audio Tracks

Demo Tracks

Chapter	Track #		Fig. #	Content
2	2-1	(0:00)	4	minor pentatonic with blue 3rd
		(0:34)	7	minor pentatonic with blue 3rd and ♭5th
		(1:09)	9	minor pentatonic with blue 3rd, ♭5th, ♭7th
		(1:24)	10	blue-note pentatonic phrase
3	3-1		Ex. 1	one-bar call-and-response
	3-2		Ex. 2	two-bar call-and-response
4	4-1	(0:00)	1	hammer-on triplets ascending
		(0:12)	2	pull-offs triplets descending
		(0:24)	3	combining hammer-ons and pull-offs
	4-2		4	picking with dynamics
	4-3		5	the slap
	4-4		6	the rake
	4-5		7	bare-finger picking
5	5-1		1	sliding
	5-2		2	whole-step bends
	5-3		3	bend-and-release
	5-4	(0:00)	5	two-step bends
		(0:18)	6	bending and releasing to chord tones
	5-5		7	phrasing with wide bends
	5-6		8	vibrato exercise
6	6-1		3	phrasing with the 6th
	6-2		5	phrasing with the 9th
	6-3		6	phrasing with both 6th and 9th
7	7-1	(0:00)	6	pattern #4 lower octave: transposing from upper octave
		(0:30)	7	pattern #4 lower octave
	7-2		9	pattern #5 Albert King-style phrases
	7-3		10	pattern #5 blues tonality phrases
	7-4		11	connecting patterns #4 and #5
	7-5		13	pattern #1 B.B. King-style phrases
	7-6		14	pattern #1 blues tonality phrases
	7-7		15	connecting patterns #1, #5, and #4
	7-8		17	pattern #2 phrasing
	7-9		18	pattern #2 blues tonality phrases
	7-10		20	pattern #3 blues tonality phrases
	7-11		21	shifting/sliding through patterns ascending
	7-12		22	shifting/sliding through patterns descending
	7-13		23	one-string melody

Chapter	Track #		Fig. #	Content
8	8-1		6	12-bar call-and-response solo
	8-2		7	12-bar blue-note pentatonic key-center solo
	8-3	(0:00)	8	I7–IV7: 3rds and 7ths
		(0:26)	9	I7–V7: 3rds and 7ths
	8-4		10	"Three Seven Blues"
	8-5	(0:00)	11	"St. Louis Blues" chord-tone solo
		(0:31)	12	"St. Louis Blues" key-center style
	8-6		14	pickup blues
	8-7		15	combining phrasing skills
	8-8	(0:00)	18	traditional turnaround
		(0:14)	19	traditional turnaround
		(0:28)	20	traditional turnaround
		(0:43)	21	traditional turnaround
	8-9	(0:00)	22	single-note turnaround
		(0:14)	23	single-note turnaround
		(0:29)	24	single-note turnaround
		(0:43)	25	single-note turnaround
	8-10	(0:00)	26	blues ending
		(0:16)	27	blues ending
	8-11	(0:00)	29	blues intro
		(0:16)	30	blues intro
9	9-1		1	Jimmy Reed-inspired solo
	9-2		2	Freddie King style
	9-3		3	Billy Butler style
	9-4		4	Albert King style
	9-5		5	Pat Hare style
	9-6		6	two-chorus solo
10	10-1		4	12-bar solo with 3rds
	10-2		6	12-bar solo with 6ths
	10-3		8	12-bar solo with chords
	10-4		9	Chicago-style solo
	10-5		10	solo with chord accents
	10-6		11	low-register solo
	10-7		14	open-position solo in A
	10-8		16	open-position solo in E
	10-9		17	solo in E combining open and moveable patterns
11	11-1	(0:00)	2a	phrasing over ♯IV diminished
		(0:10)	2b	phrasing over IV minor
		(0:19)	3	more IV phrasing ideas
	11-2	(0:00)	5	phrasing over I–VI–II–V
		(0:20)	6	phrasing over I–VI–II–V
	11-3		7	12-bar solo over uptown changes
	11-4		9	"How Long" 8-bar solo
	11-5		11	8-bar solo over substitute changes
	11-6		13	"Highway" 8-bar solo
	11-7		15	"Nobody Knows You" 8-bar solo
	11-8		17	16-bar blues solo
	11-9		19	minor blues solo
	11-10		20	one-chord solo

Appendix III: Audio Tracks

Chapter	Track #	Fig. #	Content
12	12-1	3	slow blues solo
	12-2	5	"Stormy changes" slow blues solo
	12-3	6	jump solo
	12-4	7	Gatemouth-style jump solo
	12-5	8	one-chord boogie solo
13	13-1	1, 3	soul-blues groove and solo
	13-2	5, 6	smooth blues groove and solo
	13-3	8	Latin blues solo
	13-4	9	rock 'n' roll blues solo

Play-Along Tracks

Chapter	Track #	Content
3	1	One chord medium shuffle
8	2	I7–IV7 (two bars each) medium shuffle
	3	I7–V7 (two bars each) medium shuffle
	4	12-bar slow change medium shuffle in A (two choruses)
	5	12-bar quick change medium shuffle in A (two choruses)
	6	turnarounds: last four bars (4 times)
	7	endings: final four bars (4 times)
10	8	12-bar shuffle in A 66 bpm
	9	12-bar shuffle in E 66 bpm
	10	12-bar shuffle in E 100 bpm
11	11	IV7–♯IV diminished and IV7–IV minor changes
	12	I7–VI7–II7–V7 change
	13	12-bar medium shuffle, uptown changes
	14	8-bar "How Long" medium shuffle
	15	8-bar uptown medium shuffle
	16	8-bar "Key" medium shuffle
	17	8-bar "Nobody" ballad
	18	16-bar shuffle
	19	12-bar "Onions" minor shuffle
	20	16-bar one-chord shuffle
12	21	12-bar quick change slow blues
	22	12-bar "Stormy Monday" slow blues
	23	12-bar jump blues
	24	one-chord fast boogie
13	25	12-bar soul-blues
	26	12-bar minor smooth blues
	27	12-bar Latin blues
	28	12-bar rock and roll blues

About the Author

Keith Wyatt has been performing professionally and teaching blues guitar since the late 1970s. Since 1996, he has toured internationally and recorded with renowned Los Angeles-based "American Music" band The Blasters. For over thirty-five years, he taught blues guitar and a variety of other subjects at Musicians Institute in Hollywood, where he also directed the world-famous guitar program (GIT) and served as Vice President of Programs. He is the author of numerous books, including *Blues Rhythm Guitar*, *Harmony and Theory: the Essential Guide* (with Carl Schroeder), and *Ear Training for the Contemporary Musician* (with Carl Schroeder and Joe Elliott). His best-selling instructional videos include *Rockin' the Blues*, *Electric Blues Guitar*, *Electric Slide Guitar*, *Acoustic Blues Guitar*, *Getting Started on Guitar*, and many others. For over twenty years he has been a regular columnist for guitar magazines including *Guitar World*, the best-selling guitar magazine in the US.